INTRODUCTION TO
FRENCH LOCAL GOVERNMENT

INTRODUCTION TO

French
Local
Government

BY

BRIAN CHAPMAN
M.A., D.PHIL.
Lecturer in Government
University of Manchester

GREENWOOD PRESS, PUBLISHERS
WESTPORT, CONNECTICUT

Library of Congress Cataloging in Publication Data

Chapman, Brian.
    Introduction to French local government.

    Reprint of the 1953 ed. published by Allen & Unwin,
London.
    Bibliography: p.
    Includes index.
    1. Local government--France. I. Title.
JS4883.C45 1978   352.044   78-19030
ISBN 0-313-20538-8

This volume was prepared at the instigation of
THE INSTITUTE OF PUBLIC ADMINISTRATION
76a New Cavendish Street
London W.1

First published in 1953.

Reprinted with the permission of George Allen & Unwin Limited

Reprinted in 1978 by Greenwood Press, Inc.
51 Riverside Avenue, Westport, CT. 06880

Printed in the United States of America

10 9 8 7 6 5 4 3 2 1

To W.J.M.M.

PREFACE

In a book such as this the English reader, due to the peculiar nature of English local government, expects to find considerable space devoted to the history of the subject. The nature of French local administration renders this unnecessary in a book of this size since the whole system has remained structurally almost unchanged since the Napoleonic Constitution of 1800. Whereas it is impossible properly to understand English local government without some knowledge of the Justices of the Peace or the Boards of Guardians, it has seemed to me quite feasible to discuss the work of Prefects, Mayors and local councils after only a bare outline of their historical background.

Local government in England has hinged on the development of particular services in local areas, whereas in France the emphasis has been on the evolution of local institutions. I have therefore not attempted to deal separately with particular services such as Public Health and Education, but have followed the French practice of regarding them as aspects of the work of departmental and communal councils. To impose an English preconception on foreign political institutions would be in this case, as in most others, highly misleading.

I am deeply indebted to the Institute of Public Administration for sponsoring this book and for generously assisting me to undertake the travelling necessary for collecting material. I must particularly thank Professor W. A. Robson, lately chairman of its research committee, and its Director, Mr. Raymond Nottage. I also received invaluable aid from the research fund of the National Association of Local Government Officers.

Professor Mackenzie of this University and Mr. William Pickles of the London School of Economics have unstintingly given me the benefit of their experience, and without their encouragement and advice this book would have been less accurate and less readable. I should also like to acknowledge the many useful suggestions made by my colleagues Mr. Campbell and Mr. Spann.

If a work like this is to have any value, it must involve personal contact with many members of the French Administration. I have found the members of the Prefectoral Corps and of the local authorities unfailingly ready to assist me with their individual experience and with unpublished documents. They are too numerous for me to thank them all by name, but I am particularly indebted to MM. Bertaux, Goguel, Pisani, Virenque, and to Professor Laferrière and Senator Léo Hamon. Finally, I was greatly helped by my wife's constant aid, company and encouragement.

B. C.

Manchester.
July 1952

CONTENTS

CHAPTER ONE

Introduction

THIS introductory chapter is intended primarily for the English reader who has little acquaintance with the structure of French local government. Later chapters will deal one by one with the elements of local government mentioned here, but two general matters are best cleared up at the outset. First, to sketch the main areas of French local administration and to introduce the *dramatis personae* of local government. Second, to underline the differences between French and English administrative law. It will be necessary in later chapters to assume some understanding of these two things.

THE AREAS AND PERSONNEL OF
FRENCH LOCAL GOVERNMENT

The principal difficulty met with in this study is the tendency to identify certain French offices and areas with a supposed English equivalent ; to assume, for example, that the French *département* is really an English county transposed to the continent. This is particularly dangerous where the titles are the same, as with the French *maire* and the English Mayor, and it may lead to a complete misunderstanding of the continental conception of local " government ". If comparisons must be made it is more satisfactory to compare modern French local administration with *mediaeval* England, for the differences between the latter and modern English local government are sufficiently well known to obviate the danger of false analogies.

Consider the following statement :

". . . . The country was predominantly engaged in agriculture . . . the population was widely scattered . . . and an

extensive system of local government was necessary. The
country was for this purpose divided into counties, at the
head of each of which stood the Sheriff appointed by the
Crown, and possessed of such wide powers that Maitland
could speak of him as a 'provincial viceroy'. Each county
was governed by a county court composed of all the freemen
of the shire. . . . In turn the county was divided into hundreds,
each governed in a similar manner by the hundred court
composed of the freemen of the area under the presidency
of the bailiff.[1] "

Three points in this require stressing. First, that widely
scattered agricultural populations are best administered by a
decentralised system of government; second, the existence of
two levels of local administration, the county and the hundred;
third, the combination of a state official and local citizens in
the government of each area, and the predominant weight at the
county level of the officer of the Crown. It is these three points
that form the basic elements of French local government today.

In the first place France is still a predominantly agricultural
country in which less than half the working population is
engaged in industry, and in which, as a consequence, local
administration is based to a large extent on small rural communi-
ties scattered throughout the country. Indeed, about two thirds
of the basic areas of local administration in France, the Communes, have less than five hundred inhabitants. This is so unlike
modern England that to appreciate it requires a conscious
effort of will. Further, although modern systems of communications have been as effective in France as in England in bringing
all parts of the country nearer the centre, the distances involved
in France and the surprisingly wide variety of climate, agriculture, industry and local tradition, still raise problems which are
little known to the present day English administrator. The
French solution is roughly on the lines followed in mediaeval
England: state officials are found in all local government areas,
and these areas are in turn of a far more uniform structure
than is the custom in England today. These last two points
will be examined now in more detail.

[1] Hart : *Introduction to the law of local government and administration.*
3rd edition. D. J. Beatty. London, 1946. pp. 9-10.

The basic areas of French local government are the Communes, and these are combined together into Departments.[1] Both these areas were created during the French Revolution in order to give France a uniform and rational structure. Before 1789 French local administration had been a highly confused and unco-ordinated pattern of local autonomies, rights, dues, monopolies and privileges. Feudal fiefs existed alongside charter towns, provinces and ecclesiastical domains jostled each other, and each individual unit had distinct rights, duties and status. The Commune was introduced by the Constituent Assembly to replace all existing " primordial " unities, while the Departments were created to supersede all the greater local areas and especially to remove all trace of the old Provinces in which resided the seeds of federalism and separation. The Departments, therefore, were in origin more or less artificial areas, whose boundaries were the result of reason and expediency rather than history and geography. The Commune, on the other hand, was the natural basic entity, and as such it covered not only the small hamlet in the Alps but any urban area which formed a naturally cohesive unit.

There is no point here in elaborating the vicissitudes and changes that have occurred in departmental and communal areas over the last hundred and fifty years. It is sufficient to say that the principle of sub-division remains the same, and that the Department and Commune are today the essential units of local government.

We come now to a vital point which will affect all the later part of this book, and the best way to explain it is to return for a moment to the " hundred ". The quotation at the beginning of this section did not tell the whole story of local administration in mediaeval England, as it did not mention charter towns with their own rights, privileges and duties. The " hundreds " were essentially rural districts, and the enclaves formed by the charter towns introduced from a very early stage the conception of different standards for town and country ; they foreshadowed

---

[1] The anglicised version of the French *département* will be used throughout this book. When there is any possibility of ambiguity, e.g. " a government department", the word "division" will be used to describe the bureaucratic sub-division.

the present County Borough and contributed to the chaotic sub-divisions of English local administration. These distinctions have no place in French local government. The Commune in France is the only primary area for local government: it is as if all the mediaeval charters had been swept away and all the mediaeval English towns had been converted into " hundreds " with exactly the same status and powers as the rural community.

Only Paris in the whole of France has any individual form of local government.[1] Everywhere else, whether it be Marseilles (population 636,264) or Lucelle (population 92), the basic area is the Commune, and all have the same system of government. There are rural, urban, agricultural and industrial Communes, but the adjective is factually, not legally, descriptive : only the Commune as such is legally recognised, politically constituted and administratively organised. This uniformity is helpful to the lawyer and the writer, but very confusing to the English reader. The questions which inevitably arise from the idea of the meanest hamlet in the Pyrenees being governed according to the same set of rules as the city of Lyons must be left over to the next chapter, but they obviously affect the whole character of French local administration.

There are 37,983 Communes in France ; of these 22,665 had, in 1946, under 500 inhabitants, close on 16,000 had less than 200 inhabitants, and there are 581 Communes in which there are fewer than 50 people. Ten Communes are officially classified as " uninhabited ". Clearly from these figures no plausible generalisations can be made about the territory and wealth of Communes as a whole. Indeed, a Commune with a very small population may cover a larger area than a town like Lille; for example, an alpine village extending the length of a valley with uninhabited mountain reaches included within its boundaries. Again, it is not very illuminating to state that in 1948 the average income of a Commune was £3,500, and the average expenditure a slightly higher figure; there are enormous variations—several Pyrenean Communes had budgets of £25

---

[1] For purposes of internal administration, Lyons has some slight peculiarities. These are dealt with below, p. 89. The Constitution of 1946 makes provision for the enactment of special charters for large towns, but so far none have been elaborated.

or less while Strasbourg and other large urban Communes spent several million pounds. This sort of thing is inevitable if a formal legal structure is applied rigidly over the whole of a country as large and diversified as France, and it threatens from the outset to render generalisations somewhat misleading and even dangerous. But the generalisations must be risked, and the safest way is perhaps firmly to grasp the legal nature of the Commune and subsequently to examine the different realities to which the law can be accommodated.

Communes are grouped together into a Department, which is a corporate body with interests particular to itself and transcending those of the constituent Communes. In present-day France (including Corsica) there are ninety Departments,[1] each of which takes its name from a geographical feature such as a river or mountain range rather than from the name of a town. On an average there are some 426 Communes in each Department, but this figure is doubled in the case of the Department of the Pas-de-Calais (capital Arras) where there are over 900, while at the other extreme in Belfort[2] there are only 106 Communes, and in the Bouches-du-Rhône (capital Marseilles) 117.

The Department corresponds broadly to the mediaeval English county, but there are real differences, principally in size. France, which is nearly three times the size of England, has 90 Departments as compared with England's 50 administrative counties. The average French Department has an area of 2,363 square miles ; the average English county 1,107 square

---

[1] In addition to the Departments of France proper, there are three Departments in Algeria—Algiers, Constantine and Oran—and four overseas Departments (*départements d'outre-mer*)—Guadeloupe, Guyane, Martinique and Réunion. These Departments come under the Minister of the Interior and have a prefectoral administration, but their local administration at the communal level is quite different from that in France proper, in order to deal with special problems. This book does not pretend to cope with these issues, which require a detailed knowledge of French colonial theory and practice.

[2] Strictly speaking Belfort is a *Térritoire*, rather than a Department, since after the Franco-Prussian War the Alsatian part of it was ceded to the Germans and the rump was made into the *Térritoire de Belfort* to commemorate its fine war record and to invoke in the future the memory of France's mutilation. It has kept this title, but is nevertheless a Department.

miles. The largest single county—the West Riding of York-shire—is 2,775 square miles in area; the largest Department—the Gironde (capital Bordeaux)—is nearly twice as large, 4,140 square miles. At the other end of the scale Rutland, the smallest county, has 152 square miles, while the Seine (Paris) covers 185 square miles.

The most densely populated part of France is the centre of industrial activity, the Nord (capital Lille), which has close on two million people at an average density of 860 to the square mile. Belfort has the lowest population with 86,648, but the most sparsely populated Department is the Basses-Alpes (capital Digne) where there are only 30 people to the square mile; in this case it is remarkable that these few people are scattered in 245 Communes each with an average population of some 350 people. The Nord and the Basses-Alpes are the extremes, but the average population of the Departments, 406,000 inhabitants, gives a false impression as a small number of densely populated areas raise the national average.

No legal distinction is made between Communes of varying size and importance, but Departments are classified into four groups.[1] The 15 most important Departments in France are classified as *hors classe*, and as one would expect, amongst these are the Departments in which are situated the principal cities of France: for example the Gironde (Bordeaux), Bas-Rhin (Strasbourg), Haute-Garonne (Toulouse), Alpes-Maritimes (Nice) and Nord (Lille). Next to these are 19 " first class " Departments, and this list sounds like the roll of the provincial capitals of France; the Puy-de-Dôme (Clermont-Ferrand), Loire-Inférieure (Nantes), Maine-et-Loire (Angers), etc. After these come 22 smaller but still important " second class " Departments such as Corsica (Ajaccio) and Vosges (Epinal), and at the bottom 34 " third class " Departments like the Jura (Lons-le-Saunier) and the Haute-Marne (Chaumont).

These classifications have been gradually established over a period of years, but generally they are self-evident. For example, when Strasbourg was returned to France after the 1918 war,

[1] This classification in no way affects the legal status, powers, organisation and duties of the Department; it is an administrative device, the significance of which will be shown later.

its strategic and political importance was such that the Department of the Bas-Rhin was placed in the *hors classe* category. Sometimes changes occur which bring such increased importance to a Department or to its capital that its classification has to follow suit. In former times an insurrection was sufficient to lose a Department its name and to change its status and capital city. Such down-grading has not occurred recently, but a notable change in the upward direction occurred in 1948 to the Department of the Côte d'Or (Dijon). This was for a long time a second class Department, but after the reorganisation of the French security forces in 1948 the Prefect of the Côte d'Or was given special regional powers over the police. He, rather than any other Prefect in the region, was chosen because the Army had its Command Headquarters in Dijon. These special police powers were granted to eight state officials throughout France, all of whom ranked as Prefects of *hors classe* Departments, and to avoid obvious discrepancies the Department of the Côte d'Or was raised to *hors classe* status. Thus there is no hard and fast rule about the classification of Departments, but on the whole it is a general guide to their relative importance.

There are two other areas of local administration which must be mentioned here, the *arrondissement* and the *canton*. Both are sub-divisions of the Department; the *arrondissement* is important enough to warrant closer examination, but the *canton* can be dismissed in a few words. It is a collection of Communes which for certain administrative purposes are best grouped together. On an average each Department has about 35 *cantons*, but Corsica and the Nord have over 60 and Belfort and the Pyrénées-Orientales (Perpignan) have less than 20. The principal administrations based on the *canton* are the Army and the Judiciary, and therefore as an area of government it has no place in this book; it is, however, also an electoral area for local government elections in the Department.

The *arrondissement* is of much greater importance in French local administration. It is distinguished from the Commune and the Department in that it is a purely administrative sub-division with no corporate personality and no elected council. Its principal function is to ease the burden on the departmental

B

administration. On an average a Department is divided into
three or four *arrondissements*. Belfort has no such divisions and
the Rhône (Lyons) has only two. On the other hand the Bas-
Rhin (Strasbourg) has eight *arrondissements*. The latter is,
however, a special case as it reflects the Government's desire to
allow that area as much localised administration as possible,
for the autonomist movement in Alsace has always reacted
strongly against centralisation.

In general each *arrondissement* has between 100 and 150
Communes within its borders, with about 100,000 inhabitants.
The capital town of the Department and the surrounding area
is always one *arrondissement*, and the capitals of the other
arrondissements are generally the towns next in importance to
the departmental capital. For example, Lille is the capital of the
Nord, and Douai, Cambrai, Dunkirk, Valenciennes, and
Avesne-sur-Helpe are the capitals of the *arrondissements*. There
are exceptional cases where this system is reversed owing to
special considerations. For example, Draguignan is the capital
of the Var while Toulon, which is incomparably more important,
is only the capital of an *arrondissement*; this is because the
latter is an important naval base with a resident naval authority[1]
who, although possessing no civil powers, could yet be an em-
barrassment if Toulon were used as a centre for departmental
administration.

Like the Departments, the *arrondissements* are divided into
four classes, and their classification generally reflects the relative
importance of the towns and areas within the Department.
In extreme cases such as the Nord all the *arrondissements* are
hors classe, but a more usual pattern is that of the Somme where
the departmental capital, Amiens, is a first class *arrondissement*,
Abbeville ranks as second class and Montdidier as third class.

These are the principal areas of government which will be met
with in the coming pages. It is necessary next to consider the
officers who serve in the local administrations of the Commune,
arrondissement and Department.

It will be remembered that in mediaeval England the Sheriff of
the county was what we should now call the executive authority,

[1] The *préfet maritime*. The flag officer commanding the coastal zone:
the same position arises at Cherbourg and Brest.

and the freemen of the shire were associated with him in the government of the county. Departmental administration in France offers a rough parallel to this, with the Prefect acting as the executive authority and the *conseil général* as the consultative body of citizens. The same division of responsibility found in the " hundred " between the bailiff and the freemen is now found in the Commune between the Mayor (*maire*) and the *conseil municipal*. There is one further point in this parallel which is worth mention: the Sheriff was an officer appointed by the Crown and responsible directly to the King's Court, whereas the bailiff was a local figure nominated for his local prestige or position. The Prefect in modern French administration is also a state officer appointed by and responsible only to the central Government, while the Mayor is a local figure of some eminence whose contact with the central Government is always indirect.

The parallel between mediaeval English and modern French systems will not bear much further strain; this is principally due to the complexity of continental administrative law, which will be dealt with in the next section of this chapter.

The French Mayor has considerably greater personal prestige and personal power than has his English counterpart. He is head of the administration of the Commune, a prominent local political figure and also in some respects a state official. He is a figure in local administration whose status may be compared to that of the German Burgomaster but not to that of the English Mayor.

The growth of the Mayor's influence can be traced back over the last hundred and fifty years. After some experiments in local autonomy during the 1790's, Napoleon, in 1800, redrafted the whole system of French local government and gave it roughly the shape that it has today. The adventures in local autonomy during the previous decade, during which local men exercised much independent authority, were superseded by a more rigid system. At first the power of the executive was all-important, (partly as a reaction against previous abuses), and all the Mayors and the *conseils municipaux* were nominated by the central Government, with the Mayor as the communal executive and the *conseil* as a purely consultative body.

During the next eighty years this system was subjected to

continual modification. In 1831 the *conseil municipal* was made an elected body; a few years later it was granted certain powers of decision, so that in a limited number of cases the Mayor could not act without the prior approval of the *conseil*. Eventually, as a result of the democratic pressure exerted after the foundation of the Third Republic in 1871, the Mayor ceased to be nominated by the Government and became in 1881 an elected officer chosen by and from the *conseil municipal*. Three years later the *conseil municipal* came into its full inheritance when the law on communal administration of 1884 laid down that the *conseil municipal* was to have full powers of decision in all matters of purely communal concern,[1] and therefore that the Mayor required the sanction of the *conseil* before he could act in such matters.

This law of 1884 is the basis of all modern communal government and will be dealt with in detail in later chapters. The modifications which it has undergone in the last seventy years or so have altered the essentials surprisingly little. A point which should be emphasised here is that the Mayor is bound by the decisions of the *conseil municipal* in all matters of purely *communal* concern. But, as has already been mentioned, the Mayor is also a state official and he performs certain acts on behalf of the State. His powers under this latter head are personal to him and no other communal body can interfere with them. That part of the Commune's administration devoted to carrying out duties delegated to it by the State is therefore outside the control of the *conseil municipal*. This means that the Commune has to be regarded not only as an area of local government but also as the basic unit for certain parts of the state administration. This dual character of the Commune and the dual responsibility of the Mayor both to the *conseil municipal* and to the State, present complications seldom encountered in English local government and both points will require elucidation in some detail later on.

In the same way as the Commune, the Department is both an area of local government and an area for state administration. The difference between the administration of the two areas is

[1] This statement must not be taken at face value: the *conseil municipal* is in practice subject to many checks. See below, p. 43 seq.

that in the Department there are decentralised offices of the central Ministries living alongside the departmental administration. At the head of each of the state administrations is a state official appointed from Paris and directly responsible to his Minister. Most Ministries, from the Post Office to the Army, have departmental offices, but those which will occur most frequently in this book are those concerned with education, finance and civil engineering.

The educational system of France is on a regional basis. Each region, the *académie*, has its centre in one of the seventeen university towns, and at its head is the *recteur* of the university, who is the president of the University Council and the highest authority in the region on secondary and higher education. He holds a watching brief over the elementary educational institutions in the area. The *recteur* is represented in the Department by the *inspecteur d'académie*, who is effectively the administrative educational authority in the Department. Elementary school teachers are nominated on the advice of the *inspecteur d'académie*, and he, together with the Prefect and certain educational administrators, elected members of the *conseil général*, and teachers elected by their fellows, form the departmental *conseil* for primary education, with disciplinary powers and advisory duties.

The senior financial official in the Department is the *trésorier payeur général*, an officer of the Ministry of Finance, who is responsible for the proper administration of the revenue offices in the Department. He is assisted by state-appointed officials, the *receveurs particuliers des finances* in each *arrondissement*, and *receveurs-payeurs municipaux* in all Communes with more than 10,000 inhabitants. The influence of all these officials in local administration has considerably increased in recent years.

Finally mention should be made of the *ingénieurs des ponts et chaussées* and the *ingénieurs des mines*, because although they will not figure prominently in this book they are persons of some influence in the Department. The former are specially trained civil engineers organised into a national *corps* under the Minister of Public Works and recruited and administered by the State. Their job is to direct and supervise all public works concerning state or departmental highways, ports and port installations and certain other highway systems. The latter are the State's mining experts and they are responsible for the observance of safety regulations in the mines and for the prevention of accidents.

We can now turn to the administration of the Department itself. At the head of the departmental administration and the hierarchic superior of all state officials in the Department, no matter what their seniority or status, is the Prefect. He is appointed directly by the Government by Decree, and he is the personal representative of all the Ministers, whether or not they have members of their own administrations in the Department. He is the only legal representative of the State, and consequently he alone can authorise the payment of sums from public funds or represent the State in legal actions. He is not *primus inter pares*, but the clear and lawful superior of all the administrations, whether state or departmental, within the Department.

The Prefect, like the Sheriff in mediaeval times, has a body of citizens to assist and advise him.[1] In the Department this body is the *conseil général*, which originally, in 1800, was a purely consultative body and unable legally to influence the Prefect's administration of the Department. During the nineteenth century, however, the *conseil* gained increased power and influence, and a gradual transfer of powers of decision from the Prefect to the *conseil général* redressed the balance between the elected body and the executive authority. In the first years of the Third Republic the powers and status of the *conseil général* were laid down approximately as they are today. In 1871 the *conseil général* was made the final authority on all decisions affecting matters of purely departmental concern, and the Prefect, as the executive of the Department, was bound in these cases to carry out the wishes of the *conseil général*. There have been certain modifications to the powers of the *conseil général* since 1871, but the fundamentals are precisely as they were then and the organisation of the Department rests principally on the law of 1871.

[1] Articles 87, 88, 89 and 105 of the Constitution render the whole relation between Prefect and elected authority difficult to determine in law. For the practice see below, pp. 73-78.

During the periods when the *conseil général* is not in session a special body elected by and from the *conseil* takes over certain of its powers and duties. This body is the *commission départementale*, and for the time being we can regard it as in effect the standing committee of the *conseil général*.

The Prefect is assisted in his duties by certain officers who are members of the *corps préfectoral*. Firstly, he has a personal assistant, who is the most junior member of the *corps*, called the *chef de cabinet*. His right-hand man in the Prefecture is the Secretary-General, who is the head of all the administrative organisation of the Department, and who also has certain responsibilities for the *arrondissement* in which the departmental capital is situated. In each of the other *arrondissements* in the Department there is a Sub-Prefect (*sous-préfet*) to assist the Prefect. The Sub-Prefect has certain powers in his own right, but his principal task is to ensure the proper functioning of the state, departmental and communal services in the *arrondissement*, and to him are generally delegated some of the Prefect's powers for that area. These four kinds of official, Prefect, Sub-Prefect, Secretary-General and *chef de cabinet*, form the *corps préfectoral;* although the post of Secretary-General is recognised by law, he is always in fact a Sub-Prefect performing special duties, and what applies to the Sub-Prefect in the remainder of this book will automatically apply to the Secretary-General unless the context or an explicit statement indicates otherwise.

An important point about the career of the *corps préfectoral* is that there is no automatic direct line of promotion from the ranks of the Sub-Prefects to those of the Prefects. It has already been stated that the Prefect is appointed by the Government, and there are no limits to the Government's discretion; it has an absolutely free choice in the man it appoints. Therefore, although in practice many Sub-Prefects reach the eminence of Prefects, not all Prefects have been Sub-Prefects. The career of Sub-Prefect is today comparatively clear and straightforward, with entry as *chef de cabinet* and promotion by steps to the grade of *hors classe* Sub-Prefect. There it may stop. An *hors classe* Sub-Prefect may or may not achieve promotion to Prefect.

It will be remembered that Departments and *arrondissements*

are graded into four classes. The Prefect or Sub-Prefect in a
given Department or *arrondissement* takes his personal rank
from the grade of the area in which he is serving: that is, the
Prefect of Gard (Nîmes) is a first class Prefect because Gard is a
first class Department, and the Sub-Prefect of Saint-Jean-
d'Angély is a third class Sub-Prefect because his *arrondissement*
is in that category. The way of promotion then is to be transferred from one area to another of a higher classification;
but again there is nothing to prevent the Government appointing, for example, a third class Prefect straight to a first class
Department, whereupon he automatically jumps a grade.[1]

In conclusion some mention must be made of the place of the
region in local government in France. Some central Ministries
are organised regionally, but these do not concern us here.
We have only to consider the region as it is used in local government administration.

There is a long history of regionalism in France stretching
back to the last days of the nineteenth century, and it has been a
recurrent theme of political scientists; their case for regional
government rests on the inadequacy of the Department for some
purposes, and on the continued existence of local patriotism
towards the old Provinces of France which were abolished as
political and administrative entities by the Constituent Assembly
in 1789. In addition the French regionalist can point to the
varying and overlapping regional areas which have been set
up by the individual Ministries with awkward administrative
results. Each region comprises several Departments, but a
Department may belong to one region for one service and to a
different region for another service. The regional capitals for
the various services also differ. For example, the Department of
the Aisne (Laon) has its judicial assize court and its regional
economic headquarters at Amiens (Somme), its educational
centre and military headquarters at Lille (Nord), its administrative tribunal at Châlons-sur-Marne (Marne), its Bishop at
Soissons (Aisne), the centre of its *police judiciaire* at Rheims

---

[1] In certain circumstances, if a Prefect remains for four years in the same
Department he may be promoted to a higher grade as a personal concession, without reference to the classification of his Department which
will remain as before.

(Marne) and its water board at Compiègne (Oise). This confusion is made tolerable in France only by the local centralisation offered by the Prefecture at the departmental capital—and not always then.

It is obvious that such confusion presents difficulties even in ordinary times: in times of danger and emergency it can endanger the whole fabric of government by dispersion of responsibility. Such periods of acute danger have occurred on three occasions in the last decade, and each time the government of the day has reacted by creating Prefects with powers extending over several Departments. The first such occasion was immediately after the collapse of France in 1940, the second at the time of the Liberation in 1944, and the third late in 1947. Each period was marked by very difficult economic conditions combined with a real political and military threat to the integrity of the State. The three different kinds of regional Prefect have, therefore, all possessed special security and economic powers.

Under Vichy, France was divided into 18 regions, 12 in occupied and 6 in unoccupied territory. The Regional Prefects were those who happened to be resident in (or appointed to) the Prefectures in the departmental capitals of the regions. Special economic powers were delegated to the Regional Prefects by the central Ministries and they acquired special authority over the police by the virtual dispossession of the ordinary departmental Prefects of their normal police powers. In a short time these Regional Prefects became the effective, although not the legal, superiors of the ordinary Prefects, and there grew up around the regional capital a bureaucracy specialising in regional affairs. This first experiment in regional government was not an unqualified success even from the administrative point of view. The regional movement under Vichy had been inspired in large part by nostalgic reactionaries like the *Action Française*, and writers of dubious reputation like Maurras. Politically, therefore, the region was labelled as an authoritarian device, smacking of Vichy, Laval and repression.

This reputation was ignored at the time of the Liberation for the very good reason that the needs of law, order and economic rehabilitation were even more urgent than under Vichy. De Gaulle, in agreement with the internal Resistance, replaced the Regional Prefects by *commissaires de la république;* their regions roughly coincided with the Vichy Regions, but the total number was increased to 18 by the inclusion of Alsace-Lorraine and the reorganisation of the whole of the former prohibited zone (zone C). These *commissaires* were, for a short time, enormously powerful, with authority to suspend laws; annul prison sentences; reform or cancel previous acts of the Vichy administration; arrest, detain and investigate all suspected collaborators; and purge professional, administrative and technical bodies. They were further covered by a blanket authority empowering them to take all measures necessary for the maintenance of good order and public safety, which could and did include wide interference in economic and political affairs. The powers of the *commissaires* gradually fell into disuse as the Minister of the Interior in Paris succeeded in extending his control over the various parts of the country, and in May, 1945, they had their duties restricted to controlling, stimulating and co-ordinating the actions of the Prefects. In this field they did valuable work; but as communications were restored and the central Government increased its hold over the country their *raison d'être* became less obvious, and they were subject to increasing attacks from the Left as being De Gaulle's agents. Eventually, in May, 1946, the post of *commissaire de la république* was abolished, together with those regional services still in existence. The ordinary Prefects then resumed their pre-war powers.

Within two years it was found that too much had been swept away, for when, in November, 1947, there were widespread strikes and a threatened insurrectionary movement, the ordinary Prefect proved to be far too isolated to cope with hostile movements covering several Departments and bestriding important communications. The Government then realised the danger of dispersed and unco-ordinated security forces, and in March, 1948, the Minister of the Interior introduced a Bill in Parliament which authorised him to create eight *inspecteurs généraux de l'administration en mission extraordinaire* (IGAME) whose task was to reorganise all the security forces of France —police, military and militia—on a regional basis, and to assume control of such forces at all times of grave civil or military emergency. The regional centres were the eight towns in which the Army had its Command Headquarters. In the first instance four of the IGAME were resident in Paris and had no departmental duties, while the other four were the Prefects already resident in those towns.

These IGAME are the new " super "-Prefects with whom we shall have to deal later. It should be noted that they are in no way comparable with the former regional Prefects, since their powers are strictly circumscribed and they are not the hierarchic superiors of the ordinary departmental Prefects: but they undoubtedly enjoy extra prestige.

After this summary of the principal officers met with in French local administration we turn to consider some general points of legal principle which distinguish French local administration from English local government.

THE PRINCIPLES OF FRENCH ADMINISTRATIVE LAW APPLICABLE TO LOCAL GOVERNMENT

Two important differences between French and English constitutional law and their implications must be touched upon here, since they affect all local government.

The first point is that French local authorities are in a real sense organs of the State; they are a part of the hierarchy of administration with special duties. Whereas, however, the powers of most of the principal state organs (like the National Assembly) are defined in the Constitution, the powers and rights of the local authorities are not. In technical language Parliament, or the Council of Ministers, or the President of the French Republic, are " immediate " organs of State drawing their authority from the Constitution, local authorities are "mediate" organs depending on a constitutional authority for their grant of power. If the rights of the National Assembly are altered, the act is unconstitutional; if a higher body changes the terms of reference of the local authorities then that is entirely within its discretion. In several instances the competent higher authority is Parliament, but when a local authority is acting as an executive agency it is subject to the Executive.

This introduces the second important point. The doctrine of the separation of powers in France means that the Executive has its own rights and status with which Parliament cannot interfere except by legislation. The Executive has its own responsibilities and sources of authority *qua* Executive and distinct from those granted to it by Parliament; the notion of execution implies some measure of autonomy. There can therefore be certain fields where local authorities are subject exclusively to the rules and orders laid down by the Executive and its agents.

The juridical authority under which the Executive issues orders can be classified under four heads.[1] First there are some actions of the Executive which are subject to no judicial or legislative control at all : these are the *actes de gouvernement*. On some occasions the health and safety of the State depend upon the Executive's right to act without warrant and due process of law.[2] These acts, by their very nature, can seldom be precisely defined in advance, and the only valid test is whether or not a court of law will agree to receive plaints based on an alleged breach of law. The conduct of foreign affairs, the declaration of a state of siege, and police measures taken by the Executive to protect the State from subversive activities in time of war, have all at one time or another been considered by the courts to fall within this category. The courts—and the politicians—are reluctant to use this concept.

Second, the head of the Executive[3] is responsible for the safety and security of the State and for the execution of the law, and to perform this duty members of the Executive have the authority to issue " police " regulations limiting the citizens' freedom to act in certain ways.

At this stage a very confusing ambiguity in French terminology must be noted. The term *police* has a double meaning: it can be used in the English sense to denote the forces responsible for maintaining public order and repressing crime, or it can mean the power to organise the community in the interests

---

[1]This is a simplification of the views put forward by M. Prélot : *Précis de Droit Constitutionnel*. Dalloz 1949, pp. 514–520 ; and L. Rolland : *Précis de Droit Administratif*. Dalloz 1947, pp. 44–67, 158–167.

[2] Rolland : op. cit., pp. 64–67.

[3] The President of the Republic under the Third Republic ; the President of the Council of Ministers under the Fourth.

of public order and security. In the one sense it is a body of men, in the other a power. In this study the word will rarely be used in the normal English sense, and when it is it will always be with the addition of the word "forces". This is unfortunate, but inevitable. The use of "police powers" in France is so widespread and of such broad significance in local government that it is impossible to find a real alternative.[1]

The Executive has a monopoly of police powers: it alone is entitled to issue orders calculated to enforce or maintain public order, public hygiene and public morality. The Mayor, as a member of the Executive, can therefore order the repair of unsafe property, the Prefect can decide when the hunting season shall open in his Department, and the Minister of the Interior can forbid the carrying of weapons in public. Police power, in this sense, is not restricted to the repression of crime: it is also directed to its prevention. It is used to prevent circumstances arising in which public security is liable to be jeopardised, public morality disturbed, or public hygiene (*salubrité*) affected. All these activities are grouped under the heading of *police administrative*, and they are the responsibility of the Executive. There is also the *police judiciaire*, which is a body of men responsible for repressing and detecting crime and apprehending offenders; and in the ordinary way the members of the Executive whom we shall consider here, the Mayor, Sub Prefect and Prefect, are also members of the *police judiciaire;* this is an interesting source of authority and has, in the case of the Prefects, interesting results, but the *police judiciaire* has no proper place in this study.

A third source of Executive authority is that the organisation and discipline of the public services is the constitutional duty of the Executive. Thus examinations for entry, disciplinary measures taken for disobedience, the organisation of the offices and so on, are the concern of the Executive alone.[2]

Finally, the Executive has on many occasions been authorised

---

[1] The use of "police power" in this sense is common in the United States, and will present no difficulties to those acquainted with its institutions.

[2] Individual Deputies and Senators do sometimes interfere, but this is a political matter and does not affect the legal argument.

by Parliament either to organise services which Parliament has created, or to use its own discretion in elaborating the details of a scheme already broadly sketched by Parliament. In this case the Executive is limited by the original terms of reference and cannot legally go beyond them. This form of delegated legislation is well known in this country and its principles require no elaboration here.

Two major points relating to local government emerge from this. Every member of the Executive is subject to the hierarchic control of his administrative superior. When the Mayor acts as a member of the State's administration, he can be instructed to perform certain actions by the Prefect; similarly the Prefect is under the direct control of the Minister of the Interior. Second, because local authorities are organs of the State, peculiar only in that they have a special task to perform and a special mode of recruitment, the State has certain powers over them and over local councillors. Local authorities can be dissolved if they are found incapable of carrying out their duties properly, or if they violate the laws or refuse to perform duties legally incumbent on them. In addition, many of their decisions and actions are liable to the scrutiny and approval of a state authority, without which the decisions are null and void. This form of prior consent and general supervision over local authorities is called tutelage.[1]

The individual councillors of the Commune and of the Department occupy a curious legal position somewhere between the national representative of the people and the *fonctionnaire*, the public official. The way they attain their position (viz. election) marks them off from the *fonctionnaire* proper, but because the Commune and the Department are legal entities within the corpus of state institutions elected councillors are individually as well as corporately liable to the general rules laid down by the State, and they can be dismissed from office by members of the Executive for certain offences; they can also be required to perform certain public functions under pain, ultimately, of dismissal.

The notion that local authorities are an integral part of the machinery of the State, and the doctrine of the independence

[1] See below, chapter IV.

of the Executive, are both foreign to English conceptions of law and government. A simple statement of the legal position, however, gives a false impression of the true status of the Executive *vis-à-vis* the other organs of government and the citizens, and of the independence actually enjoyed by the local authorities. In fact, the power of the Executive is limited in many ways, the most obvious of which is by the Constitution. The Executive cannot pass a law on its own account,[1] and it cannot make actions criminal; Parliament alone can do this. It cannot, as a *general* rule, deprive the citizen of privileges and liberties granted to him by Parliament or the Constitution, and only when, in particular cases, the exercise of those liberties threatens public order or the safety of the State can it interfere.

The Executive is not above the law, and no member of the Executive can break it with impunity. But in the exercise of its duties the Executive is administratively (though not politically) independent of both Parliament and the Judiciary. This means that the actions of its servants, when acting within the scope of their employment, are not subject to the same courts as those of the ordinary citizen. If a postman knocks down a citizen with a post-office van, the Judiciary, in the sense of the ordinary civil or criminal courts, will refuse to receive a claim for damages. Instead, there are special administrative courts whose job it is to deal with such matters.

These administrative courts were originally set up by Napoleon to advise him, and to deal with questions of law and conduct concerning the administration. This was prompted by his distrust of the conservative character of the ordinary courts—a distrust he shared with the revolutionaries of the 1790's. Actions of the Executive were to be subject to the Executive's courts, and they alone were empowered to judge conflicts arising between the Executive and the citizen, and between the various branches of the state administration. In addition a person who held a *fonction publique* was protected from ordinary judicial warrants by the nature of his employment. When he was acting for the Executive, only the Executive's courts could judge his actions.

[1] Although the juridical distinction between the *loi* and the *décret* is very difficult to formulate except by reference to the promulgating authority.

Napoleon set up the *Conseil d'État* as the senior administrative court of the land, with administrative, judicial and
legislative functions. It was modelled fairly closely on the
Conseil du Roi which had existed under the *ancien régime*.
Since 1800 the *Conseil d'État* has undergone a complete change
of climate and of role but not of numbers. Originally its principal duty was to tender advice to the First Consul, and to
ensure the proper formulation of laws and administrative
obedience to the regulations. Now it has emerged as the pro-
tector of the rights of the citizen against the Executive, as the
most authoritative and decisive voice in the technical preparation of laws, and as the unsleeping conscience of administrative
practice. Its untiring and courageous work has, in the last
fifty years, made it the paragon of all French institutions.

The *Conseil d'État* is the senior court of administrative law
in the country, and from its decisions there is no appeal. It is
the appellate court for the subordinate administrative courts
throughout the country, the *conseils de préfecture*. These
courts also trace their descent from the Napoleonic constitution
of 1800, when they were established in each Department to
assist the Prefect. They were principally consultative bodies,
but they acted as the administrative courts for all actions placed
within their competence by law. Such actions were not numerous
at the beginning, but they have expanded since.

Since 1800, the *conseils de préfecture* have undergone considerable change both in function and in composition; their advisory
and consultative functions have almost disappeared and they are
now almost entirely concerned with cases of administrative justice.
In the first place, they were composed of active administrative
officials and presided over by the Prefect himself, but they have
gradually become specialised courts recruited from university
graduates and taking little part in administrative life; they are
no longer presided over by the Prefect. This change was partly
dictated by the feeling that justice was sometimes abused when
administrators were judges in their own case, and partly by the
increasing complexity of administrative practice during the late
nineteenth and early twentieth centuries, which left active
administrative officials insufficient time for both functions.
Nevertheless, transformation was slow, and was complicated

by the entry into the *conseils de préfecture* of many local councillors who had neither knowledge nor skill.

For a long time the *conseils de préfecture* had a bad reputation, and appeals from their decisions were commonplace. On grounds of economy and efficiency, therefore, in 1926 Poincaré decided to regroup all the *conseils de préfecture* into twenty-two *conseils de préfecture interdépartementaux*, each covering several Departments. Many councillors were relieved of their posts and those remaining had their pay increased; entry to the new *corps* was henceforth by special examination, and standards rapidly rose with the rise in pay and status. The primary administrative courts in this study are properly speaking the *conseils de préfecture interdépartementaux*. Although the primary administrative courts, they do not decide all cases of first instance, since they are assigned their jurisdiction by law, and when the law is silent the *Conseil d'État* alone is competent, and then it acts as the court of both first and last instance.

Proposals to widen the jurisdiction of the *conseils de préfecture interdépartementaux* are at the present moment under consideration ; it is recommended that these courts should be the courts of first instance in all cases, and that the *Conseil d'État* should be the court of appeal. From the point of view of speed and efficiency this reform has much in its favour.

CHAPTER TWO

The Work of the Elected Bodies

THE elected bodies to be considered in this chapter are the *conseil municipal* in the Commune and the *conseil général* and the *commission départementale* in the Department. The elected executive in the Commune is the Mayor, and his relations with his *conseil municipal* will be discussed here, but his duties as a member of the state administrative hierarchy will be dealt with in the next chapter.

CONSEIL MUNICIPAL

Composition

Every Commune in France[1] has a *conseil municipal* elected by the enfranchised inhabitants of that Commune. In Communes with more than 9,000 inhabitants, the election is according to party lists (*scrutin de liste*), but the elector has the right to transfer his vote from individual candidates in one party to individual candidates in another (*panachage*), and to state a preference (*vote préférentiel*) for particular members in any one list. Seats are apportioned between lists according to the votes gained by that party divided by the quotient obtained after dividing all the votes cast in the election by the number of seats to be filled. If some seats remain unfilled because the remaining votes for any one list do not make up the quotient, those seats are filled by awarding each successively to the list to which the

---

[1] The *Ville de Paris* and the Department of the Seine have a unique system of local government. A special chapter is devoted to their administration, and they are always implicitly *excluded* from any of the general rules about communal or departmental government laid down in the next two chapters.

award of one further seat would give it the biggest average number of votes per seat (*plus forte moyenne*). The Commune is treated as a single constituency.[1]

In Communes of under 9,000 inhabitants the elections are a simple form of *scrutin de liste*.[2]

The number of councillors is determined by law, ranging from eleven in the smallest Commune to thirty-seven in Communes with over 60,000 inhabitants. Special arrangements are made in the largest towns like Lyons whereby the Commune is divided into several wards which elect altogether some sixty councillors.

Subject to several exceptions regarding eligibility as candidates, any French citizen over twenty-one possessing property or residential qualifications in the Commune is entitled to vote in the communal elections and to stand for election. The exceptions are those categories of citizens whose work is of such a nature as to make it undesirable for them to present themselves for election in a particular area : consequently, members of the *corps préfectoral*, magistrates, police officers, certain administrative officers of State and Department, and the paid employees of the Commune, are ineligible.

Communal elections are held every six years on the same day in May throughout France, and unless one of three special conditions is met there can be no by-elections. The first condition is that if in Communes under 9,000 inhabitants, through resignation, removal or death, a *conseil municipal* falls below two-thirds of its proper number elections must be held at once to fill the vacancies.[3] In the second place, new elections can be held if a *conseil municipal*, or a large proportion of its members, resigns as a political protest against some action of the Prefect, the Government, or its own Mayor. Mass resignations of this nature are not uncommon, as will be seen: certain things can

[1] Law of September 5, 1947, and Decree of September 18, 1947.
[2] This is in fact the *scrutin de liste majoritaire à deux tours;* i.e. the elector casts one vote for a list of candidates and the list getting an absolute majority is elected *in toto*. If there is no absolute majority, then a relative majority operates at a second ballot held a week later.
[3] Unless the local elections for the whole country are due within three months. In Communes with over 9,000 inhabitants a vacant seat is filled by the next name on the list of the previous councillor.

only be done by the *conseil municipal*, and an appeal to the local electorate against the decision of a higher authority assumes the nature of a referendum, and triumphant vindication at the polls is regarded as a warning, and is certainly a moral set-back, to the Administration.

Third, the Government itself can dissolve the *conseil municipal* by a Decree made on the advice of the Minister of the Interior. Such a right is a direct consequence of the fact that the local authorities are integral parts of the machinery of State. If the *conseil municipal* is unable to function, grossly abuses its powers, or threatens to cause a breakdown in public services or local administration, the Government can act. The numerous political parties and the personal nature of local politics often make it extremely difficult to find a stable majority in the local assembly: for example, the *conseil municipal* of Levallois Perret in the Department of the Seine was, before its recent dissolution, composed of 16 Gaullists, 15 Communists, 3 MRP and 3 Socialists, and no administration was possible since the balance of forces could be changed overnight if personalities clashed or a councillor was taken ill.

Special arrangements are made when a *conseil municipal* resigns *en masse* or is dissolved by the Government. A special Delegation of between three and seven members is appointed by the Minister of the Interior, its size depending on the size of the Commune. The Delegation is restricted to administering current business, and it is expressly forbidden to interfere with communal finance or to commit the Commune to any new plan or contract. Any decision it has to take as a matter of urgency can later be over-ridden by the new *conseil municipal*.

The mere fact of holding communal elections at the same time throughout the country is sufficient to give them some national importance. In France, though less than in this country, the growth of national parties and the development of national programmes and machines have tended to distort the real issues at stake in a local election.

French local election campaigns centre round national party names, but they are really concerned with local issues and personalities, and party titles are often appropriated by local politicians merely to indicate their general bias. In parts of the

South bodies of electors vote for the party furthest to the Left: consequently, although some councils may appear to change hands over a period of time; from the Radicals of the 1870's, to the Socialists of the 1910's, to the Communists of the 1930's; the different names indicate little real change in the political dogma of the electors. Names are symbols, programmes are pious hopes, and machines are local clubs: behind them stand attitudes of mind and traditional reactions which can be traced back sometimes to the French Revolution and before.[1]

It is very difficult to generalise about French local politics. It is untrue to say that every Commune has its own peculiarities; but many Departments have, and assiduous research often shows that the " national " element in local elections is quite submerged by local issues and traditions.

There are 466,209 municipal councillors distributed unevenly between 37,983 Communes. The number of councillors to a Commune is based on population, but in such a way that the proportion of councillors to population is higher in the smaller Communes than in larger ones. For example, Communes with under 500 inhabitants have eleven councillors, with 500–1,500 inhabitants thirteen councillors, with 1,500–2,500 inhabitants seventeen councillors, and so on. For Communes with over 10,000 inhabitants there is a sharp fall in the proportion: thus, there are twenty-seven councillors in Communes with 10,000–30,000 inhabitants, thirty-one in those with 30,000–40,000, and only thirty-seven in those with above 60,000.[2] This system means that under half the total electorate, living in the Communes of under 4,000, elects over 430,000 municipal councillors.[3]

This probably has no very serious result on local admin-

[1] F. Goguel: *Géographie des élections françaises de* 1870 *à* 1951. Paris, 1951., pp. 7–10; and F. Goguel: *Esquisse d'un bilan de la sociologie électorale française. Revue Française de Science Politique*, Vol. 1, No. 3, October, 1951, p. 285.

[2] There are provisions for increasing the number of councillors in the largest towns such as Lyons, and Paris has a different system ; see below, p. 207.

[3] This fact is particularly significant because the municipal councillors send delegates to the electoral college which elects Senators to the *Conseil de la République.*

istration : the smallest Communes have enough members to ensure full discussion and the participation of various interests, and the largest Communes are not overburdened with councillors for whom there is no work.

In general, national politics are most prominent in the large urban Communes where industrial and social life encourages the formation of cohesive groups, and favours the party machine rather than the individual politician. Mass parties such as the Gaullists and the Communists find their greatest support in these towns, even though the system of proportional representation ensures that the centre parties like the Radicals, the MRP and the Socialists, are equitably represented. Even in these Communes, however, many of the Right-wing groups have no proper local organisation, are built up round a prominent local figure, and live only during the election period. Such " parties " are extremely fluid and liable to disintegrate, but they can rely on a hard core of conservative sympathy, and by proportional representation they can acquire some influence.

In the smallest Communes personal influence is much more noticeable. Even when, as often happens, national party labels are used, the issues on which the elections are fought are of the parish pump variety. In other places the local personalities and their supporters choose the party labels which seem to them appropriate to local circumstances. Yet again, joint lists of parties and electoral alliances can be arranged for purely local reasons : Radicals and MRP may combine on economic grounds to fight proposals by the Socialists and the Communists to create a new municipal service; elsewhere, Radicals and Socialists may ally themselves against the MRP on an anti-clerical basis. Joint anti-Communist lists may be formed, especially where there is a real danger of Communists obtaining an absolute majority.

Finally, there are plenty of Communes where there are practically no politics at all in the normal sense of the word. Lists presented by the *groupe de défense des intérêts communaux* and similar tickets, in several cases genuinely non-political, are regularly returned to office.

The results of any election can be challenged for irregularity before the *conseil de préfecture* by any voter or candidate or by the Prefect or Sub-Prefect. In the past, attempts to bring pressure on the electors and falsification of electoral rolls and returns were the principal causes of legal proceedings. Present conditions have improved however, and since 1945 electoral litigation has generally been concerned with the eligibility of candidates, since post-Liberation legislation made those convicted of collaboration ineligible for public office. The national political climate has changed since 1945, and many former politicians find local elections the simplest method of bringing this continued " discrimination " to the public notice. A recent case at Dax suggests that in rural areas some ineligible candidates are held in considerable favour, provided that they are far enough to the Right. Three times a M. Milliès-Lacroix, an ex-Senator who voted full powers to Marshal Pétain, has been elected by the citizens of Dax, and triumphantly elevated to the dignity of Mayor by the *conseil municipal*. Three times the *conseil de préfecture* and the *Conseil d'État* have declared him ineligible, and three times he has been returned again. Naturally ordinary communal administration suffers from these political games.

The *conseil municipal* holds its first session within a fortnight of the publication of the results of the elections. At this first meeting in the *Mairie* (or the *Hôtel de Ville*),[1] the chair is taken by the oldest councillor present, and the youngest member acts as Secretary. First the Mayor is elected, followed by the Assistant-Mayors (*Adjoints*). The number of Assistant-Mayors varies with the population of the Commune, from one where there are less than 2,500 inhabitants to a maximum of twelve in the largest Communes.[2]

Contrary to English practice, the appointment of the Mayor is a deliberate political choice, but the multiplicity of party groupings in many councils frequently makes his election a matter of involved internal manoeuvring.

Where one party has an absolute majority in a council, nomination will depend on the balance of forces inside that party, and this can sometimes be a complicated matter. The method of proportional representation used in the municipal

[1] The name has no legal significance: only local pride is involved.
[2] Lyons has a special right to appoint seventeen.

elections, moreover, often produces no clear and cohesive majority; two or even three ballots may then be needed, for the Mayor is elected on the first two counts only if he obtains an absolute majority, and not until the third ballot does a relative majority suffice.

The Mayor does not always belong to the majority party in the council. He may be elected by a coalition of minority parties or from a minor party with the support of a major party. For example, at Le Havre, in 1947, a Socialist Mayor was elected by 19 votes to 18: his majority consisted of 18 Gaullist and Independent councillors and himself, and the opposition of 16 Communists and two other Socialists.[1]

To complicate the issue still further, the national standing and personal prestige of some Mayors is so great that even when his party is in a minority in the council his opponents deem it wise not to challenge his re-election. M. Herriot, Mayor of Lyons, for example, was elected by 16 Radicals (his own party) and 6 MRP; the 23 Gaullists and 13 Communists abstained.

Herriot's career raises a further point of some interest in local politics ; that a local political career is commonly regarded as the proper and natural step to a national political career: it is significant that over a third of all the present Senators are also Mayors in their own Communes, and that most Ministers have local government connections. This extremely healthy activity at the bottom has two unfortunate results in national political life; local issues become too important for individual legislators to risk losing local favour on grounds of national responsibility; and it seriously hinders the creation of new cadres of young political leaders, since local influence often depends on seniority alone and it seldom comes without a lengthy struggle against jealousy and prejudice.

The *conseil municipal* has a free hand in choosing its Mayor and Assistant-Mayors, with two minor exceptions; they must not be members of the state financial administrations, and the Assistant-Mayors must not be employees of the Mayor. The Mayor and the Assistant-Mayors together form the *municipalité* of the Commune.

[1] D. M. Pickles: " Trends in French Politics: the Municipal Elections analysed," in *The World Today*, Dec. 1947. pp., 529–537.

Within twenty-four hours of the election of these communal officers, the results must be proclaimed by a notice on the doors of the Town Hall, and the Sub-Prefect must be notified under registered cover. Objections to the election can be made by any voter to the *conseil de préfecture* within five days of promulgation. At the end of that time the *conseil municipal* and the communal officers are in full possession of their powers.

Organisation

The *conseil municipal* must now meet at least four times a year (February, May, August and September), each session lasting a fortnight, to deal with communal affairs and to prepare the communal budget. When necessary, the Mayor can convene extraordinary sessions to discuss urgent business, and a third of the *conseil municipal* can insist on such a meeting being called whether or not the Mayor wishes it. The Prefect or the Sub-Prefect can also convene extraordinary sessions. Such sessions are common, and they are occasioned by a variety of reasons: it may be the refusal of the Government to allow a grant for the new drainage scheme, the question of joint protest at the creation of an ammunition dump outside the town, or the arrangements necessary to succour an area devastated by a forest fire.

The Mayor must give at least three clear days' notice of his intention to convene an extraordinary session and a quorum of a half is necessary. If the quorum does not appear at the first summons, a new session is convened three days later at which decisions are valid irrespective of the number of councillors present. These precautions help the Mayor to resist the temptation to call hurried sessions without informing his political opponents of his intentions.

A point of some importance in internal organisation is that a councillor is allowed to delegate his vote to another councillor if he is unable to attend a meeting. Only one proxy can be held by any one councillor and it cannot be exercised for more than three consecutive meetings unless the councillor's absence is due to ill-health. Naturally, the right to use another councillor's vote is always revocable at will.

On all occasions but one the Mayor can preside over meetings of the *conseil* if he wishes, and in his absence the senior Assistant-Mayor takes his place. The Mayor is forbidden to take the chair at the session at the end of the financial year when the Mayor's accounts are presented to the *conseil* for discussion and vote. For this special occasion a temporary president is elected. The Mayor may be present during the discussion of the accounts, and frequently councillors, especially of the opposition, call upon him to justify items of expenditure. The Mayor must withdraw from the council chamber before the accounts are put to the vote.

The internal organisation of the *conseil municipal* is directly affected by its legal status. The English committee system is entirely unknown. There is no history of independent *ad hoc* authorities, with legal status and statutory powers, dealing with specific branches of local services. The *conseil municipal* is the only body recognised. It is responsible for all communal services, and no committee can be granted powers of decision; these belong in their entirety to the parent body. The *conseil* as a corporation has a monopoly of power, and any decision taken must be taken in its name by an absolute majority of the councillors voting.

This does not mean that there are no committees in French local government, but merely that they owe their existence to the will of the *conseil* itself. Committees are normally formed for one of two purposes. Some are formed to give continuity to communal government when the *conseil* itself is not in session; others are set up to allow for the specialised examination of specific problems. The committees can meet whenever they like, both during the sessions of the *conseil* and in the interim periods. Committees are never public, and they provide an opportunity for detailed and unprejudiced discussion; consequently, even though the *conseil municipal* may go into secret session if the Mayor or more than a third of the councillors desire it, it seldom does so (except in the case of communal appointments), since the committees afford ample privacy when desired.

There are no statutory committees, and therefore no guide can be given regarding the number found in any particular Commune. In the smallest Communes few committees are formed except to examine proposals from neighbouring Communes for the joint provision of services. Schemes involving loans or applications for state assistance are also normally assigned in the first instance to an *ad hoc* committee. In larger Communes there are likely to be standing committees for specific subjects; for example, for general administration, for the Municipal Theatre, for public assistance and so on. Generally all proposals for future expenditure, plans and schemes will be remitted to a committee for examination and report; its recommendations will then be presented to a full session of the *conseil municipal*.

In all cases a committee draws its powers from and owes its existence to the will of the *conseil municipal*, and it has no more influence or authority than that body allows it. No delegation of function is allowed in local government practice; the *conseil municipal* can never give to another authority its own powers of decision, nor can the execution of communal affairs be entrusted by the Mayor to any other body. The classic statement of this is in the judgment of the *Conseil d'État*[1] in a case arising out of the decision of the *conseil municipal* of Castelnaudary which proposed to grant to an association of landowners the power to recruit and organise a rural police force to protect property, in place of recruiting an ordinary police force. The landowners were willing to pay the force, so that the Commune would have been saved money, and it would probably have also been more efficient; but no such delegation of authority was permissible, and the *Conseil d'État* annulled the decision of the *conseil municipal*.

Powers

The Law of April 5, 1884, laid down the powers that were to be exercised by the communal authorities, as well as prescribing the detailed organisation of the administration described above. There have been several amendments and additions to this law, but in all essentials it remains the same, and later alterations in communal government have been within the framework of the original law.[2]

[1] *Conseil d'État:* June 17, 1932; Castelnaudary. In *Recueil des Arrêts du Conseil d'État*, known as *Lebon Chronologique*.
[2] With the exception, naturally, of the Vichy period.

The law is a curious combination of meticulous detail and precision and considerable vagueness and ambiguity. In some 163 Articles[1] it attempts to define the role that communal government is to play, who is to do what, and how it shall be done. Subjects like communal elections, which lend themselves to tight definition, are dealt with in very precise terms, but this was impossible when it came to the powers to be exercised by the *conseil municipal*. A Commune can have from a hundred inhabitants to a million, and therefore great skill is clearly necessary to avoid either gross imposition and intolerable burdens on the smallest Communes, or the rigid constriction and sterilisation of the largest.

Parliament resolved this dilemma by ordering the *conseils municipaux* to undertake (under pain of compulsion) certain clearly defined duties which were explicitly enumerated in the law, and then by giving them a general grant of power to provide for all matters " of communal interest " as they pleased. This phrase was not defined, and the natural difficulties of interpretation will be dealt with shortly.

For those matters which the law defines as obligatory the *conseil municipal* has to allow adequate sums in its annual budget. The list contained in the law includes the maintenance of official buildings and cemeteries, the salaries and pensions of communal employees, the debt service, the expenditure imposed by law on the Commune for public assistance and public education, the maintenance of communal roads, and the expenses of the rural police and other security services (for example, contributions to the fire service). They comprise the elementary provision for the basic needs and the orderly administration of the Commune; without them local administration would collapse.

On inspection the list of obligatory duties imposed on the Commune seems sensible and balanced: the law is so framed as to meet the basic needs of both very small and very large Communes. For example, in a backward mountain area official buildings would only be the church and the school: in Bordeaux they amount to a considerable estate. A small Pyrenean Commune often does no more than pay an honora-

[1] Excluding transitional provisions for Algiers and the colonies.

rium to the Secretary of the Mayor (often the local school-master), contribute to the salaries of the *receveur particulier* and the *garde champêtre* (rural policeman) who may be shared with other Communes, maintain the church and the *Mairie* (often the school), see that no communal property is in a state of collapse, and provide a rudimentary form of street lighting. This is not unduly onerous, though it provides no scope for adventure. There are cases where the total communal budget is properly balanced at £30 or even less.[1]

On the other hand, in a large industrial urban Commune like Bordeaux, these same services cover much wider ground: a sizeable administrative organisation,[2] fire services, welfare organisations, public assistance, sanitation, public health and education are all on an incomparably greater scale and demand heavy outlay each year. In larger Communes the law sometimes imposes additional duties: for example, when a Commune has more than 20,000 inhabitants it is obliged to have a *bureau d'hygiène* and a disinfection service. As the size of the Commune increases, so do its responsibilities; but as its responsibilities increase so does the revenue with which to cover them. In this way the superficial uniformity of French local government belies its real capacity for admitting extremely wide divergences. The system has obvious disadvantages, however, since when blanket phrases such as "the expenditure imposed by law for public education" are used, the exact obligation of a particular Commune may be open to doubt.

For example, there have recently been several cases of Mayors and *conseils municipaux* in Catholic Communes refusing to obey, or resigning in protest against, decisions of the Prefects instructing them to keep open the state schools when most of the children go to church schools. The Mayor of Longeron (Maine-et-Loire), for instance, resigned rather than carry out the Prefect's order to keep the school open even though it only had

[1] P. Doueil: *L'Administration locale à l'épreuve de la guerre.* Toulouse, 1948; Appendix. He gives two complete budgets where all obligatory expenditure has been met, one of £35 and the other of £200.

[2] In the larger Communes there is a state police force, but local authorities are allowed to raise their own force for local duties, known also as *gardes champêtres*.

one pupil and was costing the Commune £20 a year for heating and maintenance.[1] Behind all educational issues there lurks the shadow of the Church and State controversy, and this is very dangerous ground for apportioning praise or blame.

When these conflicts of interpretation arise the local authorities are fully entitled to go to law in the administrative courts. In a later chapter of this book the work of these courts and the rules they apply will be examined. An extremely detailed body of case law has been built up by the *Conseil d'État* which covers most contingencies likely to arise, and the problem of interpretation is not in fact (at least from the legal point of view) as fraught with difficulties as it might appear to be.

The *conseil municipal* must meet obligatory expenditure. However, the right to initiate, control, administer or terminate any service of communal interest, or to make grants to other bodies, is entirely within its jurisdiction. The vagueness of the phrase " of communal interest " allows for adjustment to fit all types of Commune; it is merely indicative of the criterion to be followed by a local authority in considering a new service. It avoids the need to legislate in detail and to grant specific powers before anything can be done. It is probably the only type of legal phraseology which would work, given the enormous span between the smallest and the largest Communes, but it is even more difficult to interpret than the test of obligation.

Normally, in the case of making grants to other bodies, the *Conseil d'État* merely asks whether, in these particular circumstances, this is or is not in the particular interest of the inhabitants of the Commune. But the great variety of cases and the complexity of the administrative case law evolved by the *Conseil d'État* on this question illustrates the difficulty of applying any one simple test. The *Conseil d'État* has never attempted to draw up a list of what it will accept; it will give only particular judgements and no prior rulings. It has refused to allow a Commune to pay subscriptions to a schoolmasters' federation, to a religious body with political aims or to a rent-payers' association. A Commune may not insure its Mayor against personal liability, use communal funds for sending ambulances to Republican Spain, nor support the activities

[1] Reported in *Le Monde:* February 7, 1950.

of the Partisans of Peace. On the other hand, a Commune has been allowed to grant money to the widow of a municipal councillor who died in a concentration camp, on the grounds that this was a patriotic example of genuine communal interest. Grants to strikers have led to many actions before the administrative courts, and nowadays such grants are usually allowed, provided that the money is distributed through the welfare centres (*bureaux de bienfaisance*), subject to the ordinary tests of need.

The question of public services of communal interest raises yet further difficulties. They can be provided in three ways: either the Commune itself runs the service as a monopoly (*en régie*), or it grants a virtual monopoly to a private contractor (*concession*), or it participates financially in a private company (*entreprise d'économie mixte*). The *régie municipale* is subject to certain well-defined rules: it must have the prior approval of a central authority, usually the *Conseil d'État*. Three-quarters of its board of administration are appointed by the Mayor and the remainder by the Prefect, and the director of the *régie* is appointed by the Mayor with the Prefect's approval. The Mayor represents the *régie* in legal actions, and the *conseil municipal* must approve major questions of policy and pass its accounts.

A *concession* to a private contractor is also subject to strict rules. In principle, the contractor operates at his own risk, and is liable for any losses incurred. The terms of the contract must enumerate the services to be provided, the charges to be imposed, and the duration of the *concession*. The contract can also grant a virtual monopoly; it may stipulate that the local authority shall refuse to grant any other concession for similar services, and if the authority should grant any permits, licences, or facilities which it could legally refuse, that would be a breach of contract. The contract may also provide for the local authority to guarantee the contractor against loss.

A Commune may participate financially in an existing private firm by taking up ordinary or debenture shares. In the latter case the Commune cannot hold more than 40 per cent of the capital shares issued, and it must have adequate representation on the board of administration.

In 1945 the Minister of the Interior set up the *Conseil National des Services Publics Départementaux et Communaux* to prepare model contracts and standard charge sheets for public services.[1] Public authorities and contractors with concessions of public services had to adjust their charges to conform to the standard rates. In the event of disagreement between the local authority and a contractor the matter was forwarded to the *Conseil d'État* for its view, and the Minister of the Interior was empowered where necessary to alter the terms of the contract. In several cases unduly onerous contracts were changed to prevent the exploitation of the citizens by the contractor, and sometimes a contractor was relieved of a contract that threatened his solvency.

Before a *conseil municipal* can set up a new public utility service in the Commune on grounds of public interest, it must obtain the permission of the *Conseil d'État*. The test of " communal interest " is even more difficult to define in this field than in that of grants to already existing bodies and institutions. The intervention of a public authority in industrial and commercial activities is beset by the snares of divergent political philosophies and local antagonisms, and to leave such decisions to the will of local authorities is to run considerable dangers. Parliament would have been faced with an impossible task had it attempted to lay down fixed terms in such an extremely varied field of activities, and with such differences in the needs and strength of local authorities. In place of detailed legislation, therefore, Parliament subordinated the decisions of the local authorities to the prior agreement of the *Conseil d'État*.

The *Conseil d'État* has approached the problem of providing commercial and industrial services in the light of two broad guiding principles. First, the citizen should never be deprived unreasonably of his right to trade and manufacture ; and second, no particular service should be created in such a way as to threaten the financial stability of the Commune.

For a long time the *Conseil d'État* was very strict in its definition of what comprised a public service, and, basing its jurisprudence on a law of 1791, leant heavily towards the right of the citizen to trade freely without the threat of competition

[1] *Ordonnance:* February 24, 1945.

from local authorities. Nevertheless, even when this doctrine was at its most rigorous, the *Conseil d'État* granted authority to local bodies to undertake services on their own account provided that one of four conditions was fulfilled: (a) that private enterprise had failed to provide the particular service in question, (b) that although private enterprise had undertaken to provide such a service, the result was inefficient and inadequate to meet the demands properly made upon it, (c) that as a matter of fact the service was already run as a monopoly, (d) that the creation of a monopoly was the only practicable method of organising the service efficiently. In the presence of any one of these conditions in a Commune, the *Conseil d'État* would be prepared to receive an application for the creation of a new service by communal authorities.

The *Conseil d'État* has greatly modified the rigour of its old doctrine in the last twenty years. On the one hand it has always been prepared to adapt its judgements to fit current social and legal conceptions; on the other hand, the legislator specifically intervened in this field to authorise local authorities to provide new services and amenities; for example, communal authorities are legally empowered to set up municipal abattoirs (very common in medium-sized Communes), to provide a communal service of *pompes funèbres*, to build cheap and medium-priced dwellings for their inhabitants, and to arrange for cheap restaurants for artisans. The *Conseil d'État* has also accepted a wider definition of public welfare and has sanctioned municipal baths, communal dispensaries, technical institutes, and has even allowed a communal cinema on educational grounds. The new doctrine now appears to be so elastic that Professor Rolland[1] notes that in recent cases the *Conseil d'État* no longer applies the test of adequate provision but of adequate and efficient provision, and if this double test is not met then the communal authorities will be empowered to enter the field and provide their own service. Similarly, the conception of public welfare is nowadays so wide that communal authorities have a general warrant to intervene whenever they feel that the needs of their inhabitants are not being met. This is naturally a great stimulus to a progressive local authority, and it is one of the

[1] Rolland: op. cit., p. 222.

D

best instances of the flexibility of the system of French local government. Today all the normal public utilities, water, the distribution of gas and electricity, transport, the disposal of household refuse, funerals, housing, and the public welfare services, are often run *en régie* by the Communes themselves: there is no general rule as to what services to expect in any particular Commune.

In all, the obligatory services are carefully defined, and so framed as to meet the needs of all types and sizes of Communes, without imposing too great a burden on the weak and yet never allowing the larger authorities to neglect the essentials of local administration. Optional services, on the other hand, are very loosely defined, and great variations are admitted between Communes. Probably this is the only method by which so rationalised and uniform a system of local government can be made to work.

Syndicat Intercommunal

The problem that remains is to ensure that the smallest and poorest authorities are able to provide those services which involve large outlay. Without such provision the small authorities would be condemned perpetually to exist with the bare minimum of amenities.

There are two means by which a local authority can undertake services beyond its individual capacity. The first is to grant a concession to a private firm or industry to undertake the service; the second is to join together with other Communes to form a *syndicat intercommunal*. The *syndicat intercommunal* is in many ways similar to the English joint board, and in rural areas of France it is an important element in local administration.

A *syndicat* is formed when two or more Communes agree to associate together to provide a particular service. This agreement is drawn up and voted upon by the respective *conseils municipaux* and is then submitted to the Prefect and the *conseil général* of the Department. This latter body decides whether or not permission shall be given to proceed. Communes outside that Department can also be admitted to the same *syndicat* provided that the constituent Communes and the other *conseil général* agree. Certain compulsory powers to force a reluctant Commune into association are now possessed by the *Conseil d'État*, and appeals can also be made to this body by the *conseils municipaux* against refusals on the part of the *conseil général*.

Once formed, the *syndicat* acquires the status of a corporate personality with its own property and revenue, and it can sue or be sued in its own name. The general direction of its affairs is in the hands of an administrative committee, composed of two delegates elected by each *conseil municipal*, regardless of size, making up the *syndicat*. There is no restriction as to who should be the communal representatives, but one is generally the Mayor.

The *syndicat* exercises over the establishments, factories or commercial enterprises included in its charge the same rights of discipline, production and planning as does the *conseil municipal* over a purely communal service. The *syndicat*'s capital and revenue consist of those enterprises handed over to it by the Communes at the time of its formation, and of contributions by the participating Communes made each year according to individual resources.

Syndicats are normally formed in respect of only one service, which in a large number of cases is water: but other services may be undertaken with the agreement of the member Communes, and in 1947 M. Blum suggested the creation of *syndicats généraux* to undertake all common services.[1] No steps have so far been taken in this direction, but it seems to offer considerable possibilities.

The *syndicats* exercise a considerable influence on local life. They include all forms of industrial, commercial and social services. In 1937 there were altogether 2,168 *syndicats*, and of the 38,009 Communes of France 24,054 (63%) belonged to at least one *syndicat;* 1,986 *syndicats*, combining together 22,903 Communes, were for public utilities such as gas, water, electricity and transport. The striking thing about these figures is the proportion of rural Communes to urban Communes, some 97 per cent. This reflects the desire of the urban Communes to cope with their own problems, and to benefit from the profits

[1] Doueil: op. cit., p. 197.

which should accrue from public services; it also reflects their suspicion that they would contribute unfairly and be openly penalised by the condition that each Commune in a *syndicat* whatever its population has exactly the same number of representatives on the administrative board.

There are several practical difficulties in the way of extending this system. The peasantry of a rural Commune have little regard for the amenities of the urban part of the Commune, and see little reason why money should be spent on, for example, providing running water in the towns. Where there are several large land owners, all communal expenditure is subjected by them to rigorous scrutiny, and economy tends to be the sole criterion. In face of this, local officials, whose task it should be to recommend beneficial measures to the attention of the elected authority, find that their councillors regard them with distrust if they are too forthright, and they are suspected of seeking favour in the eyes of the Prefect and Sub-Prefect, gentlemen whom the local politicians regard with deferential distrust. Much of the best work done in the field of *syndicats intercommunaux* has been the direct result of the personal influence of the Mayor of the big town of the neighbourhood, but success depends more often upon the importance of his contacts in administrative and legislative quarters than upon the value of the work he suggests or upon the personal esteem in which he is held.[1]

Certain *syndicats intercommunaux* have very creditable records. The *syndicat* of the Communes of Toulon and La Seyne has since the war constructed a drainage system costing over a milliard[2] francs, and various *syndicats* in the Department of Seine-et-Oise have spent more than 1,200 million francs (about £1,200,000) on schemes of modernisation. But these tend to be notable exceptions and they are all predominantly urban Communes, free from the drag of peasant opinion and apathy.[3]

From the point of view of finance, the State and the Department generally supply something between 60 per cent and 80

---

[1] Martial Charrier: *La Vie Départementale. Revue Administrative;* January/February, 1950.

[2] A milliard is a thousand million.

[3] Martial Charrier: op. cit.

per cent of the capital for large-scale schemes. This participation is exceedingly valuable, and without it the *syndicat* would frequently find it all but impossible to begin work. But even this assistance has its drawbacks, since many peasants of the rural areas regard with suspicion any intervention in communal affairs by outside authorities.

There are methods by which a Commune can be forced into a *syndicat intercommunal* against its wishes by judgement of the *Conseil d'État*, but this inevitably involves local political difficulties for the Prefect, and in the present conditions of financial stringency the Ministry of Finance hardly welcomes large scale calls upon the state budget. Two very desirable reforms would be a greater use of the power of compulsion, and the elimination of the statutory regulation requiring equal representation upon the boards of control. Several responsible writers look upon these steps as inevitable, since the *syndicat*, properly used, is extremely well-fitted to the needs of French local authorities.

Section de Commune

It is evident that on occasions an existing Commune can become too small to provide even the minimum requirements of local administration. In such circumstances, the law[1] provides that it can then ask to be incorporated with its neighbour. It becomes a *section* of that Commune, and loses its separate identity altogether, with one reservation. This is that the property possessed by the *section* when it is incorporated can only be used for the benefit of its own inhabitants, and cannot be disposed of by the Commune without the express consent of the representatives of the *section*. The *section* is represented by a *commission syndicale*, whose election can be sought either by the inhabitants of the *section* itself, or by the Sub-Prefect, should matters arise in which the *section* is required to give a corporate opinion. Such matters are all concerned with the use, disposal or acquisition of property held in the *section*'s name. If the *conseil municipal* and the *commission syndicale* disagree on a proposal, the Prefect decides. The *section* possesses a legal personality in order that it may, if necessary, sue the Commune to which it belongs.

[1] *Ordonnance:* November 2, 1945.

A *section* is created by an ordinance of the Prefect if the *conseil municipal* of each of two adjoining Communes agrees and if the opinion of the *conseil général* is favourable. In other cases the decision is given in a Decree of the *Conseil d'État*, after detailed examination of the territorial and financial questions involved, and after all the interested parties have put their case. The original request for the change can be made either by one of the *conseils municipaux* concerned, or by a third of the electors in the area under discussion.

The creation of a *section* is the ultimate way out of the impasse which is encountered when a Commune is unable to provide adequate services. In the past this power has been used very sparingly, as can be seen from the number of very small Communes still in existence. Reformers have been pressing in recent years for a greater use of the *section* in order to create strong and viable local units.

Powers of Decision

In some fields the decisions of the *conseil municipal* require no further sanction to become operative, but in several very important matters the decision is subject to the approval of the tutelage authority, whether that be the Prefect, Sub-Prefect, *Conseil d'État* or Minister. Following its general principle, the Law of 1884 precisely defined those matters which were subject to further examination, and left unspecified those free of control.

Anything concerned with the acquisition or sale of communal property; changes in street names, alignment, abolition or widening of communal roads; raising loans; setting up markets; participation in industrial or commercial services; the creation of new communal monopolies; and, most important of all, the communal budget itself, requires ratification by the appropriate tutelage authority.[1]

Two points need stressing. First, the power of initiative in all matters not made obligatory by law[2] belongs entirely to the *conseil municipal*. Thus, the creation of services, the grant of

---

[1] Who this is in the various cases will be dealt with in the chapter on tutelage.

[2] See above, p. 44.

leases, proposals to join a *syndicat intercommunal*, and so on, are dependent on the *conseil municipal*. Its decisions may eventually be over-ridden, but no one else can take the initiative. Second, communal property is always under the *conseil's* control, and (provided that obligatory expenditure has been met) no other authority can dispose of communal funds against its wishes. Between them these two points constitute the *conseil municipal's* greatest and most effective political weapon, as will be seen later.

The importance of the powers of the *conseil municipal* should not be underestimated because of the ratification and supervision to which they are subjected. Many of the services which the State would consider desirable in a perfect world are incapable of realisation on political and economic grounds because of the strength of the communal authorities.[1] Principles may be established by law, but their realisation depends on the discretion of the *conseil municipal*, which has the power to judge when, and under what conditions, construction or execution should be undertaken. The total effect of this is considerable. Something approaching 350,000 buildings are communal property, and communal authorities are responsible for 283,000 kilometres of highways and lanes. The suspicions and reaction that cause difficulties in forming new *syndicats* in rural areas also hinder necessary development.

After a *conseil municipal* has taken a decision on any subject, the resolution must be sent by the Mayor to the Prefect or Sub-Prefect (whichever is the competent tutelage authority) within a week. This is done in order, first, to ensure that an up-to-date record of all decisions is available in the Prefecture, and second, to make the Prefect (or his subordinate) responsible for deciding the category of the decision, rather than leaving that to the *conseil municipal*. Those which require ratification by the tutelage authority are thereafter treated differently from those within the competence of the *conseil municipal*.

When the decision of a *conseil municipal* does not require further approbation, it becomes executory after a fortnight;

[1] Roger Farçat: *Le problème de l'équipement des collectivités locales. Revue Administrative*, September/October, 1950 ; p. 458. M. Farçat is a *sous-directeur* in the Ministry of the Interior.

provided, of course, that it has not been challenged on legal grounds: for all decisions can be quashed if there is any legal fault with them. The decision must not be *ultra vires* or in conflict with a law or decree, it must have been taken at a properly authorised meeting of the *conseil*, and it must not have been taken in the presence of a councillor who was an interested party. If any of these rules have been broken the Prefect will annul the decision, subject to an appeal to the *Conseil d'État*.

When the decision is subject to prefectoral approval, tacit approval may be assumed if he (or the Sub-Prefect) has remained silent on the subject for a period of forty days. This procedure of consent by default is very rarely used. The decision becomes executory within a week of the Prefect's approval being given. When the tutelage authority is the Minister or the *Conseil d'État*, the period which must elapse before tacit approval can be assumed is three months, except for cases involving concessions of public services when the period is six months.

The most important part of the work of the *conseil municipal* is the preparation and voting of the budget, and consequently the Prefect's powers of tutelage over its form and content are particularly important. If the budget approved by the *conseil municipal* is not balanced, if obligatory expenditure has not been met, or if matters not properly of communal interest have been included, then the Prefect returns the budget to the Mayor within a fortnight, with a request that the *conseil municipal* make such changes in it as are required to make it acceptable. Within ten days the Mayor must call a special meeting of the *conseil municipal* to consider the budget again; within a week of this meeting the budget must be returned to the Prefect (or Sub-Prefect). If it is still presented in an unacceptable form, the Prefect can make the necessary alteration on his own authority. He can reject items of optional expenditure or reduce the credits allowed for certain items, but unless new funds have to be found to meet obligatory expenditure he cannot impose new financial burdens on the Commune by levying new taxes or raising existing rates. The ratification of the budget raises fine points of law and politics, and these will be dealt with in the appropriate chapter. Here, it is merely necessary to recall that the power of initiative belongs to the *conseil municipal* alone, and that " obligatory " expenditure by no means covers all the matters which nowadays are taken for granted in a modern community. The Prefect's task on these occasions is very delicate and fraught with political difficulties, and tutelage involves questions of policy and finesse that are often overlooked by writers on the subject.

A Prefect's refusal to approve a decision of a *conseil municipal* is always subject to appeal. If it is a matter involving legal powers the *Conseil d'État* is the appropriate higher authority, and it is from these appeals that most of the administrative case-law of local government has been developed. It is a most important factor in local government that the Mayor can, when directed to do so by his *conseil municipal*, appeal against the Executive. The Prefect's case has then to be presented in court in the same circumstances as that of the Commune, and for all the special position of the *Conseil d'État* as an administrative court, it shows the Executive little tenderness and will require the submission of all the relevant documents on pain of assuming as true the plaintiff's version of the case.

Appeals to the Minister can be made when the Prefect has in all respects acted within his powers. In these circumstances a legal axiom holds that actions involving the discretion of the administrative agent can only be over-ruled by the possession of greater powers of discretion; these reside with the agent's superior, and for the Prefect this is the Minister of the Interior. The Minister can accept, reverse or amend the Prefect's decision.[1]

Normally, an appeal can only be made to one of these two authorities; either to the *Conseil d'État* or to the Minister. Certainly an appeal to the court on legal grounds is on surer footing than an appeal to the Minister, whose views about the expediency of a measure will tend to coincide with those of his Prefect. But even when appeal to the Minister fails, local authorities are quite prepared to invent other methods of protest

[1] Sometimes a law explicitly grants the Prefect the authority to take a decision. In pure law the Minister is then unable to override his Prefect, but since the Minister can dismiss a Prefect at will it is evident that he can in fact bring considerable pressure to bear on his subordinate. In practice, it is rare for the Minister to intervene.

to make public their displeasure. For example, when the *conseil municipal* of Bayeux recently proposed to return to the local seminary as a gift a large number of books on canon law and theology which had been taken from it in 1908 and were now communal property, the Prefect refused to give his approval.[1] This was within his discretion (viz. disposal of communal property), and the Prefect not unnaturally saw the Church and State controversy influencing local politics. Immediately, the *conseil municipal* proposed to raise the grant paid by the Commune to the Church educational authorities for school-leaving prizes from £28 to £50, but the Prefect (who supervises budgetary expenditure) insisted that £28 was quite enough, and struck the new item from the budget. The *conseil municipal* retorted by declaring that no councillor would give the prizes away or attend the prize-giving ceremony at the state school, and the Mayor roundly declared that as far as it lay in his power he would suspend all work in hand which was being financed by the Commune designed to improve the amenities and conditions of the state school. The state school's lavatory was fair revenge for the seminary's library.

In many small Communes politics play a very minor role, yet even there the political basis of the *conseil municipal* cannot be completely ignored. This curious mixture of politics and administration runs right through French government, and it is especially exemplified in the person of the Mayor, who is, by virtue of his election, the political representative of the Commune, but as the executive head of the Commune is in several particulars the administrative subordinate of the Prefect.

THE MAYOR

The Mayor is the Commune's executive; and as such he has a threefold responsibility. First, he puts into effect the decisions of the *conseil municipal* and is responsible to that body for the way he acts in this respect. Second, the law makes him personally responsible for ensuring the public security, morality and hygiene (*salubrité*) of the Commune (*police municipale*). Third, he has to perform administrative tasks devolved upon him by the State, normally comprising the preparation and compilation

[1] Reported in *Le Monde*, 30 June, 1949.

of reports, statistics, and registers. In the last two cases he comes under the administrative control of the Prefect, and the *conseil municipal* cannot interfere with his activities. In this section we shall deal solely with his relations with his *conseil municipal* and with those duties for which he is responsible to that body and not to the Prefect.

The Mayor is responsible to the *conseil municipal* for administering the Commune, for putting the *conseil's* decisions into effect, and for representing its views and interests before the courts and before the administration. However, his position *vis-à-vis* the *conseil municipal* is not so simple as might at first appear, partly because for more than half his time he is acting as agent of the State independently of the *conseil municipal*. In addition, as executive head of the Commune, he is responsible for the discipline and efficiency of communal employees, he alone can draw up the Commune's budget, he can, on his own initiative, take any measures necessary for the safety and protection of communal property, and he is personally responsible for the collection of communal taxes and revenue; these facts all add to his stature. All executive power involves some exercise of discretion, and in the case of the Mayor the question is whether his discretion goes so far as to nullify in practice his legal subordination to the *conseil municipal*, or whether the *conseil* can always ultimately insist upon its will being made effective whatever the Mayor personally desires. The answer to this question brings out the subtle relations that can exist between French local authorities.

To take the example of a matter where the Mayor is subordinate to the *conseil municipal*: if the Town Hall needs repainting the *conseil municipal* must lay down the form that invitations for tender must take, it can specify the terms that must be met, and it judges between rival tenders and decides which to accept. Throughout these operations the Mayor is passive, except of course in so far as he has personal influence in the discussions, and this comes more from his personality than from his position. He is bound by the terms of reference laid down by the *conseil municipal*, and he has no option as to the terms of the contract or the choice of the successful applicant.

The position changes when the next stage is reached. If

practical difficulties arise, for example, if the contract is not properly fulfilled, then the Mayor, being responsible for the proper use of communal money, possesses sufficient authority to be able to prod the contractor into performing his work satisfactorily. His actions will be subject to later justification before the *conseil municipal* and his decisions although discretionary cannot be arbitrary. He is now no mere passive figure; he has day-to-day discretion, although subject to *a posteriori* control.

This freedom is sometimes extended a little further. The Mayor may be authorised by the *conseil municipal* to go to law in a case affecting communal interests. Once this decision is made the Mayor's freedom of action automatically increases. As the legal representative of the Commune he has to choose legal advisers and counsel, and he draws up the Commune's case with them. This is entirely within his discretion, and the *Conseil d'État* has ruled that the Mayor can even decide whether or not to carry the case to appeal without further reference to the *conseil municipal*. Even the *a posteriori* control is here wearing a little thin.

The final stage is reached when, as must frequently happen, the *conseil municipal* empowers the Mayor to decide when and under what circumstances its decision shall be put into effect. For example, the *conseil municipal* may allow a credit to repave the Rue Bonaparte and instruct the Mayor to commence operations when the surface of the road becomes too bad. The *conseil municipal* would find it very difficult indeed to question the Mayor's right to act at any particular time, since they have made their decision subordinate to his judgement.[1]

The Mayor has the same degrees of freedom as regards his financial powers. He alone can prepare the communal budget, and what he puts in or leaves out is his entire responsibility. The *conseil municipal* however has full powers to amend, reject or approve any item on the budget. The Mayor has no special authority in this matter by virtue of his office, and only his personality and prestige give weight to his voice. However, his

---

[1] For a detailed discussion on this point see J. Rivero: *Le Maire, exécuteur des délibérations du conseil municipal. Revue critique de législation et de jurisprudence;* 1937; pp. 535–605.

initiative returns once the budget is voted. He is responsible for
authorising expenditure from communal funds, and for ensuring
the legality and correctness of the Commune's financial account.
He may thus decide when and in what order work shall be
dealt with, and, although limited by the decisions of the *conseil
municipal* as to the total sum to be spent under any one heading,
he can reallocate that sum between the items under that heading
by transferring credits from one item to another.[1] This is no
empty power. The provisions of the budget will be executed
throughout the following year and it will be for the Mayor to
make any necessary adaptations to meet changing circumstances. If the Mayor does not in fact spend the credit allowed
by the *conseil municipal* the only result is that the communal
budget will end the financial year with a favourable balance, and
since the examination of the Mayor's accounts is restricted to
questioning and proving the legality of the various entries, there
is no official way of introducing the problem of the unused
credit, although ingenuity can sometimes find a way round this.

The *conseil municipal* often finds it difficult to phrase its
decision so clearly that the Mayor cannot find a loophole if he
desires. It is very difficult on some occasions to distinguish
between the additions which he makes to a motion in order to
make it properly effective, and those deliberately calculated to
change its whole tenor. The *Conseil d'État* will support a *conseil
municipal* if it can prove that the Mayor acted with deliberate
malice, but the possibility of proving this will depend on circumstances and the Mayor's astuteness. The Mayor can always
plead delays of procedure, difficulties raised by third parties
and consideration for their rights, and the financial complications likely to arise from hasty action. A judicious use of such
arguments can lead eventually to a virtual non-execution of the
conseil's wishes.[2]

Given these inherent, explicit or assumed powers of discretion, the Mayor is seldom forced into the position of blank
refusal to carry out the *conseil municipal's* decisions. If this does
happen, however, the *conseil municipal* can appeal directly to

---

[1] An example of a communal budget is given on pp. 193-4, and the
principal headings set forth.
[2] Rivero: loc. cit.

the Prefect to order the Mayor to carry out its orders, on the grounds that his refusal is a breach of duty, and as such liable to prefectoral intervention.[1] Where the issue is quite clear the Prefect or Sub-Prefect may exert their general tutelage powers and order the Mayor to do his duty: and in the face of continued defiance they can proceed to act for the *conseil municipal* on their own authority.

Alternatively, if the Mayor oversteps his authority, the *conseil municipal* can appeal to the law. It may show that the Mayor has acted *ultra vires*, and the administrative courts will then annul the Mayor's decision. Or, if the Mayor has gone much too far, the *conseil municipal* can claim compensation from the Mayor personally, by making him civilly responsible for the illegal work done on his orders. If a court finds that the Mayor has used his powers corruptly by showing personal favour or by acting maliciously, it will hold him personally liable for the cost of the work done or the damage suffered. If, however, the court finds that he has indeed acted illegally but that this was done in good faith for the Commune's benefit, it will dismiss the case and the Commune itself will have to pay any damages incurred. The test is therefore one of good faith against malice, error of judgment against corrupt intent.

The appeal to the courts and the appeal to the Prefect are the technical methods by which the *conseil municipal* can seek protection from its own Mayor. But the real balance lies in the political nature of much communal government. The *conseil municipal* can make the Mayor's position untenable; and should he refuse to resign when he loses the support of his majority the *conseil* can bring communal administration to a standstill, either by opposing all measures put forward by the Mayor or by refusing to vote the communal budget. If this happens the Minister of the Interior will have to dissolve the *conseil municipal* and hold new elections, and after these the Mayor may well not be re-elected.

The Mayor and the *conseil municipal* must live together, and

[1] The Mayor can be suspended from his function by the Prefect for failing to perform his duties, and, in the last resort, dismissed from office by the Minister. On an average ten Mayors are dismissed from office every year.

the pull of party loyalty is strong, although often obscured by local personalities. The dissolution of the *conseil municipal* or the resignation of the Mayor is, in the last resort, only likely to favour their opponents.

THE CONSEIL GÉNÉRAL

The *conseil général* is the elected body of the Department, and it has a great influence in local government. Its powers are wider, its prestige greater and its powers of decision more often definitive than those of any *conseil municipal*, no matter how important or influential the town the latter may represent.

The *conseils généraux* of France have a special constitutional status which comes near to transforming them into "immediate" rather than "mediate" bodies. After the civil war of 1870, a law of the new Third Republic laid down that if at any time the National Assembly was prevented from meeting, either because an invader had captured the capital or because Parisian extremists had arrogated to themselves the sovereignty of the people, delegates of the *conseils généraux* should be convened to form an alternative assembly either until it was safe for the National Assembly to meet or until a new one had been elected.[1]

The political status of the *conseils généraux* is curious yet important. They stand somewhere between the national legislature and the communal authorities in public interest and political activity. Between two and three hundred members of the two national Assemblies are members of the *conseil général* of their Department, and they consider the increased effort and call upon their time well worth while. Despite the presence of these national politicians, however, the internal politics of the *conseil général* are often of the parish pump variety, as is proper in a local assembly, and the influence of local personalities is very marked in all its debates, motions and elections. They form a very inaccurate guide to national political affairs, but they do provide a close reflection of the real political forces in the

---

[1] Law of February 15, 1872. No use was made of this law during or after the last war, and it may be regarded as no longer fully operative. It exists, however, and in the formative days of the Third Republic it helped to increase the real importance, as well as the prestige, of the *conseils généraux*.

country. Since the Department is used as the constituency for the national elections, no party can afford to ignore departmental affairs; and indeed the Department is the ground in which the political roots of the parties are planted. No party which hopes to win mass support can succeed unless it has a substantial number of Departments in which party loyalty is strong, and in which local party machines can provide the future cadres of the party. Many Right-wing parties and groupings have no hope of mass support, and their departmental organisation is rudimentary if not non-existent; but the major parties like the Gaullists, the Communist Party, the Socialists and the MRP all have their fiefs.

The *conseils généraux* have an even more direct influence on national politics in that they form (together with the Deputies of their Departments and representatives of the Communes) the electoral colleges for the *Conseil de la République*.[1]

Composition

The *conseil général* varies in size from Department to Department, as one councillor is elected for each *canton* and the number of *cantons* is not uniform ; thus, the *conseil général* of Ille-et-Vilaine (capital Rennes) numbers 43 members, whereas the Hautes Alpes (capital Gap) has only 24. Third class Departments usually average between 20 and 30, second class Departments between 30 and 40, and first class and *hors classe* Departments anything up to the 68 of the Nord (capital Lille). The principal tension in departmental government comes from the inequality of size and population among these various *cantons*. Their boundaries were drawn up in the nineteenth century and have undergone very little modification since; consequently, today there are heavily populated urban *cantons* having equal representation with rural *cantons* including no town of any size. This reflects the traditional battle between the town and countryside, which is in many ways the fundamental division in all French politics.

Each councillor is elected for six years, and half the *conseil général* retires every third year. After the Liberation all the *conseils généraux* were re-elected in their entirety, and the

[1] Law of September 23, 1948.

Cantons were divided into two Series; the councillors representing the first Series should have stood again in 1948,[1] and those for the second Series in 1951. Elections are held throughout the country on the same days in October; the next elections will be in October, 1954, and thereafter every three years.

To be eligible a candidate must be over 25 and have either property or residential qualifications in the Department, always provided, however, that not more than a quarter of the councillors are non-resident. Holders of various offices are not eligible as candidates in the Department where they carry out their duties; amongst these are members of the *corps préfectoral*, serving officers of the Armed Forces, magistrates, police officers, the *recteur* of the Academy, state officials such as *ingénieurs*, *inspecteurs* of education and post-office officials; and no departmental employee or contractor to the Department can hold his job or contract while he is a councillor. Finally, no one can be a member of more than one *conseil général*.

A candidate is elected if he gains an absolute majority of the votes cast at the first ballot, and then only provided that a quarter of the enfranchised citizens have actually voted. If no one is successful at the first count, a second *tour* takes place on the following Sunday, and then a relative majority suffices. In the 1951 elections there were 1,515 vacant seats, of which 814 were filled at the first *tour*. The intervening week is taken up with log-rolling and local political conversations; since 1947 the manoeuvres have been frequently aimed at discovering which of the various candidates will make the best showing against the Communists.

There are, however, many exceptions to this rule; for example, in the traditionally Catholic areas of the west, Socialists and Radicals are likely to make departmental bargains in order to present the best anti-clerical front to the MRP or the Gaullists. In the central Departments there have been significant withdrawals by Communists for Socialists and *vice versa* to fight Right wing parties, and in the south east Socialists and Radicals are often in bitter competition for seats and make compacts with other parties to defeat their most dangerous

[1] In fact the elections were in May, 1949.

E

rival. Similar instances can be found of MRP candidates with-drawing in favour of Gaullists and independents. Altogether individual local conditions determine political alignments to a much greater degree than in the national elections, and no hard and fast rules can be discovered. Joint anti-Communist fronts are most frequent when a Communist arrives at the head of the first *tour*.

As in the case of the *conseil municipal*, any elector, candidate or the *conseil général* itself, can challenge the result of an election before the administrative courts, and a person who objects to the condition or procedure of an election lodges his complaint with the Prefect. The Prefect can also challenge the results on legal grounds within three weeks. This can lead to odd actions. A M. Thiriet was defeated in a by-election for the *conseil général* of Moselle (capital Metz) by a M. Rouprich. M. Thiriet protested that his opponent had unfairly swayed the election by announcing during the campaign that he had been made a *Chevalier de la Légion d'Honneur*, when in fact he had only been proposed as a candidate for the honour. Thiriet con-sidered this behaviour passed the bounds of good taste and rectitude when M. Rouprich actually decorated himself with the honour at a public function, although he had received no official warrant to do so. The *Conseil d'État* gravely annulled M. Rouprich's election for illegally wearing the decoration.[1]

Both the *conseil général* as a body and the individual coun-cillors are specially protected against arbitrary action by the Government. In theory, the Government can dissolve a *conseil général* by Decree, but the consent of the National Assembly must be obtained at the first opportunity, and arrangements for holding new elections must be put in hand immediately. No *conseil général* has been dissolved since 1874.[2] At no time, and under no conditions, can all the *conseils généraux* be dis-solved as a general measure.[3] This is a safeguard of some importance.

Normally a councillor can only be dismissed from office by the *conseil général* itself, and then only if he has absented him-

[1] Reported in *Le Monde*, 5 September, 1950.
[2] Under Vichy they were suspended not dissolved.
[3] Article 36, Law of 10 August, 1871.

self from an entire session without good cause. There are other means of removing him from office, but their use is uncommon. A councillor guilty of illegal actions or of failing to carry out his legal obligations can be dismissed from office by the *Conseil d'État* and declared ineligible for one year. If he is present at an illegal session of the *conseil général*, and refuses to obey the Prefect's order to disperse, he can be charged before the civil courts under Article 258 of the *code pénal*, and if there found guilty he is dismissed from office and is ineligible for the next three years. These conditions are probably the minimum required by the Executive to ensure the integrity of the *conseils généraux*.

Organisation

The *conseil général* holds two ordinary sessions each year, one in April and one between August and October. The first session cannot last more than a fortnight, but the second—at which the departmental budget is prepared and voted—can last up to a month. The *conseil général* can be convened for a special session by decree, by the Prefect, on the demand of its standing committee (the *commission départementale*), or at the written request of two-thirds of the councillors. The Prefect is responsible for calling these meetings after giving proper notice to all members. No special session can last for more than a fortnight, but during this time the *conseil* is free to discuss whatever it pleases: it may be convened because war has been declared, or because urgent measures are necessary to combat the Colorado beetle, but this does not limit the action of the *conseil*. Normally all sessions are public, but if five councillors, the Prefect, or the President of the *conseil général* put down a motion demanding a secret session a vote must be taken (without debate). This is rare, except in the case of departmental awards and appointments to departmental offices; for these the *conseil* is legally bound to vote in secret.

Apart from these limitations, the *conseil général* is master of its own internal organisation and standing orders.

At its August session it elects its own President for a year, and he is eligible for re-election without limit. This office is often held by a notable public figure; several *conseils généraux* are presided over by a Deputy or Senator, and the post is coveted by aspiring politicians. The Secretary and the Vice-Presidents are also elected at the August session for one year. Election to all these offices is by absolute majority, but if this is not achieved by the third ballot, a relative majority suffices. They are, of course, conducted on political lines.

A quorum for a meeting is half the total number of councillors, plus one. If at any time during the session a quorum is not present, that day's meeting is suspended until the following day, when decisions taken are executory no matter how few councillors are present. This is to prevent any systematic boycotting of the *conseil*'s work. Should the opening day of the session be marked by a boycott, the Prefect will resummon the absent councillors; if, on the third day, there is still no quorum, the *conseil* can go ahead with its duties, no matter how few councillors are present.

Although the President of the *conseil général* controls the meetings, and is empowered to expel or arrest any person who disturbs the peace, the Prefect and the Secretary-General of the Prefecture have full rights of entry to any session. Since the Prefect is the executive officer of the Department this is a necessary condition of the *conseil*'s work. An ordinary meeting of the *conseil général* presents the following picture: the council chamber is a specially appointed hall in the Prefecture, in the chair is the President, on his right the Prefect, and on his left the Secretary-General. The councillors sit by party in the forum of the council chamber, with the Secretary of the *conseil général* and the clerks in the well. Against the wall or at the back sit the various officials in the Department and the senior officers of the Prefecture, and these officers can all be called upon by the *conseil* to furnish reports on their administration and to answer any question put to them about their organisation. They can only speak with the Prefect's permission. A part of the council chamber must be reserved for the public with space for the press. In the ordinary course of events the discussions follow the normal procedure for such debates; the Prefect, as the executive officer of the Department, presents his report, and discussion follows. There is no restriction on what the *conseil* can discuss, and any aspect of departmental organisation and administration, and any branch of the State's services working in the Department, may be fully examined and criticised. The law, however, forbids a *conseil général* to vote on " political motions ". When it becomes obvious to the Prefect that such a motion is about to be put, he warns the *conseil* that it is treading on forbidden ground and must abstain. If the *conseil général* persists the Prefect rises, followed by the Secretary-General, and, escorted by the officers of the State and departmental services, he quits the chamber. The session thereupon becomes illegal and any votes taken or motions passed are null and void in law. The Prefect has the legal authority to clear the chamber by force on such occasions, but in these days such brutality is very rare, because of the standing of the *conseil général* and of the political trouble which may follow any resort to violence.

The political importance of the *conseil général* is recognised in the legal proviso that its work must receive proper publicity. The Secretary to the *conseil* is responsible not only for the ordinary minutes of the debates but also for drawing up a summary of each day's work and debate which must be made available to every newspaper in the Department within 48 hours. Further, every elector or tax-payer in the Department has the right to examine the records of the debates and decisions. The local daily press in fact sets a good standard of informed comment on the activities of the *conseil général*, and the great importance of the local press in France enhances the value of these provisions.

Powers

The competence of the *conseil général* covers not only all departmental affairs but also some aspects of communal government. It also has a watching brief over the activities of the state administrations within the Department. This forms the most convenient starting point for summarising the powers of the *conseil général*.

The relations of the *conseil général* with the state administrations are of three sorts: first, it is required by law to provide and maintain some of the buildings in which these administrations work; second, individual councillors take an active part in some administrations; finally, the *conseil général* as a body acts on the State's behalf in organising national services. The Department is called upon to provide and maintain the Prefecture and Sub-Prefectures, the offices of educational authorities, the teachers' training college, the barracks of the *gendarmerie*, the Assize Courts, civil and commercial tribunals and some types of detention quarters. Expenditure on these buildings is compulsory, but the size of credit and the order in which repairs are undertaken is, within limits laid down by the *Conseil d'État*, within the competence of the *conseil* itself.

Individual councillors are nominated for service on several state bodies operating in the Department; for example, a councillor sits on each of the military tribunals for exemption from national service. The services operated by the Department on behalf of the State include practically all branches of public assistance,[1] from grouping the Communes into hospital areas to setting up sanatoria; in this field the *conseil général* has wide powers of discretion and initiative and is really only restricted by the need to conform to a national standard; over and above that it is free.

In other fields, too, the *conseil général* has a voice in state affairs. No Minister can make grants within its Department for the upkeep of churches, charitable institutions, kindergartens or to agricultural associations without its agreement, and it is authorised to draw up the order of priority of work to be done. If it wishes, a *conseil général* can have direct access to any Minister, and through its President (not the Prefect) it can place before him any matters of special interest to the Department, and any suggestions as to the needs of state services. Although it is formally forbidden to vote upon political motions, it has power to pass motions on economic policy and on general administration, and the dividing line between economics and politics is extremely uncertain.

Finally, convention has it that the Government shall seek the *conseil*'s opinion on matters of concern to the Department as a whole, and Ministers find it politically wise and practically convenient to obey this informal injunction.

---

[1] For the administration of the public assistance and the field covered by those services, see below, pp. 108–110.

The *conseil général* has jurisdiction over certain communal services and administrations. Its most important powers here are in the field of public assistance, where it can fix the rates to be charged by hospitals in the Department, the allowances which can be made to the indigent, and the hospital areas to which the individual Communes are attached. The administration of public assistance described in the next chapter is in large part supervised by the *conseil général*.

The *conseil* also apportions the cost of intercommunal works between the participating Communes when there is any dispute, and it designates the sectors of the highways of intercommunal importance for which each Commune is responsible. Certain special texts give the *conseil général* power to fix the charges that can be levied for maintaining communal roads. It frequently has funds raised by departmental taxation at its disposal, and in several cases it has created a departmental equalisation fund, and makes general grants to the Communes in the Department in relation to their needs and wealth. The creation in 1949 of the national Equalisation Fund (*fonds de péréquation*) has given increased scope to the *conseils généraux* in the field of general finance, since it is the *conseil général* which divides the fund between the Communes in the Department, and it has considerable discretion for evaluating needs.[1]

The influence which the *conseil général* has upon the Communes within the Department is extensive; it controls almost everything which transcends the limits of one single Commune or affects all of them, and in a large proportion of cases its decision on intercommunal matters is final. Competition for seats on the *conseil général* is consequently more than a fight between political parties and personalities, it is also a struggle for influence between local authorities within the Department.

The powers of the *conseil général* in departmental affairs are even more extensive. It has the decisive voice in departmental policy and financial matters. The Prefect, acting as its executive, may propose, but the *conseil* alone disposes. The law of 1871 lists twenty-two matters on which the *conseil* has absolute and unfettered powers of discretion. The most notable items on the list are departmental property and estates, departmental high-

[1] See below, chapter 6.

ways, all schemes which are to be financed from departmental funds, the public assistance institutions in the Department and several welfare services,[1] recourse to litigation on behalf of the Department, and several aspects of public education. Naturally, the most vital of these is the sole right to decide upon expenditure from departmental funds, but the importance of many of the other items scarcely needs emphasis.

The *conseil* exercises control over departmental expenditure in two ways. At its August-October session the Prefect presents the proposed budget for the following year, together with all necessary explanatory memoranda and documents. In the ensuing discussion, the *conseil général* has the right to any further information it may require. The budget is voted chapter by chapter, and the *conseil général* makes any changes it considers desirable, either by cutting down or increasing the amount to be spent on any particular item, or by transferring credits from one item to another. An instance of the way this works in practice is given in chapter six.[2]

During this session the Prefect gives the *conseil général* a summary of the affairs of the Department and the important events since the last meeting. At the April session he provides them with a survey of the work in hand in the Department and the policy which he recommends for the coming year. At this session, also, the Prefect presents the accounts for the previous financial year, and these are examined in detail by the *conseil;* any relevant point can be raised, and the Prefect can be asked to state his authority for particular actions.

The powers of the *conseil général* are much wider than one expects to find in the hands of a local authority in what has always been regarded as a highly-centralised State. In so far as the Prefect is the *conseil's* executive officer his authority is that of personal persuasion and not of legal superiority. He can carve for himself in the Department the same degree of extra discretion as can the Mayor in the Commune, but he has less chance than the Mayor of forceful action in face of an obstinate

[1] In fact, later laws have to a large extent codified the organisation and benefits obtainable under public assistance and the discretion of the *conseil général* has consequently been restricted.

[2] See below, p. 192.

council. He rarely stays long enough in one post to acquire complete ascendency over the elected body, but he can, by personal distinction, add to the already high prestige of his office. In fact, he draws his real authority, prestige, and influence from his position as representative of the State in the Department. He possesses in his own right no powers of tutelage over the departmental assembly comparable with those he exercises over the Communes. It is the Ministers of the Interior and of Finance and the *Conseil d'État* who hold those powers of tutelage over the *conseil général;* but it is the Prefect who initiates new measures, recommends policies, and advises the Ministers.

Control

The principal forms of control exercised over the *conseils généraux* are, first, that the budget is subject to the approval of the Minister of the Interior[1]; second that certain types of expenditure must compulsorily be allowed for in the budget; and, third, that certain types of revenue can only be raised by the Department with express permission from a higher executive authority.

The Minister's tutelage powers over the Department's budget are of the same type as those of the Prefect over the communal budgets, and the same type of problem is likely to arise. The Minister can strike out expenditure on the grounds that the *conseil général* has overstepped its powers, or because it has not allowed enough for obligatory items, or because the scheme it proposes is unworkable. If the Minister's decision involves a point of law, appeal can be made to the *Conseil d'État*, but if it involves the Minister's 'discretion' then the only challenge open to the *conseil* is through political pressure in Parliament, to which the Minister in question may or may not be susceptible.

One way of changing the Minister's mind is to work out a compromise satisfactory to all parties. For example, a Minister refused to endorse departmental expenditure on roads which were legally the responsibility of the Communes, holding that this would be sanctioning an illegal act. Arrangements were therefore made by the *conseil général* to set up a *syndicat*

[1] Until August, 1950, by an interministerial decision of the Ministers of the Interior and Finance.

intercommunal of the Communes concerned, to be financed by the national Equalisation Fund available for distribution in the Department. This solution was acceptable to the Minister on legal grounds, and the scheme was put into effect.

The quarrel in this case was a technical one, and awkward political problems do not permit of this sort of compromise. The *conseil général* of the Loire Inférieure (capital Nantes) decided to allow in its budget 400,000 francs (£400) to provide scholarships for higher education to pupils of state schools, and 3,315,000 francs (£3,315) for those attending church schools. There were 6,600 pupils in the state schools and 8,620 in the church schools, and the Minister refused to sanction the expenditure on the grounds that it evinced gross favouritism, and that scholarships should be allowed in proportion to the number of pupils attending the schools; the Minister pointed especially to the 114 pupils of state schools who had been refused scholarships. The *conseil général* replied that it had based its estimates on the number of demands for assistance it received ; further, it added that it considered that the powers of tutelage had been improperly exercised and that if it did not receive satisfaction it would appeal to the *Conseil d'État*. The Minister quashed the new decision of the *conseil général* on technical grounds, since it had not prepared its decision in the correct way. The content of the new decision was not this time openly attacked, the *conseil* having taken the precaution to base it on the greater expenditure incurred in sending children to church schools. The *conseil* tried a third time, voting a general sum of 3,900,000 francs to be divided between both church and state schools, and carefully eliminated from its decision those technical errors which had been the occasion of the previous rejection. This general credit, correctly framed, was finally allowed.[1] A compromise of sorts can be detected here, since the *conseil général* established the principle of aid to church schools and then the Minister managed to eliminate the worst marks of favouritism from the decision. It is a different sort of compromise from that in the previous instance.

The obligatory expenditure which the *conseil général* is called upon to meet is principally concerned with the provision

[1] Reported in *Le Monde* ; October 6, 1950, and December 30, 1950.

of services undertaken on behalf of the State.[1] If the *conseil général* refuses to vote the necessary amounts the credits can be written into the budget by Decree on the advice of the Minister of the Interior and the Minister of Finance. The first call is upon any budget surplus, then upon the credit for unforeseen expenditure, and finally, when these two sources are not sufficient, extraordinary local taxation can be levied without the permission of the *conseil général*. This is the only condition under which an additional expense can be written into the budget without the express consent of the *conseil*. Its disadvantage is that the Department is compulsorily liable for matters which today form only a fraction of the normal departmental services, and if the Government tries a trial of strength, the *conseil général* might be provoked into refusing to vote the budget, and then only these minimum necessities could be provided for.

The Prefect's powers of supervision over the *conseil* are in fact limited to his right to question the legal validity of the *conseil's* decisions. No decision, whatever its portent, becomes fully executory until ten days after the end of the session, and during that time the Prefect can challenge it before the *Conseil d'État* on grounds of conflict with the law. If the *Conseil d'État* has not annulled the decision within six weeks, the decision becomes effective by default.

Some control, finally, is exercised by the *Conseil d'État* and the Ministries over decisions to raise revenue or capital by certain means. The Minister's approval must be obtained when loans are sought whose date of repayment is over thirty years or when a loan is above a certain size,[2] and certain types of extraordinary local taxes require the prior approval of the *Conseil d'État*.

These forms of legal control seem to be the minimum possible, and it would be difficult to find equal tenderness for local authorities in Britain in recent years. It also seems to belie, by its emphasis on central control, the importance generally given to the local position of the Prefect. Nevertheless, the Prefect

[1] These are enumerated on pp. 70, 107. Also, for further details see sample budget, p. 191.
[2] The exact figure tends to change.

still remains the pivot of departmental life, and he is a figure of first rate importance.

This introduces a curious sidelight on recent French local government. The system described above, although legally enforced, is in conflict with several articles in the Constitution. For the Constituent Assembly, under pressure from the Left, wrote into the new Constitution an article which said that local collectivities were to " administer themselves freely by Councils elected by universal suffrage " (Article 87), and that the execution of their decisions was to be " assured by their Mayor or their President ". The Prefect's part was limited to representing the State and " supervising " (i.e. exercising tutelage over) local authorities. Therefore constitutionally the Prefect should no longer be the executive of the Department, but only the representative of the State.

The practical steps necessary to put this system into effect were to be laid down by further organic laws, but these laws have never been passed.[1] In 1947 and in 1948, draft *projets de loi* were presented to the National Assembly, one to organise the new bases of decentralised local government, and the other to arrange for the maximum deconcentration of state powers to the state representatives in the Departments. These two *projets* were taken together by the same Commission of the National Assembly (M. Dreyfus being the *rapporteur*), and a report was presented to the Assembly on February 17, 1949. M. Dreyfus suggested that both proposals be taken at the same time, but the Government, and especially M. Moch, Minister of the Interior, objected to this as the text of the revised *projet* for the decentralisation of executive powers to the President of the *conseil général* had several points " which particularly endangered the authority and permanence of the State". After a confused debate, the National Assembly refused to pass to the discussion of the details of the Bill, and the Government, holding that it had therefore been rejected, withdrew the Bill and

---

[1] Since none have been passed, Article 105 is presumably the operative constitutional article. But even this states that when the Prefect acts as representative of the Department his actions are permanently subject to the supervision of the President of the *conseil général*. This too remains a dead letter.

promised to present a new one later on. A new one has never appeared, although several individual Deputies have put *propositions de loi* before the Assembly without success.[1] This stalemate is probably fatal to the hopes of the more fervent supporters of decentralisation.

There are several reasons behind this refusal. The fundamental political motive has, in several Departments, and notably in the industrial Northern ones, been that Red " fiefs " would be created if the President of the *conseil général* exercised the powers now held by the Prefect as executive head of the Department.

Moreover, there are many valid administrative objections to the proposals. The Prefect depends for his accommodation and living quarters upon the Department, and if he had no proper hold over the *conseil*, would it not be possible for his rooms in the Prefecture to be taken over one evening for the local ball ? (A Prefect's question, not the author's.) In several instances, the Presidents of the *conseil général* have been strongly opposed to the suggestion of increased responsibilities. They would be required to undertake many administrative duties, which at the present moment demand all the attention of a highly-skilled and intelligent professional. The President of a *conseil général* often has his own business or job, and he could not do both. The removal of the steadying influence of the Prefect would also tempt local politicians to play for popularity, and to use the departmental administrative services for their own ends. Indeed, the proposed reform would only work if the Prefect had his powers of tutelage extended as state representative over the decisions of the *conseil général;* but this would defeat the purposes of the reform which is supposed to lead to greater local freedom.

In fact the *conseil général* has quite enough real power to overcome its Prefect in the event of violent conflict. The Prefect of the Var (capital Draguignan) decided on ministerial instructions to force his *conseil général* to act in strict accordance with the law, since it had been consistently exceeding its proper

[1] For details of these *propositions de loi* see J. Gandouin: *La Constitution et la Réforme de l'organisation départementale et communale.* Thesis for Doctorate ; Faculty of Law, Paris. 1950.

powers. His attitude led to many skirmishes in the council chamber and conflicts over the budget, and eventually the *conseil général* publicly accused the Prefect of acting in bad faith and being a disloyal collaborator. All parties in the *conseil* approved the statement and they decided to meet no more while the Prefect sat in the same room. Within a month the Prefect of the Var was transferred and replaced by the Prefect of Doubs (capital Besançon). Even when backed by the Minister therefore a Prefect can be forced into an untenable position by a hostile and determined *conseil*. Only a succession of forceful and authoritative Prefects can remedy such situations.

The position and status of the *conseil général* are fundamental to the whole local government system, and in its dealings with the Administration both are put to the test of sanity and realism. Departmental government furnishes the clearest example of the subtle and supple nature of French law.

THE COMMISSION DÉPARTEMENTALE

This body might be called, rather inaccurately, the permanent standing committee of the *conseil général*. It has a proper legal status but its importance is restricted by measures designed to ensure that it never challenges the *conseil général* for effective supremacy, and never competes with the Prefect in the administration of the Department. It was the child of a compromise in 1871 between the decentralisers and the centralisers: the result was a body able to keep a watching brief over the Prefect during the time when the *conseil général* was not in session, but never able to supersede either Prefect or *conseil* in their functions.

The *commission départementale* is a collegiate body elected by and from the *conseil général*, and it has from four to seven councillors according to the size of the *conseil*: where possible, a councillor is chosen from each *arrondissement*. It is elected annually at the August session, and it meets of right once a month, and more often if specially convened by the Prefect; its principal powers are those explicitly devolved to it by the *conseil général*. To prevent it from rivalling or hampering the Prefect in the course of his duties, Deputies, Senators and the Mayor of the departmental capital are forbidden to serve on the *commission*.

The powers granted to the *commission* by law are limited in number and importance; where the *conseil général* has allowed sums for unforeseen expenditure in its budget, the *commission* decides how and when these sums shall be spent, and the Prefect must have its authorisation before he can call upon this fund. It also authorises payments from the sums accruing from police fines, and from the money raised by loan at the order of the *conseil général*, provided, of course, that the purposes to which the money is put are consonant with those for which the *conseil* raised the loan. The *commission* is also responsible for fixing the order of priority in which departmental work shall be done, unless the *conseil général* has explicitly reserved this right to itself.

Its principal administrative duty is to examine the Prefect's accounts each month, and to check his expenditure against the authorisations voted in the departmental budget. He can be required to supply information and the documents relevant to such expenditure. The Prefect must also lay his draft budget for the Department before the *commission* at least ten days before the opening day of the *conseil*'s session, and the *commission* then draws up its own report on these proposals to lay before the full body. This preliminary examination enables the *conseil* to concentrate upon controversial and debatable proposals without delay, in the knowledge that its own representatives have already extracted the essence. It is in this field that the *commission départementale* can accurately be described as a standing committee; similarly, the agenda proposed for the *conseil général* by the Prefect must first be laid before the *commission*, sufficiently long in advance for it to be able to prepare its report. The *conseil général* is saved much time by this procedure, and any hasty or unconsidered action at the Prefect's instigation is entirely its own fault.

Apart from these matters, and a small number of trivial subjects, the *commission départementale* is dependent on the *conseil général* for its powers. There are virtually no restrictions upon matters that can be devolved upon it, provided that such powers are within the *conseil*'s competence, and that the powers so devolved do not constitute the *raison d'être* of the *conseil général*. The departmental budget, the ratification of the Prefect's accounts and the right to alter the budget can never be delegated. The only other limitation on the devolution of powers is that whole categories of subjects cannot be devolved, but only individual matters specified by name : that is, " the decoration of primary schools " cannot be devolved, but " the decoration of the primary school in the Rue Bonaparte " can be.

The relations between the *commission départementale* and the Prefect are peculiar. If at any time the Prefect and the *commission* disagree over the expediency of one of their decisions, the Prefect can refuse to act until the *conseil général* has discussed it; this meeting may be several months ahead and for that period no action can be taken. If the Prefect should desire, he could convene a special session of the *conseil général* to discuss the matter, and if the *conseil général* agreed with him it could dismiss its own *commission départementale* on the spot and elect a new one. The *commission*'s subordination is evident.

Even in purely legal matters this inferior status is maintained. If the Prefect appeals to the *Conseil d'État* against a decision of the *commission* on legal grounds, the appeal automatically suspends execution.[1] This (combined with reference back to the *conseil général*) gives the Prefect a moral supremacy over the *commission* unlike anything to be found in his relations with the *conseil général*, or even with a *conseil municipal*.

The *commission départementale*, despite the restrictions laid upon it, performs a useful administrative task. It does small jobs which could not possibly be dealt with effectively by the full *conseil général*, and which (short of having the elected body in more or less permanent session) would inevitably have to be included within the Prefect's administrative powers, even though they are better suited to consideration and decision by an elected body. For example, at the April, 1950 meeting of the *commission départementale* of the Department of Haut Rhin (capital Colmar), the following subjects, amongst others, were dealt with: the acquisition of land for reserve storage tanks, an appeal from the Commune of Willer-sur-Thur to be excused the repayment of part of a loan, an application by a local savings bank to increase its rate of interest, the organisation of

[1] J. L'Huillier: *Le contentieux des décisions de la commission départementale. Revue du Droit Public;* XLIX; No. 3, 1932, pp. 526–546.

anti-tuberculosis and anti-cancer campaigns throughout the Department, the ratification of a commercial agreement between a Commune and a private contractor, a revision of the jury-list in the Department, the redecoration of the Louis XIV room in the Prefecture, and consideration of the tenders submitted for rebuilding a wing in the psychiatric hospital at Rouffach. This, and similar work, could not be done by the *conseil général* without lengthy sessions, yet to allow the Prefect to decide would violate the principle of self-government contained in the law of 1871.

No substantial body of opinion suggests widening the field of autonomous action possessed by the *commission départementale*, and it is certainly wise to leave the extent of its powers as far as possible to its parent body, the *conseil général*.

F

CHAPTER THREE

The Work of
the Local Administrations

THE Mayor and the Prefect are the executive authorities in the
Commune and the Department respectively. Some of their
powers come to them as heads of the local authorities and others
by virtue of their status as state administrators. Although the
Prefects, when they are *Inspecteurs Généraux de l'Administration
en Mission Extraordinaire*, have additional police powers which
extend beyond the Department in which they are resident, they are
not executive agents for the whole Region and their extraordinary police powers are normally exercised only in an emergency.

THE MAYOR AND THE ADMINISTRATION
OF THE COMMUNE
Police Powers

The Law of 1884 made the Mayor responsible for protecting
and maintaining the public security, morality and hygiene
(*salubrité*) of the Commune (*police municipale*); and for this
purpose he was empowered to make ordinances (*arrêtés*),
having the same legal force as the other regulations made by
the Executive. Since police powers are, by their very nature,
the monopoly of the State, ordinances made by the Mayor
under this head are subject to the ratification of the Prefect or
Sub-Prefect. A communal ordinance, therefore, does not become
effective until the Prefect or Sub-Prefect has countersigned it,
and the Prefect's decision is discretionary, the *Conseil d'État*
only receiving a case if it is based on a point of law, and not
attempting to control his use of discretion.[1]

[1] This is an overstatement, but the legal situation is extremely complex.
See P. H. Teitgen: *La police municipale;* Thesis for Doctorate, Faculty
of Law, University of Nancy, 1934, pp. 8–24, and below Chapter 5.

The Mayor's police power is defined in detail in Article 97 of the Law of 1884. He is responsible for the security of the highway, the maintenance of the peace, the repression of all outbreaks of mob-violence, the prevention of public calamities, the apprehension of lunatics and mad animals, the decorum and decency of burials and good order in the cemeteries, the inspection of weights and measures and the purity of goods offered for sale. In addition, the blanket term " maintenance of public security, morality and hygiene (*salubrité*) in the Commune " gives him a more general warrant to meet unexpected and unspecified circumstances. Thus, the Mayors during the 1914 war automatically assumed responsibility for feeding and housing in their Communes and for dealing with the refugees who came into the Commune, and they could naturally impose the necessary discipline.

The variety of these communal police powers and the responsibility which they carry must not be underestimated. The Mayor of Fontaine-de-Vaucluse, for example (826 inhabitants), became so perturbed by his Communist councillors' insistent demands that he subscribe to the Pact of Five, the Stockholm Appeal, Aid to China, and so on, and by warnings that unless he did something civilisation itself would be threatened, that he issued the following ordinance :

Article One : It is forbidden to carry or to make use of the atomic bomb in the territory of Fontaine-de-Vaucluse.

Article Two : The *garde champêtre* shall see that this Ordinance is obeyed.

This ordinance obviously comes within the definition of public security.[1] On grounds of public morality, the *Conseil d'État* has allowed a Mayor to forbid a boxing match in his Commune, on the grounds that the brutal and savage character of such contests was harmful to public morale. On grounds of public *salubrité* the Mayor can prohibit factories from creating noxious smells.

The *Conseil d'État* decides whether or not a particular ordinance is authorised by the general police power. Its tests are entirely empirical: what maintains the peace in one Commune may well cause a breach of the peace in another. The Mayor

[1] *Revue Administrative:* May, 1950, p. 301.

always has to make sure that his ordinances do not conflict with fundamental rights and that they impose the minimum restriction on the citizens' freedom. The *Conseil d'État* admits that more stringent regulations can be made for the conduct of citizens in public places than for behaviour on private premises, and it accepts the principle that more stringent measures can be imposed temporarily than can be accepted in a general and permanent ordinance. A Mayor is certainly entitled, for instance, to order a works to close on grounds of public order when there is a strike or lock-out which presents threatening possibilities; but if he attempts to close a factory without good cause, or if he tries to order the factory to remain permanently closed because its labour relations are repeatedly causing trouble, his ordinances will either be scrapped by his hierarchic superior, the Prefect, or, on appeal to the courts, by the *Conseil d'État*.

There are three further points of importance about the Mayor's police powers. First, if the Mayor refuses or neglects to take the steps necessary to ensure order, etc., in the Commune, the Prefect or Sub-Prefect can make the orders themselves, after having warned the Mayor that they would assume his powers unless he acted promptly. Thus, a Mayor who refuses to divert the traffic from the main square on the day when the President of the Republic intends to review troops there, will be warned by the Prefect to do so, and in default, the Prefect will issue the order himself.

Second, the Prefect has the authority to make general ordinances which are applicable to all the Communes in the Department; these supersede any previous ordinances made by Mayors on the same subject, and are applicable in Communes where previously there had been no regulation. The Prefect also possesses wide powers of discretion when public peace is threatened in more than one Commune; he can then assume the Mayor's police powers and take the necessary steps on his own authority.

Third, in recent years many Communes have been deprived of their police forces, and the Mayors dispossessed of certain police powers. Even during the nineteenth century in Lyons and Paris, the Prefect of the Rhône and the Prefect of Police respectively exercised police powers normally possessed by the

Mayor. In Paris all the police powers were under the Prefect of Police,[1] and in Lyons those concerned with " repressing breaches of the peace, riots, disorderly quarrels, tumultuous assemblies and mob disturbances " and " maintaining good order in crowded meeting-places, fairs, cafés, public ceremonies, churches and public entertainments " were under the Prefect of the Rhône. The police forces in both towns were recruited and deployed entirely by the State and its officers, and the Communes concerned were required to pay a proportion of the expenses. This system of state police forces and prefectoral control of municipal police powers was extended, at various times before 1939, to ten more of the most important Communes of France ; among them were Strasbourg, Bordeaux, Marseilles, Nice and Toulon. During the war several changes were made in this system, and eventually it was extended to all Communes with over ten thousand inhabitants, and the state police force was organised on a regional basis.[2] Nowadays, therefore, the Mayors in Communes with over 10,000 inhabitants are no longer responsible for repressing public disturbances or maintaining public order; it is then the Prefect's duty. The Mayor, however, retains all the other municipal police powers. These Communes are not debarred from having a communal police force, but in general the Mayor relies upon the state police to enforce his ordinances. The Minister of the Interior has several times sharply called the state police to order for being lax and unco-operative in assisting the Mayors, and has instructed them to regard the Mayor as their superior when he is regulating matters within his legal competence.

In the Communes with under 10,000 inhabitants the old order remains, with the police forces organised and paid by the Commune and under the orders of the Mayor. The appointment, dismissal, or suspension for more than a month of policemen is subject to the approval of the Prefect. In many Communes the police " force " consists of one or two *gardes champêtres* (rural policemen). The real police force for all the country districts is the national *gendarmerie*, organised and recruited

[1] See below, chapter 7.
[2] See B. Chapman: The Organisation of the French Police. *Public Administration*; Spring, 1951.

nationally by the Ministry of Defence, but deployed for police work under the supervision of the Ministry of the Interior. The *gardes champêtres*, however, act as enforcement officers for communal ordinances, do much of the administrative routine work such as checking motor licences, and, of course, prevent, if so instructed, the use of the atomic bomb.

The most effective instrument for ensuring that the Mayor performs his police duties efficiently is that in France, as in England, the local authority is responsible for damages caused by an outbreak of mob-violence, whether armed or not. The Mayor, under such circumstances, will be required to show that within the limits of available resources he has taken all reasonable measures to prevent and suppress the disturbance, and if he can show this, the Commune can sue the State for the damages involved. The precise legal liability of Communes which have state police is not yet clear, but recent judgments of the *Conseil d'État* make the State rather than the Commune liable.

State Services

The Mayor is responsible to the Prefect or the Sub-Prefect when he or the Commune's administrative services act for the State. The duties he has to perform are principally concerned with such matters as the collection of statistical information, registering births and deaths, compiling agricultural statistics, and keeping the military conscription lists of the inhabitants of the Commune. The Prefect can always intervene if the Mayor fails to perform his duties correctly in these matters, and in broader terms the State can lay down its own conditions as to how they shall be dealt with, and leave the Mayor with the minimum of discretion. The Mayor must publish the laws and keep a record of all those applicable to the Commune. He must grant a certificate of *bonne vie et moeurs* to any entitled person who asks for it, and such certificates and references are indispensable to qualify for entry into most official posts and educational institutions.

Communal Administration

As the head of the administrative services of the Commune, the Mayor is responsible to the *conseil municipal* and not to the

Prefect. The scope of these services varies enormously with the activity of the *conseil municipal* and the size and importance of the Commune. In the largest Communes there is a highly complex administrative structure, but in the tiny mountain hamlet only the most elementary organisation is found, often amounting to no more than one room where the Mayor or the local schoolmaster tackles the forms sent from the Sub-Prefecture. The budget will frequently be discussed and indeed practically drafted in the Sub-Prefecture, whither the Mayor naturally turns for advice, and virtually the only current administrative business in such a Commune will be the provision of relief to destitute persons.

As the size of the Commune increases so its administrative structure becomes more and more a matter for permanent employees under the direction of the Mayor and several Assistant-Mayors, each charged with the supervision of one or more sub-divisions. The Commune of Colmar has a well-organised and rational system, and a chart of its administrative services illustrates its scope. Colmar is the capital of the Department of Haut Rhin and it has a population of some forty-six thousand inhabitants, and a budget of some 625,000,000 francs (£625,000).[1]

The Mayor in Colmar is assisted by six Assistant-Mayors, one of whom is Vice-President of the *Conseil de la République*, the upper house of Parliament. It has ten Divisions which are divided between the permanent paid heads of the communal administration, the Secretaries-General, for supervisory, technical and disciplinary purposes. The Assistant-Mayors are, however, closely associated with the detailed administration of several *bureaux*. For example, one has under his jurisdiction the Legal Office and the Industrial Arbitration Tribunal in the Central Division, as well as the municipal medical service, public health, school hygiene, the school dental service and the sanitary inspectorate of the Division of Public Health. In this way all the detailed administration is under the supervision both of one of the Secretaries-General and of an elected member of the *conseil municipal*. The Mayor has reserved to himself all the matters in the Central Division not dealt with by the

[1] In 1948.

Records & Statistics	Registrar's Duties Statistics and Census Electoral Organisation

RECORDS & STATISTICS

Registrar's Duties
Statistics and Census
Electoral Organisation

POLICE MUNICIPALE

Regulation of Administrative Affairs
                Industry and Commerce
                Rural Affairs
                Building
                Fire Services
Military Conscription and Recruitment
Residential Register
Nationality
Civil Defence

CULTURAL

Education
Church Matters
Art, Letters and Science
Municipal Library
Museums
Theatre
School of Music
Municipal College of Arts and Music

SOCIAL

Social Welfare Services
Municipal Youth Organisation
Public Assistance
Charitable Institutions
Unemployment

PUBLIC HEALTH

Municipal Medical Service
Public Health
School Hygiene
School Dental Service
Sanitary Inspectorate
Municipal Sports Organisation

TECHNICAL

Secretariat of Technical Depts.
Accounts
Municipal Architect's Dept.
Highways Dept.
Car Park
Maintenance Dept.
Land Survey
Public Land Register
Photography Dept.

ECONOMIC

Secretariat of Economic Co-ordination
Agriculture, Winegrowing and Breeding
Industry, Commerce and Crafts
Fairs and Markets
Municipal Tourist Bureau

MUNICIPAL ENTERPRISES

Municipal Industrial Concerns
Public Baths
Abattoirs
Winegrowers' Institute
Publicity

FINANCE & PROPERTY

Finance Dept.
Government and Municipal Taxes
Accommodation Service
Communal Property and Land and Forest Holdings

CENTRAL

Secretariat, Personnel and Administrative Organisation
Survey and Planning Centre
Legal Office
Arbitration Court
Works Dept.

DEPUTY SECRETARY-GENERAL

SECRETARY-GENERAL

MAYOR AND ASSISTANT MAYORS

Organisation of a Commune.

Assistant-Mayor, the entire Cultural Division and several isolated subjects from other Divisions which are related to the matters already under his control; for example, the Finance Department in the Finance and Property Division. In this way the delegation of responsibility to individual elected members is combined with the technical assistance of the experienced bureaucrat.

The administrative organisation of Lyons will serve as a second example. It is the capital of the Department of the Rhône, and has a population of nearly half a million inhabitants, and its importance is incomparably greater than that of Colmar, both politically and economically. However, its administration is marked by a difference of degree rather than one of kind; the whole organisation is on an immense scale compared with that of Colmar, but this is principally because business is divided in more detail between more numerous administrative units.

Lyons is in some ways peculiar since it has one *Hôtel de Ville* and seven *Mairies*, scattered through the town, one in each communal *arrondissement*.[1] The titular head of each of the *Mairies* is an Assistant-Mayor elected by the *conseil municipal* of Lyons and appointed to a *Mairie* by the Mayor. Each *Mairie* has its own staff, recruited by the Commune and under the authority of the Mayor for discipline, pay, promotion, etc. The *Mairies* have nothing to do with ordinary communal administration. They are concerned only with performing in their respective areas the services devolved on the Commune by the State: the registering of births and deaths, army recruitment and the compilation of conscription lists, the preparation of the electoral register, the rating book for the property in their areas, the registration of addresses, foreigners' requests for naturalisation papers, and so on. They are also compelled to issue, or countersign, the numerous forms of official declaration required in France for births, entry to universities, marriages and deaths.

Communal administration, properly speaking, goes on in the *Hôtel de Ville*, where there is also a central co-ordinating

[1] Not to be confused with the *arrondissements* of the Department, in each of which is a Sub Prefect.

bureau to keep the *Mairies* in line. The *Hôtel de Ville* is organised into four main Divisions: General Administration, the
Police Administrative, Finance and Communal Works, and
Social Affairs. Each Division is sub-divided into *bureaux*. For
example, in the Division for Social Affairs, there are three
bureaux, the first of which comprises offices each dealing with
one of the following subjects: the labour exchange, social
questions, municipal rest homes for workers, trade unions,
unemployment insurance and workers' contributions, labour
accidents, the social security services, co-operative societies,
craft and technical institutes, municipal parks and gardens,
workmens' dwellings and council housing, and, finally, the
municipal library.

Besides the Assistant-Mayors appointed to supervise the
work of the seven *Mairies*, there are several others responsible
for the work of the *Hôtel de Ville*. The paid officials number
several thousand under the control of the Secretary-General.
They naturally form the backbone of communal administration,
and some account must be given of their position.

Communal personnel

Until 1930 communal officials enjoyed little security; despite
various measures between 1919 and 1929 intended to regulate
their conditions of service, they remained almost entirely
subject to the *conseil municipal*, and were commonly dismissed
on political grounds when the *conseil municipal* changed its
political complexion. The law of March 12, 1930, however,
enacted that in every Commune with permanent full-time
employees the *conseil municipal* must draw up a proper statute
governing their conditions of entry, promotion and dismissal.
In default, the Prefect could promulgate in its place a standard
form of statute drawn up by the *Conseil d'État*. The *conseil
municipal* still decided how many employees the Commune
should have, their scales of pay (which could not be above
comparable grades in state and departmental services), and
whether or not there should be a pension fund. A disciplinary
council was formed to cover several Communes, presided over
by the *juge de paix* and including representatives of the elected
authorities and of communal employees in the area; a Mayor

had to consult it before he could take disciplinary action against his officials.

Despite this law and further decrees, the status, pay and number of communal officials employed varied enormously from one Commune to another. In 1943 the Commune of Sète had one official for every 574 inhabitants, while a few miles away at Béziers there was one communal official for every 1,788 inhabitants.[1]

Under Vichy attempts were made to impose a more coherent system regarding scales of pay, legal status, standardisation of posts, and equivalent status between communal, departmental and state officials. The Vichy laws regulating these matters were annulled at the time of the Liberation and replaced by a new *Ordonnance* of May 17, 1945, and several later decrees, regulations and laws, which after several years' discussion were codified in a General Statute for communal officials, the Law of April 28, 1952.[2]

This law is based in part on a general statute for all state officials, and in part on two post-war measures introduced by Ministers of the Interior. The first measure had established equivalent status between state, departmental and communal officials : for instance, by 1948 a Secretary-General of a Commune of from 40,000 to 80,000 inhabitants ranked with a *chef de division* of a prefecture,[3] and the Secretary-General of a Commune of from 10,000 to 20,000 inhabitants ranked with an *attaché* of a prefecture.[4] The second measure was a Decree of November 19, 1948, regulating the qualifications required of communal officials: the *conseil municipal* could not fill a communal post which required technical or administrative ability comparable to that for a post in the state administration, unless the candidate possessed equivalent paper qualifications to those required from his counterpart in the state administration.

By 1948, therefore, the pay and recruitment of communal

[1] Doueil : op. cit., p. 208.
[2] *Statut général du personnel des communes et des établissements publics communaux. Journal officiel;* April 28/29, 1952.
[3] In charge of a Division in a prefecture: the most senior post in the prefecture after the members of the *corps préfectoral*.
[4] In charge of a *bureau*, and formerly called a *chef de bureau*.

officials had been to some extent standardised. The General Statute of 1952 laid down a general pattern of pay, recruitment, discipline, and conditions of employment, for all permanent communal officials.[1]

The law introduces two important structural changes in communal administration. First, new advisory councils, composed of municipal councillors and communal officials, have been set up to advise *conseils municipaux* on staff matters. Second, all Communes employing fewer than 40 permanent officials are compelled to belong to a *syndicat intercommunal*, which will have a joint advisory council to advise the *bureau* of the *syndicat* on this subject.

The disciplinary councils have been strengthened. Where such a council covers several Communes it is composed of three Mayors and three communal officials, and where it deals with a single large Commune it has three municipal councillors and three communal officials. In all cases it is presided by the senior *juge de paix*. On no account may the disciplinary council include an official of lower rank than that of the official appearing before it, nor must any member have been involved in the affair under consideration or have been previously called upon to give an opinion upon the official's conduct. Although a Mayor may, subject to some safeguards, suspend an official immediately for apparent grave misconduct, he can impose no serious penalty without consulting the disciplinary council, and if he decides to inflict a heavier punishment than that proposed by the council, the official may appeal to the departmental disciplinary council. This body is composed of three Mayors and three communal officials chosen by lot, and is presided by the President of the Civil Tribunal in the departmental capital.

The qualifications required of a communal official have been formalised: he must be a French citizen, in full possession of his civil rights, free from infectious disease, and (except for juniors) have completed his military service. Subject to certain exceptions he must not be more than thirty years of age when he is recruited.

---

[1] The smallest Communes have no permanent officials; the Secretary to the Mayor is a part-time appointment, usually filled by the *instituteur*, who is paid an honorarium for his services.

The *conseil municipal* retains the right, subject to prefectoral approval, to determine the size and the conditions of service of the communal staff, but this has been limited by the standard qualifications which the Minister will require from all grades which have an equivalent in the state administration. These are not explicitly stated in the General Statute, but they will probably closely follow those contained in the Decree of November 19, 1948.

The 1948 Decree laid down that the Secretary-General of a Commune of over 20,000 inhabitants must have a degree and be over 35 years of age, and where the communal staff was large enough to contain *chefs de bureau* they too must be graduates. The Secretary-General of a Commune of under 20,000 inhabitants must have the qualifications required of a *rédacteur de mairie*. The latter are recruited by a national examination held under the auspices of the Ministry of the Interior. Candidates must possess a certificate comparable to the General Certificate of Education in England (either the *baccalauréat* or the *brevet supérieur*) or a diploma from the *École d'Administration Municipale* attached to the *Institut d'Urbanisme* of the University of Paris. These preliminary paper qualifications are not needed by junior officials (*commis*) who have served for three years although they must still pass the examination to become *rédacteurs*. The *commis* are recruited by an examination agreed to by the Prefect, and they must have the school leaving certificate from a primary school or the intermediate certificate from a *lycée*. The heads of the technical services in Communes must hold the engineering or architectural diplomas required for entry to the State's technical *corps*. Master craftsmen, foremen, firemen, food and sanitary inspectors, must also hold special qualifications for their jobs. Communal officials already in office who do not possess the necessary qualifications at the time when this law is passed are not required to obtain them; they will be classified at an appropriate level in their present employment.

Promotion may be either within one authority by an increase of salary in the same post or by advancement to a higher post, or by transfer to another authority. The compulsory *syndicats intercommunaux* for all Communes employing fewer than 40 permanent officials are very important in this respect, since they will allow promising officials to transfer easily to another Commune at a higher level. Promotions to a higher grade are made annually from a list presented by the Mayor or Mayors concerned to the advisory council for staff matters already mentioned. Three candidates must be presented for every two vacant posts; vacancies depend upon the number of officials employed in each category, which is fixed by the *conseil municipal* or by the *bureau* of the *syndicat intercommunal*. Increases in pay within [the same grade are accorded as of right.

It is too early to assess the effects of this General Statute, but it is the culmination of a lengthy movement to raise the status of communal officials and to attract more promising recruits to local administration. It meets most former criticisms of the system.

An examination of the administrative services of the Commune of Strasbourg provides a practical example of the way in which local government officials are graded and of the numbers employed. The Commune has a population of 175,515. Excluding manual labourers there are 782 *titulaires* and 308 *auxiliaires* (including officials on special contracts). Communal employees are divided into four different cadres: an administrative cadre, a technical cadre, a special or miscellaneous cadre, and manual workers. The first group contains all those to be found in the ordinary offices of the Commune, from the Secretary-General, the Directors, the Sub-Directors, the *chefs de bureaux*, the *rédacteurs* to the clerical assistants and office boys; each category is classified into several grades for financial advancement and promotion within that category. The technical cadre includes the various types of engineers, the architects, the master-craftsmen, the foremen and inspectors, and in addition, the clerical assistants specially recruited for these offices. The special or miscellaneous cadre varies from Commune to Commune according to the special forms of communal activity to be found. In Strasbourg this group includes veterinary surgeons and food inspectors in the *abattoirs*, several types of medical and health practitioners engaged in school, social and public health services, laboratory workers and sanitary engineers and inspectors, the *gardes champêtres*, the firemen, and the specialists appointed on a permanent basis to the library, the archives and the museums. Finally there is the body of municipal workmen, which is divided into various groups—foremen, skilled men, unskilled men, and so on. In all, the figures for the four cadres in Strasbourg are 420 administrators, 138 technical personnel, 205 miscellaneous specialists, and 1,607 manual workmen, a grand total of 2,389.[1] This represents one communal employee for every 75 inhabitants. In addition to all this, a Commune the size of Strasbourg will probably have a *conservatoire de musique*, an orchestra, and a special school of fine arts; strictly speaking their staffs should also be included among the communal employees.

The first important difference between French and English local government service is that a sharp distinction is drawn between officials who serve in Departments and those who are employed by Communes; they are organised, recruited, disciplined and, in some respects, paid, differently.[2] There is no strong national association of local government officials comparable to NALGO, partly because of this distinction between the two types of local government officials, and partly because of the lack of strong national ties and interests; in local administration, as in so many other fields of French life, local sympathies take precedence over national interests. Considerable hostility to strong unions is still apparent in many places, especially in rural areas.

The second point of importance is that the Secretary-General of a Commune is not, like an English Town Clerk, *primus inter pares*, but is specifically the official paid head of the Commune's administration. The heads of the various Divisions are responsible to the Secretary-General, and thus indirectly to the Mayor, for the work of their Divisions and services. This is one of the effects of having no committee system in the English sense. In France committees of the Council have no powers to act; only the Mayor and by delegation the Assistant-Mayors can do so. Consequently all the measures requiring execution

[1] The slight discrepancy in the figures is due to the inclusion of some of the retired communal employees who still hold nominal posts.

[2] See below, p. 117 for conditions of service of departmental officials.

must pass through the hands of the communal executive. This naturally increases the power of the Secretary-General.

The senior appointments in communal administration are rarely made from outside, and in very few cases indeed is a Secretary-General a technical expert, for example a qualified solicitor. The career is essentially an administrative one, with promotion coming from transfers between authorities or advancement through the various grades inside one authority. Thus, communal administration is far more an instance of administration by professional administrators than is normally the case in English local government. This is not true in the smallest Communes, and there are very many of these; here the schoolmaster does what work there is, but as soon as the Commune has a staff of any importance, professionalism is a general rule.

A Mayor determines what influence his officials shall have. Many Mayors are unqualified to deal with some of the administrative matters placed before them, and they naturally turn to their senior officials for advice. But officials cannot demand attention, and only very rarely can they obtain the ear of the *conseil municipal:* there are no committees on the English pattern through which they can propose policies discreetly, and the Mayor personally leads the discussions of the *conseil municipal.* In the largest Communes many of the councillors, and probably the Mayor, are active and ambitious politicians who will not welcome suggestions from subordinates. In the smaller Communes the Mayor is more likely to seek advice from the Sub-Prefect than from his officials. In the very smallest Communes where the Secretary to the Mayor (the only communal official) is the local schoolmaster, his voice has more chance of being heard, but only because he is the local intellectual, and not because he is a communal official. The type of influence exercised by senior officials like the Town Clerk in this country comes in France from the Prefectures and Sub Prefectures and not from local communal officials.

THE CORPS PRÉFECTORAL

Departmental administration is based upon the *corps préfectoral,* whose members in each Department are the Prefect, Sub-Prefects (including the Secretary-General of the Prefecture) and the *chef de cabinet*. All these officers are appointed by the Government and are in theory liable to instant removal should they lose the confidence of the Government of the day.

Recruitment to the *corps* has only recently been formalised, as the principle that members of the *corps* could be removed at will by the Government hindered the development of a clear method of entry and promotion. There is now a reasonably clear course from *chef de cabinet* to Sub-Prefect, *hors classe*, but there is still no legal reason why this should lead to promotion to Prefect, or why a new Prefect should not be chosen from outside the ranks of the Sub-Prefects. In practice the tradition of the last twenty-five years has done much to stabilise the personnel of the *corps* and a " prefectoral career " is firmly established; yet the principle of absolute government discretion is still upheld, and under Vichy and the Liberation the right was freely exercised. The war has brought a serious attempt to formalise entry to the lower grades of the *corps* while yet leaving the Government freedom of decision at the higher levels.

A formal Statute has been drawn up in which the conditions of entry, pay and promotion have been !aid down.[1] Three quarters of the entrants to the *corps préfectoral* at the lowest level of *chef de cabinet*, must be graduates of the *École Nationale d'Administration*, a post-graduate college for training all higher administrative civil servants. It was created in 1945, and candidates for entry must already possess a university degree or have passed through various branches of the ordinary civil service by a certain age. Entry is by examination and the course lasts three years, during which the students are trained in many branches of law, politics, economics and languages: training under a senior administrator in the field is an integral part of the curriculum. At the end of the course the students are graded and the senior posts open in the various Ministries and *corps* are filled in accordance with the wishes of the students in order of merit.

Chef de Cabinet

A graduate who chooses the Ministry of the Interior may go

[1] Decree No. 50–699; June 19, 1950: "*portant règlement d'administration publique et relatif au statut particulier du corps préfectoral*". Published in the *Journal Officiel;* June 20 and 22, 1950.

either into the Ministry in Paris as an *administrateur civil*, or he may go into the provinces as *chef de cabinet* in a Prefecture. The wishes of any particular Prefect are taken into account, and a young man may be able to start in a higher class Prefecture if his academic and professional record justify it.

In the Prefecture the *chef de cabinet* is the personal *aide* of the Prefect. He is the head of the Prefect's personal " cabinet ", in which there will be a senior *attaché*[1] of the Prefecture and other assistants. The cabinet deals with all private and confidential affairs, with political reports on the happenings in the Department, the reports on departmental and state personnel under the orders of the Prefect, the secret files, and such delicate matters as reports on political parties and requests to hold public demonstrations. In addition, the Prefect's cabinet is his personal secretariat, and it automatically deals with his private correspondence, together with any reports or documents he requires.

In very large Prefectures like Toulouse or Bordeaux, the *chef de cabinet* is replaced at the head of the cabinet by a *directeur du cabinet* who is a Sub-Prefect of some experience.

The *chef de cabinet* can hope that after two or three years in that post he will be appointed as a third class Sub-Prefect in charge of a third class *arrondissement*.[2] In the ordinary way he can expect thereafter to be moved every four to six years to a higher grade *arrondissement*, or to gain individual promotion through the various grades on seniority. A wise Sub-Prefect will try to get back for some time to the Ministry in Paris in order to increase his reputation and his chances of selection to the rank of third class Prefect.

The Sub-Prefect

Before that stage is reached, however, the Sub-Prefect in an *arrondissement* will be called upon to fufil a variety of duties calculated to test his tact, discretion, and administrative ability.

---

[1] See below, p. 117.

[2] Four fifths of all Sub-Prefects must come from the ranks of the *chefs de cabinet*, and the remainder can enter from other state administrations in which they hold an equivalent rank. The Statute has a detailed list of these equivalents.

The *conseil d'arrondissement* which existed before the war has now passed into oblivion, and its duties and powers have been assumed by the Sub-Prefect. This means that although the Sub-Prefect is not bothered by the presence of an elected body, he does not have the moral support that such a body can give. He is an isolated figure depending on his Prefect's support rather than on that of his *arrondissement*.

He has a number of duties in his own right, such as sanctioning the appointment of certain communal officials including the *garde champêtre* and other communal police; he receives and passes on official papers, documents and orders from the Prefect to the Communes; and he arranges the mechanics of elections. He also has tutelage powers over the Mayors in the *arrondissement*, especially over their police ordinances and their budgets, and the Prefect can delegate additional responsibility to him for a wide range of subjects.

His most important task, however, is as adviser to the Mayors. A large part of the time of a Sub-Prefect is taken up with ensuring the prompt and accurate performance of the Mayors' duties, and with helping them to find a path through the maze of technical detail which surrounds administrative action. In many cases the Mayors of small Communes ask for assistance in drafting the Communes' budgets, and in all the variety of difficulties which can arise in communal administration—from the technical detail of compulsory land purchase to the right of the *garde champêtre* to have a pension—the Sub-Prefect is expected to act as guide, adviser and technical consultant to the Mayor.

He is also, by force of circumstances, the Government's adviser on political conditions within the *arrondissement*, and he is required to put into effect government or prefectoral policy in his area. A successful Sub-Prefect may enjoy a certain amount of popularity but only under very favourable circumstances; generally he bears a heavy burden of responsibility with little thanks.

If instead of going to an *arrondissement* a Sub-Prefect becomes a Secretary-General to a Prefecture he has a dual task: to act as Sub-Prefect for the *arrondissement* in which the capital town is situated and to ensure the efficient administration of the Prefecture and of the departmental services. The Secretary-General is essentially the Prefect's second in command, and unless orders explicitly state otherwise he takes over the Prefect's powers when the Prefect is absent from the Department. This is a job for a good administrator rather than for a public personality or an astute politician. Departmental administration is a complex matter reaching up to the ministerial level and down to the details of communal work; it is concerned with the provision of services, the administration of property and the maintenance of order and security; the Secretary-General's task in organising, administering and disciplining the many services attached to the Prefecture is wide and complex, and the size of staff alone makes the administrative side more burdensome than for the Sub-Prefect in an *arrondissement*. The Secretary-General however enjoys more peace of mind because of the relative anonymity of his position, and the close presence of the Prefect on whom public attention is directed.

A Sub-Prefect who has had experience both in various *arrondissements* and as Secretary-General is an extremely well qualified official of wide and varied experience, both as an administrator and as a public figure, and these are the qualities most necessary in the Prefects themselves.

The Prefect

The sole legal restriction upon the Government's choice in appointing a Prefect is that he should be a French citizen possessed of ordinary electoral rights.[1] Other public officials in France must possess many paper qualifications; a Prefect requires only the trust and confidence of the Government. There can therefore be no security of tenure nor any right to permanency in his post. In the nineteenth century this doctrine entailed widespread " massacres " of Prefects at every change of regime or cabinet reshuffle, and the Prefects were often hard pressed to avoid the suffocating embrace of the local Deputy. Readers of Bodley will remember the instances he gives where a Deputy was able to bring pressure to bear on the Prefect of his

[1] If he comes from the ranks of the Sub-Prefects, however, he must be first class or *hors classe*, and in the former case have at least four years seniority.

area by threatening to use his influence with the Minister to cause his dismissal: by these methods Deputies managed to acquire considerable influence in the appointment of local officials, in communal and departmental politics, and in the " arrangement " of elections.

Gradually, however, a small *corps* of professional Prefects developed, and the last great massacre of Prefects on political grounds under the Third Republic was under the Radical government in 1924. Since 1939 there have been many changes. All Prefects who were in office at the time of the Normandy landings were suspended from office until their war records could be examined. In their places General de Gaulle appointed members of his own forces or prominent local leaders of the Resistance. Over half of these newly-appointed Prefects have subsequently been revoked, and several of those suspended have since come back. The present Prefects fall into three groups: those who had served under the Third Republic but who either withdrew to de Gaulle's side during the war or chose the highly dangerous course of serving the Resistance from the Prefecture[1]; others who had been only junior administrators during the war but whose merit and records justified rapid promotion; and finally a number of outsiders who have come from the liberal professions or were Resistance leaders.

The refurnishing of the *corps préfectoral* after 1945 has led to the very rapid promotion of the most able and brilliant of the younger men, and this has caused some concern for the future of the *corps:* for there are now nearly a hundred and fifty Prefects for some hundred posts (including the overseas Departments and Algeria), with the result that many must take appointments in other administrations or remain on paid leave. The question of the Sub-Prefects' future has also occasioned misgivings.

Normally today the Prefect is not retired from office without compensation; various expedients of half-pay, prolonged leave and outside appointments are substituted, in the humane tradition of the British civil service. Ex-Prefects are to be found

[1] The first national leader of the internal Resistance was Jean Moulin, Prefect. He and several other Prefects were executed by the Germans, and others were deported to concentration camps.

as Directors of Hospitals, as *trésoriers payeurs généraux* and in other central administrations: in 1939 more than half the outside appointments to the *Conseil d'État* were ex-Prefects.[1]

This tradition of government appointment, interchange between services and the introduction of outsiders, has allowed the *corps préfectoral* continually to take advantage of the experience and peculiar talents of men from other disciplines and fields of activity; and there is little doubt that French administration is much the healthier for it.

The discipline inherent in the liability to instant dismissal is very strict. A Prefect's loyalty towards the Government and the Government's trust in a Prefect must be absolute. Not only must he obey his Minister's orders but he must also obey their spirit, and in times of crisis act as the Minister would wish if he were at the Prefect's shoulder. As the subordinate of the Minister of the Interior, all his actions and decisions are liable to examination and reversal by the Minister. The Prefect cannot leave the Department to which he is appointed without the Minister's express consent, and several of the tougher politicians have disciplined their Prefects ruthlessly, the most notable being Clemenceau, whose fury was legendary. The French argue that men of no little personal power are required to govern a Department, and any slackening in the principle of political obedience would lead to French government being carried on without the politicians; some are inclined to believe that this has already happened, but the politicians would certainly not agree.

The compensation a Prefect gets for the burden he bears is a high salary,[2] free accommodation and transport at the Department's expense, and an immense amount of influence within the Department. He is the representative of the State in the Department and as such he is the direct representative of every Minister, not only of the Minister of the Interior; all ministerial directions and requests should go through his hands even though they are to be carried out by members of another admin-

---

[1] This last, however, was a real and not an Irishman's rise.

[2] Though only in relation to French civil servants' salaries. The Prefect of the Seine gets about £2,200 plus free and luxurious accommodation and an expense account.

istrative service. He is therefore titular head of all state services within the Department, whether technical or administrative. The departmental chiefs of these services, such as the *inspecteur d'académie* (education), the *trésorier payeur général* (finance) and the Civil Engineers, may propose, but the Prefect decides. Even the most senior service heads can never for long deny their subordination to the Prefect; and although during and after the war some Ministers incited their local officers to by-pass his authority, the abuse has by now been largely rectified at the insistence of the Ministers of the Interior. This subordination is the best way of blocking centralisation in France, for the possession of authority at the centre of each Department over all branches of state life ensures that the Prefecture effectively remains the centre of departmental government. The Prefect has to try to keep a balance between his duties as state official and ministerial representative, and his interest in championing the demands and needs of his Department. Usually, though not always, the Prefecture is strong enough to defend local interests against the centre.

The Prefect has been given at different times by different laws an undetermined number of functions, reckoned by experts to be about 5,000.[1]

1.   The Prefect has extensive police powers, and is responsible for maintaining public order, public morality and public hygiene in the Department, for the security of the State, and for executing the laws (*police générale*). Consequently, he has authority to issue ordinances covering the whole Department in these matters, and he is the chief of the police forces within the Department. The uniformed state police are now on a regional basis, but within the Department the Prefect directs their activities and all interesting information acquired is sent to the Prefecture prior to transmission to the regional capital. The movement and operations of the agents employed by the counter-espionage directorate of the *Sûreté Nationale* (DST) are outside his jurisdiction, but he should, as a matter of courtesy, be informed of their peregrinations.

[1] M. Bonnaud Delamare, Prefect of the Aisne, has recently compiled a complete list.

2. In the field of counter-espionage and public security, the Prefect possesses special powers as an officer of the *police judiciaire*. Article 10 of the *Code d'Instruction Criminelle* authorises him to arrest, search and seize without warrant any persons or documents which he believes to endanger the internal or external security of the State. This Article has been severely criticised in the past and was for a time annulled, but the pressure of events over the last fifteen years made necessary the grant of discretionary power to some state officer, and the Prefect was the obvious person. His exercise of these powers has been hedged around with devices intended to protect the liberty of the citizen; he must inform the *Procureur de la République* (public prosecutor and attorney for the State in the Department) within twenty-four hours, and any police officer ordered by the Prefect to perform such duties is legally obliged to inform the state magistracy at once.

3. The Prefect has considerable powers of control over communal officers and administration. As the tutelage authority of the Communes he has power to suspend Mayors for a month for grave breaches of conduct, to sanction communal budgets and write into them obligatory expenditure if it has been omitted, and to approve or annul a Mayor's police ordinances. From the point of view of local government this is the most important reserve of power which the Prefect possesses.

4. The Prefect directs all the administrative and technical services of the State in the Department, and in this capacity he appoints many junior officials to their posts and is responsible for their discipline and conduct. He is also the State's *ordonnateur* in financial affairs, which means that money can be paid from the State's funds only on his authority; recent years have seen some departure from this principle, but it is gradually being re-established. The Prefect represents the Department in all litigation in which it is involved, except that between the Department and the State; in this event the Prefect, as the representative of the State, acts on behalf of the senior authority, and the Secretary General of the Prefecture acts on behalf of the Department.

Finally, all state contracts for work within the Department require the Prefect's signature.

5. The Prefect acts as the channel for the collection and transmission of information required by the Ministries. For example, should the Minister of Finance wish to estimate public reactions to a possible new loan he will ask for the Prefect's report. Alternatively a strike in a munitions factory might be the subject of a prefectoral enquiry. The collection of data will be undertaken by the appropriate subordinates of the Prefect, but important aspects of the report will be the work of the Prefect himself, and he will always of course be held responsible for any document forwarded in his name. The Government always starts with the assumption that the Prefect is the best-informed man in the country for the internal affairs of the Department. If he is not then he should not be the Prefect.

6. Finally, the Prefect is the executive of the *conseil général* and is responsible for putting its decisions into effect.

The Prefect is continually faced with conflicting duties and loyalties, and he must have unusual political tact and administrative subtlety. Support of his Department's interests must be tempered by knowledge of his Minister's mind, and he must know instinctively what measures are not only technically possible but politically feasible. The Minister has every right to personal loyalty regarding his policy, and yet a Prefect who fails to inform him of the disadvantages and obstacles in the way of his policy not only neglects his duty but also stores up trouble for himself in the future, when he may be compelled to implement policies unsuited to his Department's circumstances.

The Prefect is also forced on occasions to arbitrate (in the Department) between the services of other Ministries. He may then have to resolve conflicts between divergent policies, but must do this in a way that will not provoke the Ministries in Paris to elevate a local conflict into a struggle between rival administrations with Ministers' reputations at stake. Similarly, he may be called upon to placate local authorities in his Department whose schemes have been turned down by, for example, the Minister of Finance or the Minister of Public Works.

Conflicts of interest or policy may set neighbouring Communes at each other's throats, and he is called upon to arbitrate, and resolve them with the minimum of ill-feeling. National Deputies or Senators may try to gain favours for their constituencies, and if some of them happen also to be Mayors or councillors this adds another pressure to the Prefect's task.

If the Prefect can solve these problems without too much discord, and not cause difficulties for the Minister, and not antagonise his *conseil général*, and not provoke recalcitrant Communes to outrageous actions, he can still expect no peace. For the Prefect is the most exposed administrative figure there is. His is an isolated post that requires not only the aplomb and *panache* of the politician, but the reserve of a diplomat, and the internal stability of a colonial Governor. His duties win him little popularity, yet they forbid him to seek the bureaucrat's anonymity. He is the power of the State incarnate, and his person may be threatened by those who hate the State. He is surrounded by the *mystique* of his office, which is popularly believed to be endowed with secret information and hidden reserves of influence; therefore, although regarded with cordial distrust, he is sought after, and his interest solicited in personal, corporate and economic matters. His social life is dominated by public functions, and he cannot escape from private entreaties. On more than one occasion the safety of France has depended upon the strength and authority of Prefects isolated in their Departments. He must live, therefore, so as to be always ready for an emergency.

The reward for the strain is simple: it is power and the right to create. If few administrative posts offer such tension, equally few offer such opportunities for self-expression. At the end of a prefectoral career, a Prefect can chart his progress through life by what he has done; and very few administrators can do that.

THE ADMINISTRATION OF THE DEPARTMENT

The Department undertakes departmental and state services; it is also responsible for helping and supplementing the work of the various Communes within its boundaries. Thus, in the Prefecture there are Divisions which are concerned with departmental services and others concerned with communal administration; in addition, attached to the Prefecture, there are the offices of the various state services in the Department.

National Services in the Department

Certain state administrations are organised on a regional basis, but use the Department as the principal subordinate area of administration. The most prominent of these are the armed services, the judiciary and the State's judicial administration, the judicial police (*police judiciaire*), the Post and Telegraph services and the Ministry of Ex-Servicemen. The Prefect has some powers in relation to the officers of these administrations but they are all of an exceptional nature; his right to arrest persons suspected of espionage without judicial warrant, for example, and his right in times of emergency, to require the local military commander to provide him with armed support. He can also challenge a court on grounds of jurisdiction if he has reason to suppose that the case under its consideration should properly be dealt with by an administrative tribunal. By a special process of law he can cause the suspension of the case, and bring about its transfer to the *Tribunal des Conflits*[1] for that body to decide which court is competent.

The other state services are those which help the Department to provide everyday services. The most important of these were mentioned in the introduction; education with the *inspecteur d'académie*, finance with the *trésorier payeur général*, the *ingénieurs des ponts et chaussées* responsible for highway repair and development, and the *ingénieurs des mines*. Health, agriculture, economic planning, certain branches of public assistance, taxation, information, statistics, labour and others, are all dealt with by special offices in each Department. The head of each of these administrations is appointed by his own Minister, but he is required by law to regard the Prefect as the proper channel for communicating with Paris, and the Prefect must be kept informed of all problems, directions, actions and general policy in each sphere.

This is not the place to discuss the organisation of the various

[1] See below, p. 149.

decentralised state administrations, except in so far as the Department exercises powers on their behalf. The important ones from this point of view are (i) public assistance, (ii) educational administration, (iii) highways, and (iv) town planning, which, although of lesser importance, should be mentioned here.

(i) The development of social services in France dates back to the Revolution when the Communes were made responsible for succouring paupers in their area, the necessary money coming from a tax on entertainments. In 1873, every Commune had to set up a *bureau de bienfaisance* (Welfare Centre) to organise the distribution of public aid, and to supervise entry to, and the financial affairs of, the various charitable institutions in its area. Twenty years later the first big step was taken towards the organisation of free medical service to the needy sick and to expectant mothers who were unable to provide for their own needs. The Communes were responsible for granting aid and securing entry to one of the hospitals or hospices to which all Communes are attached. The Commune in which the poor person was registered as a resident was responsible for the money spent, and the relieving Commune could sue the Commune of residence for the return of the money. In each Commune a *bureau d'assistance* organised relief work, and the *conseil général* of the Department was given the responsibility for organising the service and for establishing a rota of doctors and midwives to deal with the patients.

By 1905 Parliament had accepted the right to assistance of any person who was destitute, over 65, suffering from an incurable disease or from a permanent physical disability; the Department was the area in which the administrative organisation was set up, and in 1906 it was decided that the whole cost of the service should be borne on the budget of the Department, against which were set the contributions of the State and those of the Communes within the Department.

Finally, in 1935, the branches of public assistance which had been the subject of enactments at different times were all brought together, and the scales of benefits for each one, which had up till then varied, were standardised. The Decree Law[1] listed the

[1] Decree Law, October 30, 1935.

following services as being within the competence of the
conseil général to regulate, with the Department as the area of
administration :

1. Free medical assistance.
2. Assistance to the old, infirm and incurable.
3. Family allowances.
4. Allowances to women in childbirth.
5. Free milk allowance.
6. Hospitalisation of destitute lunatics.
7. Education of sub-normal children.
8. Social protection of the blind.
9. Tuberculosis dispensaries.
10. The organisation of anti-tuberculosis campaigns.
11. The social protection of children.
12. Assistance to neglected children.
13. Aid to children in moral danger.

The *conseil général* in each Department each year fixed the
allowances and benefits to be paid by each Commune to anyone
seeking assistance on any of these grounds. This law also
made the Department rather than the Commune the relieving
authority, and a Department which assists a person registered
elsewhere can claim a refund from the responsible authority.

Since 1935 most activity in this field has been in the organisation of anti-tuberculosis and anti-cancer campaigns, in the
repeated re-framing of the scale of allowances, and in the
development of family allowances where the father is unable to
provide adequately for the health, education or protection of
his children.

All these public assistance services are organised by the
Department, and in each Prefecture a Division is devoted to
their administration, and to the supervision of the institutions
and establishments through which care and aid are given. The
State contributes between 28 per cent and 90 per cent of the
finance, and the Department and the Communes the remainder.[1]
Departmental officers supervise the communal administrations
operating the machinery, but there is ultimate state control
through the Ministry of Public Health over the regular and

[1] The Department can take over the Communes' share.

orderly conduct of the system as a whole. Thus, in this, as in other services, the Department stands between the Commune and the State.

Hospitals are (with the exception of some national institutions) either communal, intercommunal, or departmental; they can only be created or suppressed by a decree of the *Conseil d'État* countersigned by the Minister of Public Health, after consultation with the Ministers of the Interior and of Finance. The regional director of the Ministry of Public Health and the Prefect of the Department decide on the area to be served by a particular hospital; if the Communes served find the arrangement unsatisfactory, they can, with the permission of the same two officials, be attached to another hospital. New constructions and extensions are authorised by the Minister of Public Health if the cost is met by grants from public authorities, and by the Prefect if the hospital is financing the work itself. The Minister of Public Health is empowered to alter the character of the hospital by transforming it, for example, from a specialist hospital to a general one.

Communal hospitals are, within the limits of their own resources, required to treat free of charge the indigent, old, incurable, and pregnant mothers who reside in the Commune. If necessary the Commune pays a standard daily charge per head. Intercommunal hospitals have to treat free of charge the needy sick in the participating Communes, and the departmental hospitals those who reside in the Department when no other provision is made for them; they can be required to provide accommodation for wards of the Department and for children in need of protection. All these hospitals can receive paying patients.

A hospital is run by an administrative commission usually presided over by a Mayor, with two members elected from local authorities and four nominated by the Prefect. Administrative supervision is by the Prefect, and technical control by the regional director of the Ministry of Public Health. The hospital's permanent Director is appointed by the Prefect, and the administrative and hospital staff by the administrative commission on the Director's recommendation. The hospitals have their own estates and a fair degree of autonomy in using their funds and in the daily operation of the hospital.

(ii) Educational services are organised regionally. France is divided into 17 *académies*, under the direction of the Minister of National Education assisted by a *conseil supérieur de l'éducation nationale;* these *académies* are based on the universities scattered throughout France. At the head of each university is the *recteur*, appointed on grounds of academic distinction by government decree; he, with a *conseil d'académie*, is responsible for the administration and conduct of higher educational institutions within the area of the *académies*. In each Department within this region the *recteur* is represented by an *inspecteur d'académie* who is responsible for the discipline and teaching in secondary schools, and for recommending the appointment of teachers to primary schools. Primary education is organised by the *inspecteur*, the Prefect and a *conseil départemental de l'enseignement primaire*, a body composed of two school inspectors nominated by the Minister, four members of the *conseil général* elected by that assembly, and four primary school teachers (two of each sex) elected by their fellows. This body has some powers over the number, size and situation of primary schools, syllabuses, and over the discipline and recruitment of teachers. When it decides that a school must be opened, the Commune where it is to be built has to find the sums necessary to build[1] and furnish it, and after its completion the Commune must pay the cost of heating, stationery, lighting and the schoolmaster's residence.

The Department as such is responsible for many of the administrative expenses of this system; in addition it has to provide a training college for teachers and maintain the building and its furniture. It also bears the salaries of technical teachers in primary technical schools. The Department has no responsibility for the *lycées* which are created by the State and are financed by it with the help of contributions from the Communes served.[2] The law of September 28, 1951 set up in each

[1] The State in fact provides a substantial part of the cost of construction, in some cases as much as 85 per cent.

[2] Communes also sometimes have their own secondary schools, the *collèges:* these are set up and financed by the Commune itself, with contracted state assistance. The *lycée* is under the control of the *recteur*, the *collège* (subject to state inspection) is under the Commune. The Minister may, if a Commune is unco-operative, request the assistance of the *conseil général* in setting up a new *collège*.

Department a special fund (*caisse départementale scolaire*) financed by the Treasury to assist local authorities to meet some of the ordinary expenses of public education, such as the cost of equipping and maintaining schools. This fund is under the control of the *conseil général*.

(iii) There are three types of highways in France: the national routes, and departmental and communal roads. The State pays the cost of building and maintaining national routes, although in some cases the Department served may offer to find some of the money. There are 265,000 kilometres of departmental roads, and although the cost of their maintenance is the Department's entire responsibility, the cost of new construction or by-passes is shared between the State and the Department, with the possibility of voluntary contributions from the Communes served.

Communal roads are of various types: ordinary roads (of which there are 375,000 kilometres), urban roads (36,000 kilometres), and rural roads (of which 200,000 kilometres are classified and 500,000 unclassified). The Communes are responsible for the cost of maintaining these roads, although the Department sometimes contributes, and there are instances where *conseils généraux* have re-classified communal roads as departmental roads. The cost of new construction and very large repairs is shared between the Commune, the Department and the State. Both Department and Commune can levy a special tax in their areas called the *prestation* to cover the cost of highway repairs.[1]

Since 1930 the State has increasingly assumed additional responsibilities for the highways. It has increased the amount of state assistance available to local authorities not only for new construction but also for repairs when these resulted from the abnormal lack of maintenance during the war. It has also reclassified as national highways many roads previously the responsibility of the Department.

Finally, in 1951 a special highway fund (*fonds d'investissement routier*) was created to finance improvements for all types of road. In principle, this fund is not to be used for ordinary

[1] See below page 182.

repair work or for the reconstruction of badly worn roads. There are however already signs that this principle will not be fully respected.

(iv) Town planning first came into prominence in France with the law of March 14, 1919, at the time of the reconstruction of the devastated regions. Several modifications followed in the next decades, the most important being the introduction of planned regional development in 1935, with special measures for the Paris region in 1936. A Vichy law of June 15, 1943, codified and consolidated these various measures.

The Vichy system was based on 18 planning regions, including Paris; but these regions were swept away after the Liberation, and now the Department serves as the basic unit of planning, with the exception of the Departments of the Seine, Seine-et-Oise, Seine-et-Marne, and parts of Oise, which together form the Paris region.

Planning and reconstruction are now under the control of the Minister of *Urbanisme et Reconstruction*. The Minister has a technical staff in Paris, and there is a part-time national advisory committee which he must consult on all schemes of town planning. In all Departments (except the Paris region where there is a local advisory body, the *comité d'aménagement de la région parisienne*), there is a *comité départemental d'urbanisme*, on which local authorities are represented.

Plans must be drawn up by all Communes with more than 10,000 inhabitants, by those destroyed or in large part damaged by flood or fire,[1] by Communes specially classified as being of national interest on tourist, architectural or health grounds, and by Communes included in a special planning zone (*groupement d'urbanisme*). A planning zone is formed by grouping together for planning purposes several contiguous or neighbouring Communes with joint interests. These zones are created by the Minister at the instigation of the Prefect, and his decision must be ratified by a Decree of the *Conseil d'État*. The individual plans of the Communes within a zone must conform to the terms of the plan for the whole zone.

[1] Those devastated by the war come under a different system, since building and planning go hand in hand, and heavy state expenditure is involved.

H

Plans are drawn up by a qualified architect appointed by the local authority concerned, and they must contain a detailed scheme marking proposed highways, open spaces, and industrial and housing areas. Attached to this plan is a programme in which are set out the aesthetic, building and sanitary rules to be observed in future building, and any special rules applicable to particular areas.

The plan is examined and approved by the departmental committee and forwarded to the Minister. There then follow consultations between the Minister's technical officers, the Prefect concerned and the local authorities; a programme of execution is drawn up stating the priority to be accorded to the various elements of the plan, and when the plan concerns several authorities the division of expenditure between them must be added.

The completed project is then reforwarded to the Minister for approval, and he presents it to the national advisory committee for consideration; it is finally approved by a Decree of the *Conseil d'État*.

The Prefect plays a large part in putting the plan into effect. He can prevent any construction which is not in accordance with the plan, and when the plan requires the compulsory purchase of property his role is predominant.[1]

The Department ought therefore to act as the centre of activity in town planning, but for several reasons little has been done in this field. The reconstruction of war-devastated areas has naturally been given priority over other forms of construction, and the financial situation of the country has not allowed the diversion of energies to improvement schemes. The French people have little natural taste for plans and schemes, and in practice the extensive powers of compulsory purchase granted to the executive are used very cautiously and with a high regard for the rights of private property. It is probably fair to say that planning amounts to finding housing sites on which private contractors can build, to ensuring that their schemes conform to local needs, and to making the best use of ground left free either by slum-clearance or by war damage.

[1] See Articles 12–14 of Decree Law, August 8—October 30, 1935.

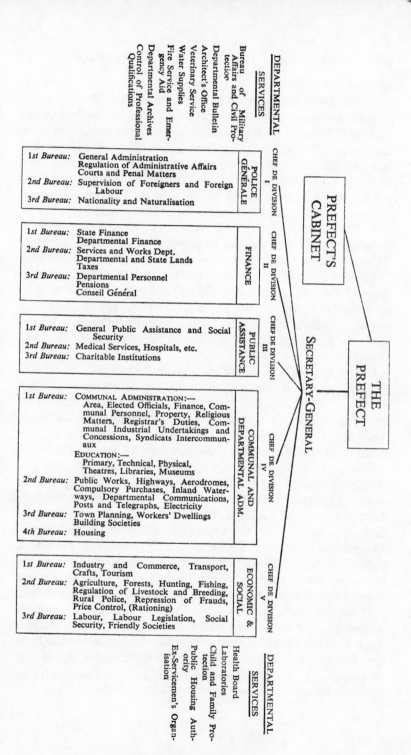

Organisation of a Prefecture.

Internal Organisation of the Prefecture

Before 1940 the Prefect was free to arrange with the *conseil général* the number of *bureaux* and Divisions in the Prefecture, and the allocation of functions between them. Until that time there was only one law laying down a general standard, and this law (of 1920) merely prescribed that each Prefecture should have at least two Divisions. On several occasions between the wars the *inspection générale* of the Ministry of the Interior attempted without success to systematise prefectoral organisation.

In 1940 a Ministerial Circular ordered conformity to a general pattern according to the size of population in the Department. Those with less than 300,000 inhabitants were to have two Divisions, those with between 300,000 and 450,000 were to have three Divisions, and between 450,000 and 800,000 there were to be four Divisions. In the seven Departments with a greater population than this a fifth Division could be created at the Prefect's discretion and an additional Secretary-General could then be appointed.

In practice no serious effort was made to conform to this circular, and it was not until a further Ministerial Circular of June, 1945, that action was insisted upon. Since that time all Prefectures have in theory been brought into line, although there are still examples of unorthodox practice in the smaller Prefectures where personal considerations have some effect.

The best example for this study is a Prefecture with five Divisions, since it has enough *bureaux* to show the scope of the work undertaken.[1] The titles of the five Divisions are General Administration, Finance and Departmental Administration, Economic and Social, Communal Administration, and Public Assistance. In smaller Prefectures with only four Divisions, Public Assistance is amalgamated with the Economic and Social Division; where there are only three, Communal Affairs are merged with General Administration; and finally, where there are only two Divisions, one deals with Departmental and Communal Affairs and the other with Finance and Social Affairs. Besides these Divisions there are departmental services housed outside the Prefecture, each of which is under the authority of the

[1] This is a composite picture of the Prefectures of Toulouse (Haute Garonne), Bordeaux (Gironde) and Rennes (Ille-et-Vilaine).

Prefect. At the head of each of these departmental services are the technical chiefs, such as the departmental architect, the *archiviste*, and the medical authorities.

The work of the first and part of the second Division does not come under the jurisdiction of the *conseil général*, although that body has full powers of enquiry, and can require any information about the services which it may desire. These are concerned with the Prefect's powers as a representative of the State. Regulations made by any branch of the departmental administration must be promulgated by them; and in fact most prefectoral ordinances (other than technical ones) are actually drawn up in one of these *bureaux*. The Secretary-General is authorised to sign ordinances in his own name for many matters of ordinary administrative concern; but a specific warrant delegating such powers of signature is always necessary before this procedure can be followed, and the terms of reference must be clearly delimited. It is an obvious time-saver in a busy Prefecture.

The affairs of the *conseil général* are dealt with in the Prefecture in a special *bureau* of the second Division. This forms the permanent Secretariat of the elected Assembly, keeps in touch with the individual councillors, and is at the service of the President of the *conseil général* and of the President and members of the *commission départementale*. The preparation of reports, the administrative organisation of the sessions, and the clerical work entailed in all these matters, is under the permanent direction of a senior *attaché de préfecture*.

Departmental Personnel

The Law of November 2, 1940, and the *Ordonnance* of August 14, 1944, made the personnel of the Prefectures and Sub-Prefectures into a state cadre, and they have since been given their own statute.[1] There are three senior grades, *chefs de division*, *attachés* of the Prefecture, and *secrétaires administratifs* of the Prefecture. The *secrétaires administratifs* comprise the majority of the officials in the medium ranks of the Prefecture, and the *attachés* and the *chefs de division* are the highest posts, immediately under the Secretary-General of the

[1] Decree, July 4, 1949.

Prefecture, and responsible for the organisation and work of the *bureaux* and Divisions.

The *secrétaires administratifs* are recruited either by national examination of about first year university standard, or by special examination from those members in any lower rank in the state administrations who are over thirty-five and who have at least five years service to their credit. They are subject to the Minister for serious disciplinary offences, but they are under the day-to-day control of the Prefect, who keeps their record cards, pays them from the funds made available by the Minister, and has certain disciplinary powers over them.

The *attachés* are recruited either by a national examination of degree standard held by the Ministry of the Interior, or by promotion from the ranks of the *secrétaires administratifs*. Eight-ninths of the *attachés* must enter by examination and a *secrétaire administratif* must, to be eligible, have had at least fifteen years service; consequently there is not much movement upwards.

The *chefs de division* are chosen by an administrative commission of the Ministry of the Interior from the ranks of the *attachés* of the first class (there are four classes). They are responsible to the Prefect and the Secretary-General for the work and organisation of a Division in a Prefecture. *Chefs de division* and *attachés* of the Prefecture can enter the *corps préfectoral* as Sub-Prefects under specially favourable terms (not financially).[1] Personnel may be required to move from one Prefecture to another; in practice many officials stay in the same Prefecture for long periods, but the national character of the posts serves to avoid the stultification of ambitious and able officers who are not prepared to wait for dead men's shoes, and also to allow officials in the central Ministries to go into the provinces.

Besides these officials there are a number of *auxiliaires d'état* and supplementary staff. These are temporary officials and this branch of the service is in process of dissolution; most of them were recruited in wartime, and those who have not yet been offered a permanent post will never be now. The number of

[1] M. Oeuvrard: *Le service du personnel dans une préfecture. Revue Administrative.* July, 1950.

temporaries in a particular Prefecture varies with the need. Their records are kept in the Ministry, but they are disciplined by the Prefect or, for severer offences, by a Disciplinary Council of the most senior *chefs de division* presided over by the Secretary-General of the Prefecture.

Finally there are all the lowest ranking personnel, the typists, clerks, book-keepers, and so on, who are appointed and paid by the Department and are generally recruited on a six-monthly contract. These officials are outside the control of the Minister, and they are subject entirely to the Prefect. The *conseil général* decides how many of these posts are necessary and votes the necessary expenditure in the budget.

REGIONAL ADMINISTRATION

Regional organisation has been allowed by law since 1871 in the sense that *conseils généraux* were then granted authority to join together into *syndicats* to undertake services of mutual interest. Little use was made of these powers, and both in 1926 and in 1930 further laws were passed to encourage the development of the economic resources of the country along regional lines. Again, little advantage was taken of them; *conseils généraux* consistently opposed the idea of sinking the identity of the Department in a *syndicat* and consequently losing complete control of part of their Department's resources as well as lowering their own prestige and influence. The reason generally offered was that regional organisation would weaken the whole principle of departmental government; a principle already under fire from various quarters. Where *conseils généraux* did combine, the services undertaken were transport, irrigation, reservoirs, sanatoria and forest development.[1]

The main difficulty facing regional administration in France is that, on the one hand, many central Ministries have developed their own areas of administration, none of which coincides with any other, and which create the utmost confusion on the map; on the other hand, there is no general agreement as to whether a region is intended to be primarily an economic unit or a socially homogeneous one, and these two aims are nearly

[1] Legrand, J.: *Les essais d'administration régionale.* Doctoral Thesis for Faculty of Law; University of Paris, 1950.

always in contradiction in a country as diversified as France.

However, the events of the last ten years have shown that regional administration of some sort is eminently desirable, firstly for economic planning, and secondly for public security and emergency government. The Regional Prefects of Vichy and the *Commissaires de la République* of the Liberation, were mentioned in the introduction. Both these posts were created under the strain of economic disintegration and political stress, and their holders were flanked by two special subordinates charged with special police duties and with economic powers (*intendants* under Vichy, *secrétaires* under the Liberation). Many difficulties arose under these systems.[1] Although regional authorities were recognised, the Region as such had no corporate personality and no regional budget, and naturally the ordinary Prefects were hostile to the whole idea and showed their hostility whenever possible. These factors were more harmful under Vichy than under the Liberation, but in both cases they seriously affected the public attitude towards the Region. Politicians especially suspected that power was passing from the hands of the Ministers to regional officers and distrusted the trend both on personal and on national grounds.

In 1946, therefore, after a scrappy debate, the *Commissaires de la République* were abolished and the pre-war system of unco-ordinated Prefects reinstated; as a consequence the regionalised state police forces were redivided between the 89 Departments (excluding the Seine) and the guiding control from the regional capitals was lost. It was with this fragmented system that France faced the big insurrectionary strike wave of November, 1947. The result was nearly disastrous, as the isolation of the Prefects from Paris, the inadequate forces under their control (which they jealously conserved, often to the detriment of their immediate neighbours), and the discordant and indecisive measures adopted by the ill-informed Ministry in Paris, all combined to favour the strikers and to spread the strikes. At one time the position became so grave that the Ministry considered withdrawing all the security forces in the South into Marseilles and Montpellier, leaving the countryside

[1] B. Chapman: A Development in French Regional Administration; *Public Administration.* Winter, 1950.

to the Communists until sufficient strength could be built up to challenge them.

Eventually the police prevailed, with the assistance of the army, but the organisational weakness had been so apparent that M. Moch, Minister of the Interior, proposed to create eight posts of *Inspecteur Général de l'Administration en Mission Extraordinaire* (IGAME), whose primary duty should be to re-organise the police services within the areas of the eight military regions, the capitals of which should be the new administrative regional capitals. The IGAME were to assume complete control of all security forces, both civil and military, in any time of emergency, and in such an event all the other authorities were to place themselves entirely at the disposal of the IGAME. This proposal was accepted by Parliament[1] and the posts were filled without delay. Each IGAME was given a Letter of Service to be used in an emergency, wherein the appropriate Ministers (President of the Council, Ministers of the Interior and Defence) delegated all their powers directly and personally to the IGAME to be exercised by him within his Region. Thus, in an emergency all the requisite powers were in the hands of a single authority, and they could be exercised even if the Region were cut off from Paris. This step avoided the political dangers of the *état de siège*, the only other method of granting one man all the necessary authority to cope with a tense situation; the latter method granted all power to the military commander in the affected area.

Four of the first IGAME (Toulouse, Lyons, Rennes and Metz) were the resident Prefects, but in the other four cases (Marseilles, Bordeaux, Lille and Dijon) the IGAME resided in Paris and had no normal prefectoral duties. Since then all vacant posts have been filled by Prefects resident in the regional capitals. The IGAME has certain extra police powers, to be exercised only in an emergency. Police headquarters have been set up in each regional capital with supply, administrative and identification services attached, and they are controlled by a specially appointed Secretary-General of the Prefecture, directly under the orders of the IGAME. This Secretary-General is a member of the *corps préfectoral* and not an ordinary police

[1] Law of March 21, 1948.

official since it was thought that a civil rather than a police official should fill this potentially critical post.

The first step taken by all the IGAME after their appointment was to overhaul the police forces of their Regions, drawing up plans, redeploying forces and testing communications. The first use of the Letter of Service came during the General Strike of the miners in November, 1948. In several areas, and principally in the Gard, the IGAME personally conducted operations, assisted by the Prefects and the military authorities. Emergency powers have also been used to combat civil catastrophes. When fires swept the Landes in 1949, the IGAME of Bordeaux used his authority to co-ordinate operations.

In addition to his emergency powers, the IGAME can be specially charged with a " mission of information and co-ordination " by any Minister or group of Ministers. When this occurs the IGAME convokes a meeting of all the Prefects in his Region and asks them for assistance in drafting a report on the subject under discussion. Many problems interesting the central Government have been dealt with in this way, among them administrative reform, the floating of the national loan of 1949, price control, wages policy and economic planning. The Ministers concerned can gain from eight IGAME a clearer picture than could be obtained from 90 unco-ordinated Prefects.

In the same spirit individual IGAME have been called in by the Government to advise on matters of major political importance affecting their Regions. The IGAME of Toulouse was sent to Madrid to discuss the development of the Pyrenees; the IGAME of Metz was called in for discussion on the future of the Saar; and the IGAME of Marseilles was asked to investigate the causes of the international dockers' strike in 1949.

In many cases the pre-eminence of the IGAME is a rationalisation of previous practice, since the Prefectures of Toulouse, Lyons, Rennes, and so on, have always been regarded as the plums of the service, to be filled by the highest class Prefects. In at least one case (Toulouse) there was a long-established custom of frequent meetings between the Prefects to discuss matters of common concern under the chairmanship of the Prefect of the Haute Garonne (capital Toulouse) even before the IGAME were created. Such co-operation was conspicuously lacking in some Regions, and here the new system offers a chance for improvement.

The IGAME should not be regarded as the hierarchic superior of the ordinary Prefects in the Region. Except for the regional police headquarters there is no regional administrative cadre, and the Prefects still correspond with and receive orders from the Minister directly. Most significant of all, the Prefects welcome the new system.

There is, however, a certain moral superiority attached to the post of IGAME. His contact with the Ministry is undoubtedly more personal, and within the *corps préfectoral* the post of IGAME certainly holds more prestige than any *hors classe* Prefect, except the Prefect of the Seine (Paris) and the Prefect of Police.

Administratively, the IGAME have supplied a long-felt need. But their eminence and authority hold political dangers, for the average French politician seldom looks favourably on the creation of a centre of power over which he has little control.

Brief mention should be made of the Economic Regions, of which there are twenty. A regional approach to the problem of economic development has for some time been popular, although in France the regulation of economic affairs has not passed as much under the control of administrators as in this country: the regions used are, in fact, " private enterprise " Regions, although officially recognised by law. These Economic Regions are composed of voluntarily associated groups of departmental Chambers of Commerce; the Regional Chambers have been granted legal status and have become very influential in matters of economic policy. They are grouped round the principal provincial centres, and they form an effective pressure group with which the Prefects and the Government generally keep in close touch. Their advice is invariably sought on major issues; for instance the development of the hinterland of Bordeaux and plans connected with stimulating activity in that declining port have all been drawn up by the Regional Chamber of Commerce with the approval of the Government. The work of these Economic Regions is not however strictly relevant to a study of local government.

CHAPTER FOUR

Tutelage and Local Authorities

THE supervision and guidance of local authorities is of great importance in French local government, and, as was described in the Introduction, the principles of control are inherent in French constitutional law. The State has a general interest in orderly and honest government, and all government bodies are subject to some form of supervision. When the State grants powers of decision to state officials operating in various parts of the country, it is said to "deconcentrate" its power. These officials are subject to the supervision of their superiors, and their decisions can be reversed at will by a member of the state administration whose position gives him greater powers of discretion. This is hierarchic supervision, and is in no sense tutelage.

Tutelage, instead, begins when the State grants powers of decision to persons who are not subject to hierarchic control, but whose actions are taken in the name of a public body belonging to the corpus of state institutions. Local authorities have no existence independent from that of the State, and consequently elected authorities exercise not their own inherent powers, but those conceded to them by a higher state organ: these powers are said to be "decentralised". Decentralisation and tutelage, therefore, go hand in hand, and perhaps the best definition of tutelage is that it comprises "the totality of the powers accorded by law to a superior authority over decentralised bodies and over their actions, granted in order to protect the general interest."[1]

Tutelage has several aspects, but they can be grouped into

[1] Maspétiol et Laroque: *La Tutelle Administrative*; Vol. I, p. 10. Sirey; 1931.

two main sections; political tutelage and financial tutelage. Since 1940 there have been interesting changes in the classical system, and these will be dealt with separately. The chapter ends with a description of the Ministry of the Interior, which is nationally responsible for the work of local authorities and which is their ultimate tutelage authority.

POLITICAL TUTELAGE

Political tutelage has two facets, control over the personnel of the decentralised authorities, and control over their decisions.

Control of Personnel

The State sometimes, though rarely, has some part in the selection of the members of the decentralised bodies; for example, some of the members of hospital boards are nominated by the Prefect and some by the local authorities concerned. Also, there are circumstances in which members are nominated by an elected body, but in which the decisions require the approval of the State (for example, the nomination of members of the *Institut*); but this procedure is seldom found in local government, although certain paid local government officials, like the Secretary of the *Mairie*, are chosen by the local authority and agreed to by the Prefect.

The two principal elected local authorities, the *conseil municipal* and the *conseil général*, are chosen by the electorate without the intervention of the State, except that the rules under which the elections are held are laid down by law. Control of the personnel of these bodies is confined to (i) the dismissal or suspension of individuals, (ii) the dissolution of the whole body, or (iii) the assumption of decentralised powers by a state official.

(i) There are many instances of the suspension of Mayors for refusing to perform actions legally incumbent upon them, or for acting in a way prejudicial to good government and orderly administration. A Mayor can be suspended from his functions for a month by the Prefect; for example, the Mayor of Boucau (Basses Pyrénées) was suspended after he had published in the municipal bulletin a copy of a telegram informing a mother that her son in Indo-China was missing, although the telegram itself had not at the time been delivered to the family: a violent anti-government commentary was attached.[1]

The Minister of the Interior has power to suspend a Mayor for up to three months, or in grave cases to dismiss him from office: the Mayor of Port de Bouc (Bouches-du-Rhône) was suspended for three months after he had publicly mocked at a religious ceremony on Liberation Day from the ranks of a political procession.[2] Dismissal from office followed upon the categorical refusal of the Mayor of Eymoutiers (Haute Vienne) to obey an order to inscribe "*Mort pour la France*" against the names of two people shot in error by Resistance forces for collaboration.[3] Normally, consistent refusal to perform their duties properly comes from Mayors of Communes which are firmly in the hands of an extremist party, and suspensions or dismissal involve no change of political control, since the senior Assistant-Mayor is generally designated to take the Mayor's place. A strong majority of one Party in a Commune can make this form of tutelage extremely difficult to exercise; for example, when the Communist Mayors of seven Communes in the Department of the Seine (Paris) were suspended for three months, all the Assistant-Mayors (who were also Communists) refused to take office, and eventually the Minister of the Interior had to nominate a councillor of the opposition to look after current business.[4] Naturally, any shortcoming in local services and any failure to carry through communal schemes are used as political propaganda throughout the Commune. These examples indicate how wilful disobedience or gross neglect of duty can be punished by suspension or dismissal, but there are sanctions against abuse of this tutelage authority, and an incorrectly worded Decree of dismissal, or one promulgated for the wrong reasons, will not only raise a storm of protest (which will certainly be reflected in Parliament) but will also lead to litigation for abuse of power before the administrative courts.

The individual municipal councillor can be dismissed from

[1] Reported in *Le Monde:* February 25, 26, 1951.
[2] Ibid: September 1, 1950.
[3] Ibid: May 11, 1950.
[4] Ibid: January 28, 1951.

office by order of the Prefect for wilfully neglecting his duties or for knowingly abusing his office for personal ends. In such cases he is stated to have resigned.

An individual member of the *conseil général* guilty of neglecting his duties is not subject to the tutelage authorities; the *conseil général* alone can expel him and then only if he has been absent from two consecutive sessions without adequate cause. The civil courts can declare a member ineligible for election for three years if that court finds him guilty of breaking the law; this penalty is not within the power of the tutelage authorities, and is a further instance of the special status of the *conseil général* in local government.

(ii) The *conseil municipal* as a body can be dismissed if it is unable to function, if it deliberately abuses its power or if it refuses to perform duties legally incumbent upon it. Local politics sometimes lead to such acrimony and such cleavage into hostile groups that no clear majority is possible, and the Mayor is unable to obtain support to continue to administer efficiently or to get the communal budget voted. Nearly every week there are examples of ministerial decrees dissolving *conseils municipaux* which are unable to function, and nothing remains but the hope that the local electorate will decide to choose other representatives.[1] It is much rarer to find dissolutions for abuse of power and neglect of duties, but this is considered to be a necessary reserve power.

The *conseil général* may in theory be dissolved by a Decree of the Government signed by the President of the Republic, but in fact no dissolution of this nature has been made since 1874.

(iii) The third method by which the tutelage authorities can control the personnel of local authorities is by assuming the powers granted to the latter by law. The most important instance of this is the Prefect's power to write into communal budgets expenditure declared to be obligatory by law and

[1] On an average some 300 *conseils municipaux* are dissolved every year. The principal cause is that the numbers fall below a quorum due to the death of councillors, but sometimes it may result from an irreconcilable disagreement on policy inside the council.

omitted by the *conseil municipal*, and to balance the budget if it is not voted in equilibrium. This is tutelage by financial means and will be dealt with in the next section.

The Prefect can also require the Mayor to take steps which the Prefect considers to be necessary in the interests of public order, and if the Mayor refuses to obey the Prefect can take the necessary measures in his own name, even though the law reserves the *police municipale* to the Mayor. Several laws explicitly grant the Prefect power to intervene in communal affairs if the communal authorities fail to perform their duties. For example, *conseils municipaux* who fail to provide the necessary facilities for Public Assistance institutions or who refuse to provide accommodation for state primary schools, may find their powers of acquisition used by the Prefect. The latter provision has been a cause of frequent disturbance in the West, where there is a predominantly Catholic population which resents having to spend communal funds on state schools when it is forbidden to make grants towards the maintenance of church schools. The problem is exacerbated by the fact that in many of these areas a very small proportion of children are sent to the state primary schools. Otherwise well-administered Communes with sober *conseils* have come into conflict with prefectoral authority on such an issue, and a Sub-Prefect, supported by a squad of *gendarmerie*, has had to brave local wrath in order to extract the keys from the Mayor and let the *instituteur* into the school; he was immediately faced with mass-resignations by the local *conseils municipaux*, who used the new elections to mark popular disapproval.[1] As with all prefectoral administration, the exercise of tutelage powers over local authorities requires considerable tact coupled with firmness.

The Prefect cannot exercise on his own authority any of the powers granted to the *conseil général*. The competent tutelage authority here is the Minister, and he frequently has to obtain the opinion of the *Conseil d'État* before acting. The *Conseil d'État* itself sometimes acts as a tutelage authority, more especially in financial matters, and these will be touched on in the next section. The power to substitute administrative decisions for those of the *conseil général* is exercised if a *conseil général*

[1] Reported in *Le Monde*: October 3, 4, 5, 1951.

refuses to balance its budget or to allow sufficient credits to meet obligatory expenditure.

Control of Decisions

Tutelage can be exercised over the decisions of local authorities in three ways. (i) The simplest is the right to examine a decision for any signs of illegality, with the power to suspend its application until the administrative courts have had the opportunity to pass judgment. The second and third methods imply a certain amount of discretion on the part of the tutelage authority: (ii) Some decisions require the approval of the Prefect, Minister, or the *Conseil d'État* before they come into operation, and this approval is discretionary; and (iii) other decisions cannot be made until the tutelage authority has given permission to the local authority to deal with that particular matter.

(i) *All* decisions of the *conseil municipal*, no matter what their content or authority, have to be deposited at the Prefecture or Sub-Prefecture for a certain time before they can be put into effect. This enforced delay is to allow the prefectoral administration to examine the decisions for illegalities.

Certain decisions are inherently tainted with illegality. A decision is *ipso facto* illegal if it is *ultra vires,* or if it conflicts with a law or an administrative regulation made under law. It is also illegal to raise or spend money in a way not authorised by law or declared to be irregular by the *Cour des Comptes.*[1] Local authorities can be pitied rather than blamed for offending against this provision, since financial law is so confused that an authority may break the law in perfect faith, and then find itself burdened with heavy damages. A Commune in the Midi had to raise a special loan to reimburse tax-payers upon whom a legally non-existent tax had been levied, and a great city's public services were seriously compromised by the *Conseil d'État* ruling that a particular tax was illegal.[2]

A decision taken by a local authority at a meeting at which an interested party is present is also illegal, even though the

[1] The senior financial court. See below, p. 137.

[2] Lainville: *Le Budget Communal:* Sirey, 7th Edition. 1951, p. 25. The *Conseil d'État* and not the *Cour des Comptes* was competent in this case, since interpretation of law was involved.

I

matter itself is *intra vires*. Similarly, a decision is illegal if taken at an irregular session or one at which the required quorum was not present. These decisions, passed in proper form, would be accepted.

The Prefect can, within a specified time, annul a communal decision which he believes to be illegal, and it cannot then be put into effect; anyone who attempts to do so is guilty of a breach of the law and is subject to the civil courts. Communal authorities have the right to appeal against a Prefect's decision to the administrative courts, but until the court decides all action is suspended. Decisions of the *conseil général* may also be held up by the Prefect on legal grounds, and he may lay the case directly before the *Conseil d'État*. Action is again suspended until the judgement. There are some cases, as will be seen in the next chapter, where the illegality of a decision is not evident, but where there is reason to believe that there has been corrupt intent or abuse of power, and then the Prefect will declare the measure illegal even when he is aware that his decision will be challenged, simply in order to ensure some judicial review of the original decision.

(ii) Then there are the decisions which require approval before they become operative. In the second chapter it was seen that many of the decisions of *conseils municipaux* and *conseils généraux* were subject to ratification by an administrative authority. These decisions concern, among other things, finance, contracts, property, and the appointment of local officials. The budget of the *conseil municipal* is approved by the Sub-Prefect of the *arrondissement* in Communes under 20,000, and by the Prefect in Communes over that figure; the Minister of the Interior and the Minister of the Budget approve the budgets of Communes with more than 80,000 inhabitants when they have shown a continual deficit over the last three financial years.[1] The budgets of the *conseils généraux* are all approved by the Minister of the Interior and the Minister of Finance.

Special permission is required before loans can be raised by a Commune for the creation of new communal services of an industrial or commercial character, and for the leasing of com-

[1] Decree; August 12, 1950.

munal property for periods longer than 18 years. The sale or acquisition of departmental or communal property also requires permission from a tutelage authority. In all these cases the Prefect or Sub-Prefect is normally the tutelage authority for the Communes, but communal business involving high figures is sometimes transferred to the Minister and the *Conseil d'État* for decision, and the tutelage authority in a specific case can often be discovered only by reference to the law.

It must be emphasised that in all these circumstances the authorisation of the tutelage authority is necessary before the decision is legally valid. If permission is not given, and an attempt is made to flout the tutelage authority, all the reserve powers of the Executive come into play.

An instance which is interesting, if rather melodramatic, was furnished by a conflict between the *conseil municipal* of Saint Junien and the Prefect of the Haute-Vienne. The Commune's representatives decided to christen their new sports stadium the " Stadium Maurice Thorez " and to change the name of an adjoining street from Boulevard Gambetta to " Boulevard Joseph Stalin ". The Prefect pointed out some days before the official opening that (a) acts of public homage concerning living persons required the authorisation of the Ministry, and that (b) the renaming of streets needed the authorisation of a prefectoral Ordinance. He informed the Mayor that the Minister refused to authorise the name " Stadium Maurice Thorez " and for his part he would never allow Stalin to replace Gambetta. In the face of the *conseil municipal*'s continued defiance, he added, a few days before the opening, that if any re-naming ceremony took place, the name-plates would be removed at the Commune's expense, and the expenses of any public forces required to enforce this would be charged to the Commune's account.

The Commune went ahead, however, and the name-plates were duly substituted. In face of this flagrant defiance the Prefect carried out his threat and removed the name-plates. The following night the local party members replaced the offending plaques. The Prefect then called his reserve powers into play. All services of the State, Department and Commune would continue to call the Boulevard by its old name: any correspond-

ence, mail, telephones, etc., addressed "Boulevard Joseph
Stalin" would be returned to sender marked "Unknown": the
plaques would be replaced, and any police force necessary to
guard them would be maintained: the *Procureur de la République* proceeded to issue warrants for misbehaviour on the
public highway and for wilful defacement of public property in
violation of Article 257 of the Criminal Code: all these operations were charged upon the Commune's budget, and substantial forces were sent to the Commune to keep the peace,
also at local expense. After some more guerrilla warfare peace
descended, more or less.[1]

This storm in a teacup is striking for several reasons. It shows
the powers inherent in the tutelage authority and the way they can
be developed and expanded when met with defiance. It illustrates
the awkward political problems with which a Prefect has to
deal, and it points to the difficulties likely to be encountered
in the event of really determined local resistance. The suspension of the Mayor or the dissolution of the *conseil municipal* for
violating the laws were useless weapons in this instance since the
political complexion of this small glovemaking town made it
inevitable that those methods would only create martyrs, and
any new election would have returned the same party to power.

(iii) Lastly come those matters requiring the prior approval of
the tutelage authority, before a decision can be made at all.
Prior permission of this sort is required, for example, if the local
authority considers raising a loan to be amortised over a period
exceeding thirty years, or if it wants to impose certain types of
extraordinary local taxes, or if it is left estate in a will or wishes
to accept conditional bequests which entail some form of contract with the executors or lawyers. Thus a certain Doctor
Dubois of Lisieux left 20 million francs in his will to the *bureau
de bienfaisance* in that town on condition that a street be named
after him, and that a letter appended to his will be published by
the Commune within a month of his death. This letter amounted
to a long apologia for the life and actions of Marshal Pétain, and
the Prefect of Calvados (capital Caen) refused to give the Com-

[1] Reported in *Le Monde:* August 24, 25, 29, 31, and September 12, 1950;
and April 9, 1951.

mune permission to enter into legal relations with the executors on grounds of public interest. Lisieux, consequently, had to forego the bequest.[1]

FINANCIAL TUTELAGE

There has always been direct state control over certain aspects of local government finance; only the two principal aspects will be dealt with here, the approval of the budget and the audit of the accounts of the local authorities.

The Budget

The budgets of all local authorities must be presented in a specific way, as defined by administrative regulation, with the revenue and expenditure each divided into precise categories (e.g. Public Assistance, Debt Service, etc.) and with a clear division between ordinary and extraordinary expenditure and revenue.[2] The communal budget must be voted by September 15 in Communes with less than 2,000 inhabitants, by October 15 in those between 2,000 and 10,000, and by November 15 in larger Communes. All these measures are designed to relieve the administration of too great a strain in examining budgets. The Department's budget must be ready by the end of the Autumn session of the *conseil général*. It must be sent to the Minister for approval through the ordinary administrative channels.

After the communal budget has been approved by the *conseil municipal* the Mayor sends three copies to the Sub-Prefect[3] and he must attach to the budget his own report of the proceedings and a record of the vote taken if the *conseil municipal* has decided to raise a new tax. If the Prefect or Sub-Prefect approve the budget without amendment, one copy is kept by the administration, one is returned to the Mayor, and one is forwarded to the *receveur municipal*, the member of the state financial administration responsible for paying out sums from communal funds. If the budget is for a Commune of more than 80,000 inhabitants,

---

[1] Reported in *Le Monde:* March 1, 1951.

[2] For the technical layout of the budget see Lainville: op. cit., pp. 200–204.

[3] Or the Prefecture if the Commune is in the *arrondissement* in which the Prefecture is situated, or if it has more than 20,000 inhabitants.

and the communal accounts have shown a deficit for the last three financial years, the budget must be approved by the Minister, and it is forwarded to Paris by the Prefect for examination.

The tutelage authority can alter the revenue side of the budget either because an item is illegal, or because the receipt from it is under- or over-estimated, or because a source of revenue has been omitted in the budget. These are all fairly straightforward, but the tutelage authority may also object to an item because, although legal, he considers it inexpedient or contrary to public interest.[1] In short the tutelage authority has an almost unlimited right (technically) to strike out items of revenue. On the expenditure side, he may strike out unjustified items or reduce the size of estimates allowed; but the only expenditure which can be written into the budget is that which is declared obligatory by law. The local authority can appeal to the administrative courts for protection against abuse of tutelage power, but the *Conseil d'État* will not receive cases in which the exercise of discretion is involved, unless the local authority can show that the grounds on which it was used had nothing to do with the control and supervision of the budget.

If the local authority neglects or refuses to provide for obligatory expenditure, the necessary sums can eventually be written into the budget by the Administration on its own authority. If the local authority refuses to vote a balanced budget similar action may be taken by the tutelage authority. The communal budget is returned to the Mayor within ten days, and within a week the *conseil municipal* must make any necessary alterations; in default the budget is balanced by the Prefect. The departmental budget is returned to the Prefect after what is often, in these days, a somewhat indefinite period; if the Minister has made any alterations the Prefect presents these to the *conseil général* which then re-votes the budget.

The communal budget can also be regulated by an administrative authority if at the end of the financial year the previous budget shows a deficit of more than 10 per cent. The new draft budget approved by the *conseil municipal* is then forwarded for examination by a special Commission presided over by the Prefect or his delegate, and composed of representatives of the

[1] cf. Lainville: op. cit., p. 223.

state financial and taxation administrations (3 in all), the Mayor and two municipal councillors. This Commission makes sure that the Commune has taken all the necessary steps to rectify the deficit and prevent a recurrence. If the Commission believes that further measures are necessary, the draft budget is returned to the *conseil municipal* with its recommendations; action must then be taken within a fortnight. Failing this the Prefect returns the budget to the Commission, and the latter does the necessary re-drafting; the budget is then promulgated by prefectoral order. In these circumstances both the Prefect and the Commission are empowered to exercise the financial powers of the *conseil municipal* in order to make the new budget effective.

At face value these tutelage powers seem to present a real threat to any form of real local government, since some degree of financial autonomy is an essential prerequisite of effective action. In fact, Prefects and the Minister are very reluctant to provoke political battles over local budgets, whether departmental or communal, since it is by no means obvious who is going to win. In the last resort the local authority will refuse to vote the budget at all, and the situation then is one of some delicacy. The Minister is faced with the alternative either of dissolving the local authority and holding new elections, or of writing the budget on his own authority. In the latter case, the Prefect or Minister can only use for revenue purposes the income from the estate of the Commune or Department, the funds which come to the authority automatically, and the taxes levied in the previous year. No new levies can be made. As regards expenditure, the tutelage authority can only make provision for matters declared obligatory by law, and these do not account for anything like all the services nowadays normally provided by a local authority; for example, street lighting is theoretically an optional expense, but its disappearance would be a nuisance. Without doubt, the removal of these amenities hits the local inhabitants more than the administration, but the political capital that can be made out of such a situation, and the natural interest that the Executive has in good administration for its own sake, more than counterbalance this. In face of these difficulties, the Prefect usually tries to persuade the Mayor or the President of the *conseil général* in private to remove the objectionable items before it comes to the vote.[1] Thus the Prefect or the Minister is in practice very unwilling to use his great powers of financial tutelage, and if he does use them he may not get the upper hand in the end. When the *conseil général* of the Seine refused to vote the 1951 budget because of the drastic cuts made in it by the Minister, the Administration quickly restored a substantial part of the original credits to avoid an impossible situation.

The final barrier to autocratic administrative action is that the Minister cannot dissolve a *conseil municipal* after it has voted its budget merely because it refuses to accept the recommendations of the tutelage authority in redrafting the budget. No *conseil général* has ever been dissolved, and no Minister is likely to make a precedent over financial politics. Normally, of course, few local authorities are willing to let the administration decide their budget for them, especially when the results are likely to be serious for their electors. Since 1948,[2] the Prefect possesses a reserve weapon in the provision that if a budget is not properly voted by January 1, each year, the preceding budget can be carried over without change until the new one is passed. This gives him some freedom of manoeuvre, by allowing him to play for time. But tutelage, in practice, is nothing like the bludgeon it has been alleged to be.

The Audit

The second important element in the Executive's control of local government finance is the auditing of accounts at the end of each year. Three authorities are concerned with the technical financial operations of all public bodies; the *trésorier payeur général*, the *inspection des finances* and the *Cour des Comptes*. There is an additional check in that the elected bodies examine the accounts of the Mayor and the Prefect. This examination may cause detailed investigation into the workings of the Administration, by revealing shortcomings or fraud. For example, the seven non-Communist councillors who formed the opposition in the Commune of Losne (Côte d'Or) resigned from office in protest against the majority's decision to pass the Mayor's

[1] Lainville: op. cit., p. 232.
[2] Decree, January 6, 1948.

accounts. They alleged that the credits allowed in the budget for repairs to the church had disappeared, but no repairs had been done; the coal which had been ordered for the school had been paid for, or at least the Mayor proffered a receipt in his statement, but the school had had no coal. The resignation of these members provoked a prefectoral investigation and a complete audit of the Mayor's accounts by state officials.[1]

The supreme financial tribunal is the *Cour des Comptes*, a body originally created in 1807 by Napoleon to examine and audit the financial statements and transactions of all public authorities; it now comprises 110 *conseillers* and 34 *auditeurs*.[2] All officials charged with the accounts of public authorities are required (under penalty for default) to present their annual accounts to the Court by a date fixed by law. One of the *sections* into which the *Cour des Comptes* is divided examines these accounts to see that they have been properly balanced, that there has been no illegality, and that all sums spent are properly accounted for and backed by receipts or other legal proof. If the accounts are balanced or in credit, the *Cour des Comptes* declares them correct by an *arrêté;* if they are not balanced the *Cour* lays down a period in which the offending authority must settle its account with the Treasury. These judgements are sent for enforcement to the Minister of the Treasury.

If, in the course of its examination, the *Cour des Comptes* discovers evidence of fraud or illegality, it will communicate its findings to the Minister of Finance and to the Minister of Justice, who see that technical experts examine the whole financial situation of the authority concerned in detail, and when a conspiracy to defraud is exposed they bring the offenders before the ordinary courts for judgement. Appeals against the judgements of the *Cour des Comptes* can only be made to the *Conseil d'État*, and then only on points of law.[3]

Control over the day to day administration of local authorities' financial affairs is exercised by the *trésorier payeur général*

---

[1] Reported in *Le Monde:* February 22, 1950.

[2] Laws: September 16, 1807; April 4, 1941; May 16, 1941; October 29, 1941.

[3] L. Trotabas: *Précis de science et législation financières.* 9th Edition; Dalloz, 1949; pp. 124–131.

of the Department, and by the *inspecteurs des finances* in the Ministry of Finance. The *trésorier payeur général* is the principal financial officer resident in the Department, and is the administrative superior of all the *receveurs municipaux* and other officials of the Ministry of Finance in the Department. He is responsible for receiving direct taxes and judicial fines, and the transfer and payment from the accounts of public authorities (with special reference to state and departmental accounts); he acts for the Central Bank in the Department and ensures that the debts of all authorities are paid.[1] He has powers of investigation and discipline over the subordinate financial officials in the Department; in recent years he has far exceeded his original role of technical official, to become what has been called the " financial Prefect of the Department ".[2] The challenge he has presented to the Prefect will be touched on in the next section.

Technical auditing is performed by *inspecteurs des finances*. They belong to an old *corps d'élite*, with extremely high prestige. They are directly attached to the Minister of Finance and responsible only to him. They have full authority to examine the accounts of any public authority or official, no matter what his rank. To ensure effective control they are given a circuit in the country, through which they travel holding without notice snap audits of any public authority in their area. Any irregularities are reported to the Ministry for action.

The Report of the *Cour des Comptes*[3] for the year 1948-9 was extremely scathing. Local authorities were criticised for failing to control their subordinate officials effectively; but even more ferocious comments were directed at the other public services and at the Ministries, and it may be said that the Report casts a relatively favourable light upon the efficiency of the authorities responsible for the financial tutelage of local authorities.

NEW TENDENCIES

Since 1940 three new trends have emerged in the practice of tutelage; first the centralisation of powers by the Ministries,

[1] Trotobas: op. cit., pp. 73, 110.
[2] Doueil: op. cit., p. 253.
[3] Annexed to the *Journal Officiel* of June 30, 1950.

involving the dispossession of the Prefect of some of his powers; second, the interposition of the *trésorier payeur général* between the Prefect and the local authorities as tutelage authority; and third, the restriction of the freedom of local authorities as regards the form which their official acts should take. The two former trends have recently been reversed, but they have left their mark and must be mentioned here. The last change has introduced a new concept into local government practice, the *contrôle administratif;* it is simplest to deal with this first.

Contrôle Administratif

From time to time before the war the Ministry of the Interior and the *Conseil d'État* laid down draft or model contracts for the use of local authorities. In recent years this practice has greatly increased. Local authorities are not compelled to use these officially sponsored forms, but they are encouraged to do so. When they do the contract is ratified by a lower tutelage authority than when they do not; for example, electricity supply concessions granted by Communes or *syndicats intercommunaux* require only the Prefect's approval if an official draft contract form is used, but if it is not then a Decree of the *Conseil d'État* is necessary. Gas, transport, water, funeral undertakings and sewage are all covered by this type of prescriptive control. Approval by the local tutelage authority naturally means considerable time-saving, and perhaps more sympathetic treatment.

Another, and stricter method of administrative control over local authorities is for the Minister to insist upon uniform procedure. For example, the conditions of service, pay and recruitment for local officials must now conform, to a great degree, to national standards. The allowances to be paid to Mayors and councillors as expenses when on official business are no longer decided by the individual authority but by an administrative regulation of the Minister.

In these matters the liberty left to local authorities is largely theoretical, except for the important choice between action and inaction. If certain powers are exercised at all they must be used in ways prescribed by the State. M. Doueil[1] calls this procedure

[1] Doueil : op. cit., p. 206.

liberté canalisée, and remarks that it is one of the most striking transformations in modern administration. He may underestimate, however, the resilience and obstinacy of small authorities who prefer inaction by nature and are now reinforced in this attitude by fear of state control.

Centralisation

Centralisation was the inevitable product of the war, and its worse excesses are now disappearing; enough remains, however, to provoke the indignation both of the Prefects and of local authorities.

The whole structure of French administration makes centralisation easy, since all that is required is for the Minister of the Interior to take some powers of discretion away from the Prefect and exercise them himself. In practice, without the Prefect, centralisation would be much worse than it is, as he forms a natural centre of attraction for all the Department, and his supremacy over all other state administrations in his area ensures effective departmental government in the sense that local problems are dealt with locally. Nevertheless, during the war certain decisions had to be taken at a national level, and the Prefect was the sufferer.

There is a considerable list (which is rapidly being shortened) of inane instances of centralisation with regard to local government: the transfer of state police officials from one Department to another can only be authorised by the Director-General of the *Sûreté Nationale;* an act of public homage involving the expenditure of more than £50 requires the permission of the Minister; a public authority can only accept a bequest or legacy valued at more than £1,000 after the *Conseil d'État* has given its authorisation by Decree. The value of the prefectoral system is that it is perfectly simple to return powers to the Prefect, and this is now being done. There now prevails a much stricter conception of what is of real national concern.

For local government, perhaps the most important piece of centralisation has been control of the property transactions of public authorities. Central control was plainly necessary during the war to avoid further inflation of property values. A special control body was set up in 1943 called the *Commission Nationale des Opérations Immobilières*, composed of senior officials from various Ministries. The Liberation extended the life of this body, and so broadened its powers that it was called upon to deal with the most trivial pieces of business entered into by small Communes. Its discretion was very wide, allowing it to enter into questions of expediency and policy; but the pressure of its work was too great to allow it to be efficient. Its short-comings became so evident that in order to relieve it, in 1949[1] a subsidiary body was created in each Department to deal with work involving only small amounts. This local body, the *Commission Départementale des Opérations Immobilières* is com-posed of the heads of the state services within the Depart-ment, and at least three members of the *conseil général*, with the Prefect as president. It has jurisdiction over leases between £50 and £300, acquisition of property valued between £500 and £5,000, and compulsory purchases involving between £250 and £1,000. Appeals from its decisions can be made to the Minister, and the commission's decision can be overridden by a joint ordinance of the Ministers of the Interior and of Finance; but this is very rare.

On grounds of expediency and bitter experience, therefore, powers have been returned to a departmental body where the Prefect enjoys his former supremecy.

Competition with the Prefect

A more serious incursion into the field of tutelage has been the rise in influence of the *trésorier payeur général*. His increased influence is one result of the wartime attempt by central admin-istrations to liberate themselves from the Minister of the Interior's supremacy in local government. For some years the Ministers corresponded directly with their officials in the De-partment, deliberately ignoring the Prefect's legal responsibility for all the administrations within the Department; and some Ministers even devolved powers of decision to these officials so as to free them from subordination to the Prefect. The worst abuses have been stamped out by post-war Ministers of the Interior, though in several instances the latter had to intervene personally.

[1] Decree: August 28, 1949.

The agent of the Minister of Finance, the *trésorier payeur général*, is now the only state official who can rival the Prefect, and in one branch of departmental administration he often clearly exceeds his lawful powers. The Prefect is responsible for authorising payments from all state and departmental funds in the Department, and he does this under his own responsibility. The *trésorier payeur général* is responsible for meeting the warrants issued by the Prefect; after the financial year is over he checks his accounts against the Prefect's authorisations. These are two distinct operations, but they tend to get confused together; that is to say, the *trésorier payeur général* takes it upon himself to check the authority of the Prefect's warrants for payment, on the tacit assumption that if he finds anything amiss he will refuse payment. What was originally intended as a purely technical check on the Prefect's financial operations has developed into an illicit form of tutelage over his actions. The *trésorier payeur général* has gone beyond his role of auditor to assume the role of financial supervisor.[1]

In several fields the jurisdiction of the *trésorier payeur général* is now parallel to that of the Prefect. His permission as well as that of the Prefect is required for the employment of communal officials (except for Communes with under 20,000 inhabitants). Previously the Prefect had the decisive voice in any dispute between administrations within the Department over financial matters, now the matter is automatically transferred to a ministerial level if the *trésorier payeur général* disagrees with the Prefect, and it is decided by a joint ordinance of the Ministers of the Interior and of Finance.

A more striking instance is that the Minister of Finance recently ordered each *trésorier payeur général* to compile a list of priorities for future public works required in the Departments. They were ordered to oppose any local authorities' application to raise a loan if it was for work not in its proper precedence. The odd point about this arrangement was that the *trésorier payeur général* could only get his information from the Prefect, since no one else had a sufficiently comprehensive knowledge of the Department. There is little apparent reason for

[1] Doueil: op. cit., p. 254. M. Doueil is a member of the *corps préfectoral*, and may be a little biassed.

thus by-passing the Prefect, and administrative friction and personal conflicts tend to result from this sort of intervention.

Despite these incursions into the Prefect's powers of tutelage he remains the centre of departmental government, and a permanent obstacle to over-centralisation. There is considerable demand from local authorities that the " normal " system of prefectoral tutelage be re-established as soon as possible. The national associations of the Mayors, of the Communes and Departments, and of the Presidents of the *conseils généraux*, have all at one time or another demanded that the Minister of the Interior and the Prefect re-assume their exclusive powers of tutelage. A drive for deconcentration was started in 1949 and there has already been a noticeable improvement.[1]

THE MINISTRY OF THE INTERIOR

The Ministry of the Interior forms the apex of all services connected with the activities of local authorities throughout France, Algeria, and the Overseas Departments to which the local government system of metropolitan France has been extended.

The present structure of the Ministry has been laid down by various Decrees and administrative regulations; the most recent are the Decree of February 23, 1949, the Ordinances of February 23 and April 26, 1949, and the Ministerial Circular, Number 133, of March 26, 1949. These were all elaborated and put into effect during M. Moch's tenure of office, and they have in part eliminated the duplication and confusion experienced in the post-war years.

The Minister of the Interior is, himself, in direct and continual contact with his personal cabinet, with the heads of the *inspection générale*, the body responsible for the supervision and examination of all the Ministry's services, and with the *Inspecteurs Généraux de l'Administration en Mission Extraordinaire*, who are the personal delegates of the Minister in each Military Region. The *inspection générale* is expected to act as the

[1] One instance of this movement was the creation of the *commission départementale des opérations immobilières* (page 141) and the abolition of ministerial control over the budgets of small and medium sized Communes in favour of the Prefects and Sub-Prefects (page 130).

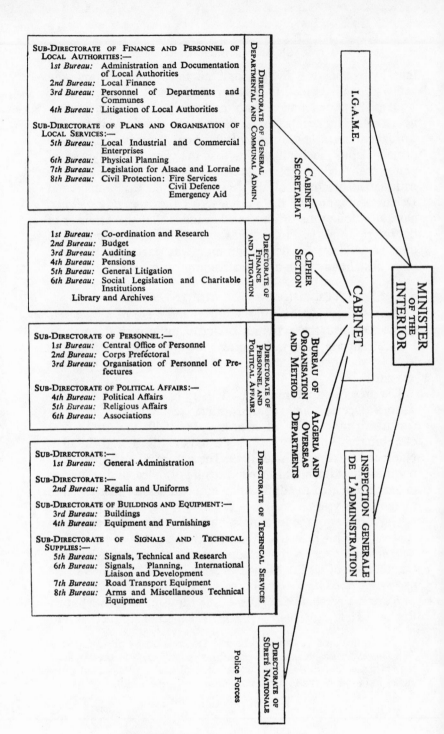

Organisation of the Ministry of the Interior.

impartial judge of the Administration, reporting personally to the Minister.

The Minister's personal Cabinet, on the other hand, is concerned with current administration. The Minister must be approached through its offices, and it must be able to present to the Minister any information required by him on any section of the work of the Ministry. It is subdivided into the Organisation and Methods section, the Cipher section, the Algerian section, and the Secretariat for the whole Ministry. The most important duties of the Secretariat are the preparation and presentation of confidential matters to the Minister, and liaison with Deputies, Parliamentary Commissions and other Ministries.

Four main Directorates deal with the various aspects of local government; local administration, personnel and political affairs, finance and litigation, and technical services. Completely distinct from these four is the Directorate of the *Sûreté Nationale*, the administrative and operational headquarters of all the French security forces, from the local state police forces to one of the national counter-espionage services. The Police Services have their own peculiar organisation and they must be regarded as a thing apart.

The Directorates most closely connected with local government and administration are the first two, local administration, and personnel and political affairs. The other two deal with certain limited aspects of local government; for example, the third Directorate supervises legal cases and acts as legal adviser to the Minister and to the Prefects, but both Directorates tend to regard the nation as their province rather than the Department or the Commune.

The Directorates of local administration and of personnel and political affairs present three important characteristics. First their organisation is based on a functional and not a territorial division of labour. The one relatively important exception to this rule is the special bureau for the legal affairs of Alsace and Lorraine. The functional approach to local government leads to serious administrative difficulties, since a single problem may require examination by two or three Sub-Directorates, and sometimes requires consideration by several Directorates. For example, a local decision concerned with the relative rights of

K

church and state schools is likely to involve the *bureaux* of local litigation, political affairs, and religious affairs. This obviously leads to delays and conflicts. A territorial organisation, on the other hand, if not matched by considerable devolution to regional capitals, would inevitably lead to a multiplication of staffs and loss of central control. In practice the introduction of a regional cadre would almost certainly mean an elaborate new organisation in each part of the country, with in Paris the same organisation as at present for ultimate control. The present functional system is by no means perfect, but it may be the best one possible.

The second characteristic of the present organisation is the division of personnel management into matters concerning local elected officials and those concerning administrative officials. Even at the highest level, therefore, this rigid distinction is maintained. There are, in fact, separate Directorates for the sheep and for the goats.

The third, and most striking, characteristic to the English observer, is the principle revealed in the very title Directorate of Personnel and Political Affairs. This very interesting Directorate is worth looking at more closely. It has two Sub-Directorates. First the Sub-Directorate of Personnel, which deals with administrative details of recruitment, discipline and pay. This has three *bureaux*, one dealing with the officials of the Ministry, one with the *corps préfectoral*, and one with the personnel of the Prefectures, the *chefs de division* and other departmental officers recruited nationally. This is not strictly a " political " division, but significantly it is linked with the Sub-Directorate of Political Affairs. In a country as politically-minded as France, it is certain that watch is kept over the political complexion and activities of the officers required to administer a ministry so strategically situated as that of the Interior.

The Sub-Directorate specifically designated to deal with political affairs is also divided into three *bureaux*. One of these is concerned with religious affairs and one with public associations: their very existence recalls the Church and State controversy, and religious conflicts can never be ignored. The third *bureau* deals with a *mélange* of political affairs, covering all branches of public political life. It is here that the electoral laws are worked out, together with an analysis of the results likely to be expected from each system.[1] Questions concerning the work of the national assemblies, the organisation of elections to the *Assemblée Nationale* and the *Conseil de la République*, and verification of the voting in those chambers, all come within this *bureau's* competence. In addition, it deals with all questions concerning local elections and local politics, from reports on violations of the law to the suspension and dismissal of Mayors and the dissolution of *conseils municipaux*. Honours, public homage and national holidays complete its supervision of matters of public interest.

Two last details are within the Sub-Directorate of Political Affairs; they are classified separately, but mean much the same thing. The first is *affaires réservées*, immediately under the Director himself, and the second is the reception of prefectoral reports and the compilation of " *synthèses* " based upon them. These reports, as was described earlier, are drawn up by each Prefect, and are designed to present to the Minister a precise picture of the political conditions in the Department, the movements of opinion or changes of political sympathy within it, and the political activities of public or private persons likely to be of interest. Secret reports on state and departmental personnel are also popularly supposed to be forwarded to the Ministry.

This is the kernel of the " policy " section of the Ministry's activities. At all times the Minister of the Interior must be able not only to describe accurately the situation of the country, but also to furnish his colleagues with a substantially true prophecy of the results in the country of any change of government policy. The network of responsible officials stationed throughout the country, each acting as a provincial viceroy, each deliberately intent upon the peaceful working of his Department, and each providing material on which to base policy, is in large part responsible for the fundamental stability of French life.

[1] In the 1951 elections their prescience was remarkable.

CHAPTER FIVE

Administrative Courts and Local Government

PUBLIC law in France is a highly-developed system with its own methods, principles, and courts. All public authorities and all *fonctionnaires* when acting within the scope of their employment are subject not to the ordinary civil courts dispensing private law, but to the administrative courts. Since all public authorities are subject to public law, the jurisdiction of the administrative courts extends over the Departments and Communes. But, and this is the difficulty, there are virtually no parts of administrative law which are peculiar to local authorities: the forms of procedure, the principles that guide the courts, and the effects of their judgements are essentially the same for cases arising out of a regulation made by a university as for those resulting from a Mayor's ordinance or the decision of a *conseil général*. It is therefore impossible to explain adequately the judicial control exercised over local authorities except by writing a comprehensive treatise on French public law. All that can be done here is to abstract from the general system the principles of law and the types of case most commonly associated with local authorities.

THE JURISDICTION OF THE ADMINISTRATIVE COURTS

Two preliminary questions must be dealt with. First, what is the dividing line between the jurisdiction of the administrative courts and the jurisdiction of the civil courts? Second, what are the respective spheres of competence of the *Conseil d'État* and the *Conseils de Préfecture Interdépartementaux*?[1]

[1] In this chapter no distinction will be made between the ordinary *Conseils de Préfecture* and the *conseil* of the Department of the Seine which

The jurisdiction of the administrative courts has been clearly stated in a famous judgement of the *Conseil d'État*. It is that " all litigation between public authorities and third parties, or between the authorities themselves, concerning the execution, non-execution, or bad execution of public services is within the competence of the administrative courts; and, in the absence of a specific legal text providing otherwise, the *Conseil d'État* is the competent court."[1] In practice the clarity of this statement is somewhat misleading. On some occasions both the civil and the administrative courts declare that they are not empowered to deal with a case, and this would result in a denial of justice if there were no further remedy. Sometimes, an official may commit so serious an offence that he must be held personally responsible for his fault; a remedy has therefore had to be found whereby he may be sued in his own name in the ordinary civil courts.[2] Finally, a plaintiff may find himself faced with judgements of the civil courts and of the administrative courts which are in flat contradiction with each other.[3]

In all these cases a special court, the *Tribunal des Conflits*, composed of equal numbers of members of both the supreme civil court (the *Cour de Cassation*) and the supreme administrative court (the *Conseil d'État*) is empowered to intervene. This court decides questions of jurisdiction and it can try the case itself if the civil and the administrative courts have arrived at contradictory judgements.

is exceptional in size, and has extra powers over the *Ville de Paris*. There is also a special *Tribunal Administratif* in Alsace Lorraine which has, in addition to the ordinary powers of a *conseil*, extra powers where local law differs from ordinary law, mainly in the fields of inheritance and taxation.

[1] From the judgement in the case of *Terrier:* February 6, 1903. Quoted by Rolland. op. cit., p. 293.

[2] The distinction here noted is between the *faute de service* and the *faute personnelle:* it is dealt with below, p. 160.

[2] For example, where a passenger in a private car is injured in an accident between that car and the vehicle of a public authority. He may first sue the driver of the private car in the ordinary civil courts, and that court may find that the entire responsibility for the accident rests with the driver of the public vehicle. He then starts an action against the public authority in the administrative courts, to find that that court holds the private driver entirely responsible. Without a further remedy, he would be unable to obtain damages from any source.

In virtually all cases in which penalties are imposed upon private citizens for breach of an executive regulation, the civil courts and not the administrative courts are competent.

The spheres of jurisdiction of the *Conseil d'État* and the *Conseils de Préfecture Interdépartementaux* are also sometimes difficult to determine accurately. The principle was stated above: that " in the absence of a specific legal text providing otherwise, the *Conseil d'État* is the competent court." That is, it may be specifically laid down that the *conseil de préfecture* is the court of first instance and in such matters the *Conseil d'État* the court of appeal; otherwise the *Conseil d'État* is the court of both first and last instance.

The jurisdiction of the *conseils de préfecture* used to be very limited, as the above principle implies; although the principle remains unchanged their jurisdiction has been greatly enlarged by case-law and statute, and the practice now is that in the great majority of cases in which local authorities are involved, the court of first instance is the *conseil de préfecture:* elections, actions for damages, litigation between a local authority and its officials, most types of contracts, and public works. Questions of powers and illegal actions, however, are normally dealt with directly by the *Conseil d'État*.[1]

ADMINISTRATIVE CONTROL OVER LOCAL AUTHORITIES

In addition to judicial control the *Conseil d'État*, and to a lesser degree the *conseils de préfecture*, exercise very important administrative control over the decisions of local authorities. It will be remembered that on several occasions cited in previous chapters decisions of *conseils municipaux* and *conseils généraux* were subject to the approval of the *Conseil d'État* as expressed by decree. To understand the distinction between administrative control and judicial control requires a knowledge of the internal organisation of the *Conseil d'État*.

The effective head of the *Conseil d'État* is its Vice-President, but when meeting in solemn session on special occasions, either the Minister of Justice or the President of the Republic presides.

[1] P. de Font Reaulx, R. Durnerin, J. Marazis: *Les Conseils de Préfecture: organisation et compétence*. Sirey, 1937; p. 48.

Next in rank after the Vice-President are the Presidents of the *sections* into which the *Conseil* is divided for ordinary work. Beneath them are 54 *conseillers d'état* (42 ordinary and 12 extraordinary), 45 *maîtres de requêtes*, and 44 *auditeurs* of the first and second class. Broadly speaking, the *conseillers* judge, the *maîtres* prepare the cases and act as legal advisers, and the *auditeurs* act as aides to the court when it is in session, and in the preparation and examination of cases.[1]

The *Conseil d'État* is divided into five *sections*. *Sections* can be joined together for some subjects, and a general assembly of the whole *Conseil* can be called to consider and decide upon certain very important matters. The first four *sections*, each of which is composed of a President and six *conseillers*, are concerned with administration and legislation. Each *section* deals with the affairs of a particular group of Ministries, joined together into *sections* of the Interior, of Finance, of Public Works, and of Social Affairs. The *section* of the Interior deals with the affairs of the Ministries of the Interior (under which come departmental and communal affairs), of Justice, of National Education, and of Information. Two or more *sections* can hold a joint session to deal with matters affecting two or more Ministries in different *sections;* for example, a proposal for rural electrification in a Department would be dealt with by the *sections* of the Interior and of Public Works.

Ministers and officials of Ministries can appear before the administrative *sections* to state the views and wishes of the administration concerned. Ministerial officials of the rank of Director and above may be appointed to act as ministerial representatives before the *Conseil* either for specified matters or for all matters affecting their Ministry. Ministers and the Vice-President of the *Conseil d'État* can call upon outside experts and specialists for their opinion.

[1] Two-thirds of the ordinary *conseillers d'état* are recruited from the *maîtres de requêtes ;* the remainder and the extraordinary *conseillers* (who are nominated for periods of a year at a time) are chosen from senior officials of Ministries, Prefects, and so on. The *maîtres de requêtes* are chosen in large part from the *auditeurs*, though direct entry as *maître* is allowed for certain types of ministerial official, and for legal experts. The *auditeurs* are recruited from the *École Nationale d'Administration* from amongst the most highly-placed students in the final examinations,

It is not easy to indicate the scope of matters affecting local authorities which require the prior approval of the *Conseil d'État*. The most important have been mentioned in preceding chapters—long-term loans, certain types of public works, acquisition of property, and the creation of municipal *régies*. Certain major administrative matters such as proposed changes in the boundaries of Communes, demands for mining rights, and some of the contracts entered into by the *Ville de Paris*, are dealt with by the general assembly of the *Conseil*. Ministerial regulations and decrees are presented to the *Conseil* for its opinion, and these may also have great importance for local authorities: for instance, those drawing up a new statute for communal or departmental officials.

The administrative role of the *conseils de préfecture* is less important than that of the *Conseil d'État*. A *conseil de préfecture* consists of a President and four *conseillers*.[1] It has no special composition for dealing with administrative questions.

The *conseil de préfecture* is required to give its opinion on any matter placed before it by a Prefect in its region; before 1926 there was one *conseil* to every Department and it had to be consulted on a variety of matters, but in that year their number was greatly reduced, leaving one *conseil* to serve several Departments. Prefects are not now required to ask their advice except on a very limited range of administrative matters—permission for a part of a Commune to accept a bequest, or for a *bureau de bienfaisance* to raise a loan when the *conseil municipal* concerned is opposed to it, and other very small matters. It also has to decide whether the *bureaux de bienfaisance* and *d'assistance* of a Commune may start legal proceedings when the *conseil municipal* concerned objects, or whether a private citizen may start legal proceedings in the Commune's name. Finally, the individual members of a *conseil de préfecture* have

---

[1] The President of a *conseil de préfecture* is recruited from the senior *conseillers de préfecture* in service. The *conseillers* are recruited from the *École Nationale d'Administration* and from comparable posts in the Ministries. Although the *auditeurs* of the *Conseil d'État* and the *conseillers de préfecture* (3rd class) are both recruited from the ENA, the personnel of these two *corps* is quite distinct; it is very rare for a *conseiller de préfecture* to reach the dignity of the *Conseil d'État*. There is marked difference between the two *corps* in pay, conditions of service and prestige.

certain administrative functions in their own right. They serve on various committees and appeals tribunals, and they can also be called upon to act as substitutes for a member of the Prefectoral Corps if occasion demands—which it rarely does.

JUDICIAL CONTROL OF LOCAL AUTHORITIES

Before dealing with the methods by which administrative courts exercise judicial control over local authorities brief mention must be made of the organisation of these courts sitting as judicial bodies, and of certain general rules governing their procedure.

The fifth *section* of the *Conseil d'État* is the *section du contentieux*, comprising a President, eighteen *conseillers* (plus some supplementary *conseillers* coming from the administrative *sections*), about 30 *maîtres*, and 28 *auditeurs*. The *section* is divided into eight *sous-sections* each of three *conseillers*. Cases involving pension rights, elections and tax-assessment are dealt with by a single *sous-section*, which both prepares the case and judges it. In other types of litigation, the preliminary examination of the case and the preparation of the report is done by one *sous-section*, but that *sous-section* joins with a second *sous-section* to pass judgement. There are ways in which very important cases can be transferred from a *sous-section* to a committee composed of the heads of all the *sous-sections* combined, and higher still to a special body presided over by the Vice-President of the *Conseil d'État*, the senior members of the whole judicial *section*, and additional members from the administrative *sections*. The judgement of any of these bodies has equal weight in law, and is promulgated in the same way as an *arrêté* of the *Conseil d'État*. Appeals against a judgement are only allowed if new evidence is disclosed or if irregularities are revealed in the previous trial or in the conduct of the parties concerned in litigation.

In the *conseil de préfecture* the President normally designates a *conseiller* to examine and prepare a report on the case, and his report is read to the *conseil* in the presence of the parties concerned; these then offer their comments. Another *conseiller* who is acting as the state representative (the *commissaire du gouvernement*) concludes with his observations, and the decision is taken. The decision must always contain a résumé of the reasoning the court has followed in coming to its decision. Appeals against the decision can be lodged with the *Conseil d'État* within two months of the publication of the judgement.

An alternative procedure, peculiar to the *conseil de préfecture*, can be used in certain cases, principally those concerning tax-assessments. On these occasions a single *conseiller* sits as judge in the nearest departmental capital and decides the case on his own. It can always be transferred to the full *conseil* if it appears to involve important issues, and appeals from this type of judgement may be made to the *Conseil d'État* within the ordinary period. This procedure is very expeditious, and is used wherever possible.

Three further points about procedure must be noticed. In the first place in all administrative courts the judge directs the proceedings, and the part played by the lawyers is reduced to a minimum. Allied to this is the rule that all evidence shall be presented in writing, so that the examination and cross-examination of witnesses is restricted; moreover, it is not the province of counsel but of the judges. In many cases administrative courts try actions in private: the *Conseil d'État* as a rule admits the public except in cases concerned with tax-assessments, but the public is not admitted to the *conseils de préfecture* unless the parties involved in litigation so request.

Second, the *Conseil d'État* only judges decisions and regulations made by the administration. In order to start an action for damages, therefore, the plaintiff must extract from the administration concerned a denial of its responsibility or a refusal to pay the damages demanded. Armed with this the plaintiff can go forward with his case. The *Conseil d'État* has decided that if a person's demand for satisfaction is not answered within a certain time, then silence means rejection. The good sense of this is obvious. The rule that only decisions form the basis for judgements does not, on the whole, hold for the *conseils de préfecture*, except in certain special cases which involve too many technicalities to be discussed here.

Third, the *Conseil d'État* can demand all the relevant documents from the administration concerned: if they are not produced within the specified time the *Conseil* proceeds on the assumption that the administration concerned admits the truth of the plaintiff's version of the case.

Judicial supervision over local authorities can be exercised by the administrative courts in three ways: (i) over their decisions, (ii) over their actions, and (iii) through having special jurisdiction over various categories of litigation, principally over local elections, litigation involving communal and departmental property, communal and departmental contracts, and public works.

(i) *Decisions*

The judicial control of local authorities' decisions must be clearly distinguished from the administrative control described above; administrative control takes the form of subordinating a decision to ratification by the court, and the decision is incomplete and of no legal force without such ratification. Judicial control is over decisions which are, or purport to be, already legally executory.

The first thing is that the *Conseil d'État* will never accept a plaint based on the harmful effect or illegality of an *acte de gouvernement*.[1] In fact these *actes* are very rare, and very rare among them are those cases involving local authorities, so that it is safe to ignore them here.[2]

The normal method for testing the legality of a local authority's decision is known as the *contentieux de l'annulation ou de la légalité*, and the action is a *recours pour excès de pouvoir*. The contention is that a particular decision or order was illegal and should be annulled. It is a test of *vires* and not an action to recover damages.

To be legal a decision must be (a) *intra vires*, (b) formulated in the proper way, and (c) arrived at not only by the use of legal powers but also in accordance with the real intention of the law. It may be held that the last two are included in *vires*, but the further division is useful for clarifying the methods employed by the administrative courts in exercising judicial control.

The clearest instance of *ultra vires* is when an authority pur-

[1] See above p. 28.
[2] The type of case which has, in the past, involved a local authority was the Prefect's supervision of the movements and activities of foreigners.

ports to take a decision which really belongs to another body:
for the Prefect to issue a departmental budget on his own
authority, instead of the *conseil général*, or for a *conseil municipal* to issue a police ordinance instead of the Mayor. It is, of
course, illegal to take a decision which violates the law, and it is
also illegal to go against a previous judgement of the admin-
ministrative courts (*la chose jugée*).

The *Conseil d'État* has also to determine the precise content
of a generally-worded grant of power. In a previous chapter[1] it
was seen how the *Conseil d'État* step by step determined what
was implied in the Commune's legal right to create services of
" communal interest "; in the process it widened the field of
decision of the *conseils municipaux* by means of judicial interpretation.

Sometimes certain conditions must be fulfilled before a
decision is taken—for example, the presence of a special
quorum, or the approval of another body; or the decision,
when reached, has to follow a specified pattern or form—for
instance, in the lay-out of a budget or in some types of contract;
or a decision can sometimes only be taken if special circumstances arise. For example, a Mayor can forbid window boxes
in places where they menace public safety; the administrative
court may then annul the decision on one of three counts: for an
error of fact (there were no passers-by to be injured), for an
erroneous evaluation of the facts (there was no reasonable
ground for supposing that the window box was likely to fall),
and for absence of cause (the window box was at ground level).

Third, a decision is illegal if it is prompted by extraneous or
personal motives. This poses more difficult problems for the
administrative courts, for here the power of decision may be
exercised by the proper authority and promulgated in the
proper way, but it will nevertheless be illegal if it discriminates
unfairly against a particular individual or corporation, or
if it is deliberately calculated to attain an illegal end.

Sometimes the discrimination is deliberate and the evidence
clear; a Mayor may refuse to license new taxis so as to curry
favour with the existing taxi-owners, or to avoid competition
with his own business. On other occasions discrimination may

[1] See above, p. 48.

be neither obvious nor deliberate. The Paris Society of Cinema Proprietors challenged an ordinance of the Prefect of the Seine, in which he allowed reductions in the entertainment tax for music-halls and theatres. They held that the law under which he acted implicitly placed cinemas in the same category as theatres and that therefore the ordinance was discriminatory. The *Conseil d'État* agreed.[1]

A more subtle abuse of power is that in which an authority uses legal powers to obtain an end which is a perversion of the real intention of the law (*détournement de pouvoir*). A classic instance of this was of a Mayor who suspended a *garde champêtre* for a month as a disciplinary measure, the maximum punishment within his power. At the end of the month the *garde champêtre* reported again for duty, and the Mayor immediately suspended him for another month. The legal warrant for the Mayor's decision was impeccable, but the *Conseil d'État* held that there was *détournement de pouvoir* as the Mayor had attempted to expand his power to suspend the *garde champêtre* for a month into what would amount in fact to a right of dismissal, a power explicitly reserved by law to the Sub-Prefect or Prefect.[2]

There is also abuse of power if a local authority takes a decision for laudable motives which are not recognised in law. A Mayor may not impose police measures to exact a higher standard of public behaviour on the Commune's property than elsewhere in the Commune in order to save the Commune expense. Nor may he in the interests of the Commune's finances levy charges on citizens for services which the Commune should provide free of charge.

The method of proceeding under the *contentieux de l'annulation* is for the plaintiff to begin an action (*recours*) for *excès de pouvoir*. A plaintiff appealing against a decision must fulfil certain conditions before his case can be heard. He must, obviously, have the legal capacity to begin litigation,[3] he must

---

[1] Reported in *Le Monde:* November 25, 1950.

[2] *Conseil d'État:* November 16, 1900. Maugras. Recueil 1900.

[3] This condition is sometimes important when the plaintiff is a corporation or a special type of authority (e.g. *bureaux de bienfaisance*), as unregistered companies sometimes have no corporate personality, and therefore cannot start litigation of this kind.

be able to show that he has a legal interest in the case,[1] he must bring his action within a certain time, and there must be no other method open to him for having the decision quashed—for example, a decision of a *conseil municipal* which violates the law can be annulled by the Prefect, and he must be asked to do so before an action for *excès de pouvoir* is begun before the administrative courts.[2]

The beginning of an action for *excès de pouvoir* does not in itself suspend the execution of the decision in question unless the *Conseil d'État* makes a specific order to that effect, which it will do if the execution would lead to serious prejudice of the plaintiff's interests.[3]

The *Conseil d'État's* judgement will be either that the decision was *ultra* or *intra vires*. In the first case it annuls the decision, and this judgement is valid not only for the particular case at issue, but also for all other similar cases and for all other persons in the same circumstances. The *Conseil d'État* cannot go beyond this and order the authority concerned to take a specific decision in place of the one that has been annulled, but it can invite it to take any steps which may be necessary to give effect to the court's judgement. If any administration in the future takes a similar decision, the court will annul it on the grounds that it is in conflict with a legal judgement.

If the *Conseil d'État* finds that the decision was *intra vires*, the decision remains valid; another party may, if the legal delays have not expired, start a similar action.

[1] There is a complex history of administrative case-law determining the conditions which must be fulfilled. Frequently in the case of local authorities it is sufficient for the plaintiff to be either an elector or a tax-payer in the Commune or Department.

[2] Of course if the Prefect refuses to annul the decision an action for *excès de pouvoir* is then open. In certain cases the *Conseil d'État* insists that the plaintiff first request a superior administrative authority to annul the decision before starting a legal action; for example, that he should appeal to the Minister of the Interior against a Prefect's decision. But the *Conseil d'État* has steadily moved away from this position, and is now generally prepared to accept an action directly.

[3] When a civil case depends upon an administrative court's judgement as to the legality of the decision, the civil court will suspend the case until the administrative court's judgement is known.

(ii) *Actions*

Judicial control by administrative courts over the actions of local authorities can be exercised in one of three ways: (a) an administrative court can award damages against an authority whose act (or that of its servants) has caused damage to a private person: this involves an action entitled the *contentieux de la pleine juridiction ou de l'indemnité*; (b) it can find indirectly that the servant of a local authority has committed an offence which makes him personally liable for the damages awarded; this uses the distinction between the *faute de service* and the *faute personnelle*; (c) it can determine the extent to which acts performed under proper warrant can interfere with the life and liberty of the citizen: this is essentially the control over the exercise of police powers.

(a) The *contentieux de la pleine juridiction* is a suit by a private individual alleging that he has suffered damage through the action of a public authority; it involves the assessment and award of money compensation for the damage caused.

Three types of circumstances can be distinguished. First, damage may be caused through the agent of a public authority being negligent or careless, though the offence itself is a normal hazard of the activities of that authority. For example, a communal vehicle may knock down a pedestrian, and unless the driver was guilty of gross negligence, such as driving when drunk, the Commune will be held responsible for the damages incurred.

Second, damage may be caused by an authority not performing its duties at the proper time and in the proper way. In 1950 the Commune of Saacy was flooded when a river overflowed its banks, and several houses were cut off. Owners of punts went to rescue stranded people and bring them to safety. Without thinking, these amateur ferrymen began to overload their boats, and the Mayor, when told of this, assumed that all would take proper precautions and refused to exercise his police powers to restrict the number of passengers. On the second day a boat sank and most of the occupants were drowned. The victims' dependents began an action for damages against the Commune because the Mayor's refusal to exercise his police powers constituted a tort. The *Conseil d'État* (confirming the judgement of the *conseil de préfecture* of Versailles) held that the Mayor's assessment of the situation had been wrong, and that his failure to use his powers was a grave error of judgement for which the Commune was liable. Damages were therefore awarded to the plaintiffs, although allowance was made for the contributory negligence of the deceased.[1]

Third, damage may be caused without negligence, but as an inevitable result of the work done by a local authority. The *Conseil d'État* has gradually developed a remedy for citizens who have been injured by a legitimate exercise of an administration's powers. If, for example, access to a man's property is made inadequate as a result of re-alignment of the road skirting his house, there is no question of negligence on the part of the highway engineer or of the workmen concerned; but by the development of a complex theory of risk the *Conseil d'État* has made it possible for the citizen affected to obtain compensation.[2]

(b) The servant of a local authority may be responsible for an offence which shows such a neglect of his duties that in justice the damages arising from his action should be his own liability. If, for example, a communal dustcart knocks down a pedestrian the Commune pays the damage: this is a normal hazard, and is called a *faute de service*. Sometimes, however, although the official was at the time acting in his official capacity the damage caused cannot be regarded as a normal hazard of the working of his service; this is the *faute personnelle*. Various formulae have been suggested to distinguish between these two types of fault, but the case-law is too elaborate to be dealt with here. There is a *faute personnelle* where the agent's " negligence is so great, his error of judgement so ludicrous, and his attention so divorced from the interests of his service that they constitute a denial of the most elementary professional qualifications."[3] For example, a Mayor took possession of a car without any of the legal preliminaries empowering him to requisition it in the public interest, on the pretext that he was moving the Commune's

[1] Reported in *Le Monde:* May 11, 1951.
[2] L. Trotabas: Liability in damages under French administrative law. *Journal of Comparative Legislation.* Vols. 12 and 13, 1930–31.
[3] Rivero: op. cit., p. 589.

papers to a safe place. The damage caused to the owner of the car was held to be the personal liability of the Mayor and not the responsibility of the Commune.[1]

In these circumstances the plaintiff begins two actions: one for damages in the ordinary civil courts against the official himself, and one in the administrative courts against the authority whose servant he is. The action must then go before the *Tribunal des Conflits* to determine whether or not the official was acting within the scope of his duties. If that court decides he was, the action for damages before the administrative courts goes forward under the *contentieux de la pleine juridiction;* the authority will then be liable for any damages awarded. If, on the other hand, the *Tribunal* believes that, if proved, the offence could not be imputed to the authority, the official himself becomes the object of an action for damages in his private capacity in the civil courts. The *Tribunal* allows proceedings against an official only if he has been guilty of gross negligence or grave misconduct.

(c) Administrative courts have also come to exercise some control over the exercise of " police powers ". The French conception of these powers is so wide that the actions of a police authority would present a real threat to the liberty of the citizen unless they were subject to judicial control. But since the French Executive is not subject, as is the English Executive, to the control of the civil courts, it would have complete discretion over the police powers if this discretion were not subject to review by the administrative courts. The *Conseil d'État* has gradually set up certain standards of conduct for testing whether or not police powers have been properly exercised, but it has resolutely turned its face against attempting to codify these standards, and categorically refuses to set up, or be guided by, absolute standards of conduct. It will never, for example, attempt to decide whether or not a particular entertainment is indecent: it will only consider whether or not a Mayor or Prefect had good grounds for considering it so in the particular circumstances. Similarly, the court has no interest in perfect worlds, and will neither allow nor require a police authority to exercise its powers with the aim of preventing a possible breach

[1] *Conseil de Préfecture* of Nancy: June 21, 1944. Tramonti. Quoted by Waline: op. cit., p. 310.

L

of the law, or to try to set up absolute standards of public behaviour. The *Conseil d'État*, therefore, insists that a police
ordinance must only ensure the *minimum* degree of public
peace normally desired or required. This may sometimes amount
to a purely passive concept, for example, that there is continued
absence of danger on the highway. Sometimes positive action
is required in order, for example, to maintain the normal moral
standards of society when events occur which present a positive
menace to that society. These standards, however, are variable
and relative; behaviour which would pass unnoticed in Paris or
Marseilles might provoke disturbances in the Vendée.[1]

At all times the *Conseil d'État* insists that the exercise of police
powers must be reconciled with the freedom of the citizen. The
discretion allowed to officials in law-enforcement varies with
the extent to which a particular liberty endangers public order
and with the esteem in which it is held by the legislature. The
court recognises that freedom of public association is more
likely to lead to serious disturbances than is the freedom to
dispose of property or to attend a church school. It is therefore
always more prepared to allow an ordinance restricting the free
passage of political processions on the public highway than one
attempting to regulate the use to which a private house is put.
At the same time a police ordinance must be proportionate to
the probability of disorder, and in the ultimate analysis the
Conseil d'État uses a doctrine which amounts to this: if a
public meeting of any sort is banned by the police authority, the
latter must be able to show that the proposed meeting was
liable to provoke disturbances of such gravity that total prohibition alone would suffice to maintain the peace.[2] In similar
circumstances in other fields the *Conseil d'État* will test an ordinance by its conception of what constitutes an " immediate
peril "; unless, as a matter of fact, the danger is imminent and
likely to be extremely serious, no ordinance will be allowed
totally to deprive a citizen of his lawful freedom.

Finally, there are limitations set upon the use of force to
ensure obedience to police prescriptions. Only in cases of

---

[1] For a detailed discussion, see Teitgen: op. cit., p. 24 seq.

[2] This is the principle contained in the case of René Benjamin: *Conseil
d'État*, May 19, 1933. Dalloz 1933.

immediate peril can the administration take the law into its own hands without proceeding by the proper judicial channels; for example, policemen can be ordered to remove a family from a house which is in imminent danger of falling down or being flooded, but if the danger is not imminent then the decision to leave or not to leave must remain with the occupants, and the proper way to proceed is by a judicial warrant directing the owner to repair or demolish his property if it does not conform to proper standards. Before force can properly be applied there must be resistance, and only so much force is permissible as is necessary to overcome the resistance. The police authority must also bear in mind that the *Conseil d'État* demands a sense of proportion, and some sort of relation between the seriousness of the offence and the amount of force used. If a pedestrian tries to run away when challenged for crossing the road outside a pedestrian crossing, he must not be shot down: a gangster escaping from a bank could be. On the other hand, the *Conseil d'État* also maintains that the essence of police action is that it must be efficacious, and that too much kindness can harm the reputation of the public authority.

(iii) *Control through special jurisdiction*

Local authorities are under the control of the administrative courts in certain special categories of litigation. These are actions for damages arising out of the public works for which they are responsible, electoral proceedings, certain types of contracts, servitudes of public interest and some types of taxation cases.

The most straightforward form of special jurisdiction is that over local elections—the eligibility of electors or candidates, illegal proceedings, and so on. In municipal elections any elector in the Commune or anyone eligible to stand as a candidate can bring proceedings before the *conseil de préfecture* within five days of the election. In departmental elections, the electors of a *canton*, any candidate, and any member of the *conseil général*, can appeal to the same tribunal within the same period. In both cases the objection is lodged with the Prefect or the Sub-Prefect who transmits it to the *conseil de préfecture* and at the same time notifies the candidate whose election is contested. The *conseil de préfecture* must pass judgement within a month. There is an appeal to the *Conseil d'État*. In the event of an appeal the Prefect sends all the relevant papers, records of the elections, and the judgement of the *conseil de préfecture* to the Ministry of the Interior, from where they are transmitted to the *Conseil d'État*. The Prefect can also start proceedings in the administrative courts on his own authority, and can appeal to the *Conseil d'État* against the judgement of the *conseil de préfecture*.

The *conseil de préfecture* deals with litigation involving the payment, assessment and collection of direct taxes; these include many of those levied by local authorities. Therefore many of the financial operations of local authorities can be subject to judicial control by an administrative court.

The law governing public works, the contracts of local authorities, and the use of public property, is very technical but it closely affects Communes and Departments which often have considerable estates.

If in the course of public works damage is caused, the action for damages comes before an administrative court. This is a simple extension of the *contentieux de la pleine juridiction*, or sometimes of the theory of risk. The case goes before the *conseil de préfecture* even if the damage can be imputed to a private contractor acting for the Department or Commune. He, or the public authority, or both, can be called upon to pay the damages incurred according to their respective responsibility. Generally, if the local authority has accepted the work as complete, the private contractor is covered.

Local authorities can enter into two types of contract; some are in all respects private contracts subject to the civil courts; others are administrative contracts and are dealt with by the administrative courts. The line between them is difficult to draw, but the practical distinction is important. An administrative contract may impose more onerous terms on the contractor than are normally encountered in private business, and the authority has powers in the public interest to alter the terms of the contract during the course of operations, to demand different standards from those contained in the contract, and even to impose heavier burdens upon the contractor without offering any extra compensation. It rests with the administrative courts to decide to what extent these powers can be used, and to interpret the terms of the contracts. Some contracts have a clause written into them explicitly stating whether or not they are administrative contracts. Sometimes the administrative courts have to decide to which category they belong, by examining the intentions of the administration concerned, the circumstances under which the contract was made, the form it takes, and the conditions it contains. If the clauses of the contract are markedly different from those normally found in private contracts—for example, unusually severe terms—the courts will decide that it is an administrative contract.

Contracts involving the use of public or private property belonging to a Commune or Department are also under the jurisdiction of the administrative courts. An authority's public property is that which is not limited to the use of one or several persons: property, that is, such as communal or departmental roads, municipal markets, and open spaces. An authority's private property is that which is restricted in use, such as houses, enclosed land, and quarries. In the case of private property and private contracts the rules used are of no special interest, but in the case of public property there is a greater need for judicial control. Mayors and Prefects can, for example, determine whether a bus company can use stopping points on communal and departmental roads, ply for hire in the town, or use ground for parking. Many Communes also possess public property which can bring remuneration to the private individual, for example, by having a stall in the communal market. Abuse of power is consequently possible; a Mayor could undermine a man's livelihood by depriving him of his licence to set up a stall. The administrative courts are sometimes faced with the problem of determining whether or not there is good reason for preventing a person using public property, for example, that the stall was a public nuisance, that the dues had not been paid, that the rules of the market had been broken. In general, to refuse a person the use of public property must be justified by the public interest or the well-being of the property, but the administrative courts have to tread delicately in this field, as they cannot deprive the authority of its right to operate its own property.

Administrative courts are also competent to deal with questions arising from servitudes on property created in the public interest: for example, the administration's right to suspend telephone wires from convenient houses, or to carry high tension wires across land.

SUMMARY

Local authorities in France are in many respects under much stricter judicial control than are those in this country. This is principally because French administrative courts, owing to their special relation with the Executive, can enter into details of decisions and actions which could not be considered by the courts in this country. The remedies provided by French administrative courts are as effective as ours, more clearly defined, more easily invoked, less expensive, and, in certain respects, more efficacious.

Injunctions are replaced by a simple procedure of appeal against electoral proceedings either by the public authority—through the Prefect—or by any interested party. In France ordinary actions for damages, or in some cases actions for *excès de pouvoir*, perform the same purpose as orders of *mandamus* in this country. Orders of prohibition and *certiorari* are replaced by two simple procedures whereby conflicts of competence between administrations are decided by the *Conseil d'État*, those between civil and administrative courts are decided by the *Tribunal des Conflits*.

Over and above these remedies, which are simple and cheap, the administrative courts provide more adequate machinery for granting compensation for damages caused by public authorities, and for preventing authorities from abusing their powers.

What is missing from the French system is simple. It lacks the simple, forthright, and fearless denunciation of attempts on the freedom of the individual which is the great distinction of the British courts. For all the attempts made by the *Conseil d'État* to keep the exercise of police powers within proper limits, it is evident that it only partly succeeds. Lord Denning can say that in this country " our procedure for securing our personal freedom is efficient, but our procedure for preventing the abuse of power is not." The exact opposite is true in France.

CHAPTER SIX

Local Government Finance

ADEQUATE financial resources, which are independent of the State, are a *sine qua non* of proper local government. Without them local authorities become mere agents of the central Government, and elected representation loses most of its point.

In recent times most democratic countries have been faced with the problem of ensuring the financial independence of local authorities in the face of rising pressure and demands for more national services. This has had a three-fold effect: the State has had to multiply its revenue many times; it has had to impose new burdens and duties on local authorities, restricting their freedom of inaction; and it has removed from their control many of their most important duties, sometimes to ensure greater efficiency, sometimes to lighten their burden. In addition, the complexity of modern administration and organisation has swollen local budgets, and inflation has persistently undermined all efforts towards stability.

Nowadays the local authorities of very few countries can balance their budgets without direct aid from the State, but quite apart from this financial dependence upon the central Government, they have come to regard state supervision of local activities as natural and even inevitable.

This chapter will begin with an outline of the background to the present system of local finance, followed by an account of the resources at the call of the local authorities. Finally the composition of the budget itself will be considered, and the principal items examined.

BACKGROUND TO THE PRESENT SYSTEM

It is by no means easy to give a clear picture of the present situation, and probably the clearest approach is through the recent financial history of local authorities, although much important evidence will have to be omitted. Local revenue is raised from many different sources; it is based upon an archaic and cumbersome system of assessment and evaluation; and Parliament has shown no great consistency in dealing with problems of local taxation.

Before 1917 there were three principal sources of revenue open to a local authority: (i) the *octroi* (for Communes only), (ii) " additional centimes ", and (iii) local taxes, imposed on a variety of goods, services and transactions specifically authorised by law. Also, since 1917, state subventions (iv) have grown in size and importance, and their history will be reviewed in this section.

(i) The *octroi* was a tax levied on all goods introduced for consumption into a Commune. The tax varied according to the type of the product and Parliament fixed maximum rates above which the tax could not go. The *octroi* was naturally attacked by critics for raising the cost of living.

It gradually fell into disfavour, as it was unfair and was expensive to collect; in 1896 Parliament drew up a list of special local taxes which could be levied by any Commune on condition that it abolished the *octroi* in its area. These new taxes were direct impositions on such things as dogs, domestic servants, balconies and musical instruments.

Many Communes took advantage of the new facilities offered and in 1926 Parliament added a further group of 23 taxes to this list; local authorities could levy these new taxes irrespective of whether or not the *octroi* still existed. It was found, however, that although the *octroi* was progressively abandoned, very few local authorities took advantage of the new list. In the Communes where the *octroi* still persisted, the expenses of collecting and assessing it were immoderately high compared with the alternative local taxes, which were collected by the state-administered offices of Direct Taxation. Eventually, in 1941, Vichy formally abolished the *octroi* in all Communes where collection expenses exceeded a certain proportion of the yield; in its place Communes were allowed to levy yet another new tax, this time on business transactions in their areas. These steps provoked a rapid decline in the number of Communes levying the *octroi*. Finally, in 1948, Parliament declared that the *octroi* was completely anachronistic and forbade it altogether. In fact this affected only two Communes, Digoin (Saône-et-Loire) and Oust (Ariège), and in Oust the tax only raised 500 francs annually.

(ii) The " additional centime " is a direct tax levied on property. Before 1918 the State had four principal taxes, on *propriétés non bâties* (unbuilt-on land), *propriétés bâties* (built-on land), *contribution mobilière* (personal estate), and *patentes* (trading licences). The taxes upon both types of real estate were based on rentable value ; for taxation purposes this value was reduced by 50 per cent in the case of built-on land and 10 per cent for unbuilt-on land, to allow for overhead expenses. The *contribution mobilière* was based on the rentable value of the rooms occupied by a family, and it was paid by the occupier. In principle every person who was not indigent was chargeable, but certain categories were exempted. The *patente* was levied on all forms of business, and was equivalent in part to a trading licence and in part to a charge on business premises. The tax was paid by owners of industrial and commercial undertakings and by members of the liberal professions.

All these taxes were voted annually by Parliament, and state taxation officials carried out the assessments and revised them whenever there were changes in the occupation or use of property. Each year Parliament decided how much the State should levy from each class of property, and the tax to be levied was expressed as a percentage of the assessed value; a natural enough method with a metric system. The sums so collected went to the national Exchequer.

Local authorities, however, were able to raise revenue from exactly the same sources, by adding centimes[1] to the State's tax. If in a particular Commune the State took 10,000 francs in tax, the addition of one centime by a local authority would give it a revenue of 100 francs. The value of one centime to the local authority could be rapidly calculated by applying the percentage voted by Parliament to the assessed value of the property in the

---

[1] 1/100th part of a franc.

Commune or in the Department, and dividing by a hundred.[1] The local authorities had no part in determining the assessed value of the property or the percentage of the State's tax to which they added their centimes, but when the value of the centime had been established each year they were authorised to raise a certain number of centimes for their own use. Some could only be raised for specific purposes, such as highway mainten- ance and public assistance, but others could be raised to meet ordinary expenditure. Provided the number of centimes voted did not exceed certain limits determined by law, the decision did not require the approval of the tutelage authority.

This system of additional centimes is still the basis of present- day local finance, but it has undergone profound modifications, and a detailed explanation of its contemporary working will be found later in this chapter.

(iii) Local taxes can be levied over a wide and varied field, from domestic servants to horses, from drains to pianos. The prin- ciple behind them has remained unchanged for over fifty years, although their number has increased and they form an integral part of the modern financial structure. They are best dealt with in the next section.

(iv) By 1939 state intervention was prominent in local finance, both in supervising financial management and in providing resources. There had been state grants before 1914, but these had been made only for specific projects of importance both to the State and to the local authority; after the 1918 war the conception of what interested the State widened, and in the inter-war period a conscious policy was followed to grant aid not only to assist essential building but also to encourage the modernisation and development of local areas. There was con- sequently a marked increase in the size of grants and in the types of scheme for which grants could be made.

By 1939 the State granted financial aid to local authorities under four headings. The first method was by direct subvention to help local authorities meet obligatory expenses, such as the grant by the State of a certain proportion of the expenditure

[1] For the way this works see below, pp. 175–6.

incurred by an authority in building a school. Many of these grants were automatic by the beginning of the war.[1]

The second method was the creation of a compensation fund from which local authorities were partly reimbursed for the expenses they incurred in the interest of the State (for example, on general administration, issuing ration books, air-raid precautions, and so on). This fund was known after its author as the *subvention Marchandeau;* it was financed directly by the State, and one-third of the fund went annually to Departments and the other two-thirds to the Communes. A complicated method was worked out to calculate the relative needs of local authorities, and to take account of differences of population, financial resources, income per head of population, length of roads, and so on.

Third, from 1931 onwards, the *Caisse Nationale de Crédit aux Communes et Départements,* financed by the State, was empowered to grant to local authorities loans at low interest rates to finance schemes of particular importance.

Finally, there were the Common Funds (*fonds communs*). The revenue of certain national taxes levied by the State was divided between Communes, Departments and State. Parliament created new common funds piecemeal as it hit upon new sources of revenue; the most notable funds were those financed by the revenue from motor-licences, the stamp duty on identity cards, and the tax on turnover (*chiffres d'affaires*) but there were many others of lesser importance. Each fund was dealt with separately, and for almost all of them a different method was used to divide up the proceeds. The original intention was to return a certain proportion of State revenue to those areas in which it had been raised, but gradually the funds became a means of bolstering up the smaller local authorities. In 1939 when the total budget of all the local authorities was 27 milliard francs, the Common Funds divided between them 1½ milliard francs, a financial contribution of some importance. The Funds were, however, subject to fierce criticism; it was alleged that they encouraged local authorities in extravagant spending, that local councils ceased to be responsible to their electors, and that their

---

[1] For a detailed survey of these see J. Boulouis: *Essai sur la politique des subventions administratives.* Paris, 1951; p. 106 seq.

autonomy was seriously threatened. They were to suffer worse in succeeding years.

In 1941 Vichy overhauled the whole system of state grants and subventions, and expenditure was drastically pruned. One result was a considerable simplification in the relations between local authorities and the State. The principal change effected by these laws was the abolition of the Common Funds and of the *subvention Marchandeau*, the two staple reserves of impecunious local authorities.[1] In their place a new single grant was made to all local authorities, called the " state subvention for expenses of general interest ". It was an automatic grant made each year from state funds; it amounted to a standard rate of 20 francs per head for each Department, and of 25 francs per head for each Commune, but this figure could be modified to take into account population and financial strength; variations from a national mean per head of population involved an increased or decreased rate for each inhabitant.

The *Caisse Nationale de Crédit aux Départements et Communes* was suppressed (Law, January 22, 1942). In its place provision was made for exceptional subventions to authorities whose population had been dispersed or whose sources of revenue had been destroyed by the war; these were based on the loss of revenue suffered between 1938 and 1941. The authority affected had to apply for these grants, but if a Commune was granted aid the Department was entitled to an analogous grant as of right.

The 1941 reforms were completed by empowering local authorities to levy a tax on business transactions (*taxe locale sur les transactions*) in place of the *octroi*. This tax amounted to .25 per cent on all retail prices, and commercial and industrial transactions. Although originally limited to Communes with over 50,000 inhabitants, permission to levy it was in 1944 extended to all *conseils municipaux*. This tax has proved exceptionally useful since its revenue mounts as inflation increases; a most important qualification for any tax in the last decade.

After the Liberation immediate steps were taken to increase the resources of the local authorities; they were simply auth-

[1] In fact three minor Common Funds remain in being to the present day. These are hunting licences, the distribution of electrical energy, and mining rights.

orised to increase the rates of existing local taxes. Those authorised by the 1926 law were in nearly all cases doubled; the tax on business transactions was raised to 1.5 per cent, and the Departments were allowed to raise a tax comparable to a local stamp duty. Finally, the State's " subvention for expenses of general interest " was more than doubled.

The law of December 31, 1945, established a more refined system of allocating state grants. 5½ milliard francs were set aside for 1946 to provide for the needs of local authorities. Grants were divided into three categories; the first was for local authorities requiring special and immediate aid, for example those with considerable war damage and not enough business or property to provide revenue. Direct application had to be made to obtain such assistance. Next, local authorities received automatic grants based on a complicated formula which reflected comparative needs; the state subvention for " expenses of general interest " was divided up according to this scheme. Finally, a new special *subvention d'équilibre* was created to aid those authorities who had exhausted all their resources and who would have to impose new and perhaps intolerable burdens on their tax-payers if additional aid were not forthcoming.

This definition covered a high proportion of all local authorities. A series of coefficients was worked out whereby the financial effort being made by each local authority could be assessed; a national mean was calculated from these returns, and as the coefficient of an authority varied from this mean so it gained or lost a point: grants were made according to the number of points awarded to an authority. The formula was exceedingly complicated, since it made allowances for all conceivable circumstances in an attempt to be as fair as possible; it surpassed all previous efforts in this direction and an " explanatory " letter sent by ministerial experts sowed so much further confusion that many local administrators were completely routed.[1] Also, practice showed that the formula chosen in fact favoured the larger local authorities and consequently those whose revenue was already the highest. This was not the experts' happiest effort; although unpopular politically and administratively complicated it remained in operation until 1948.

[1] Doueil: op. cit.; p. 269.

In December of that year a single Equalisation Fund (*fonds de péréquation*) was set up, which amalgamated the grants previously made for " expenses of general interest " and the *subvention d'équilibre*. The Equalisation Fund was financed by a new method, which although complex was intelligible, and local authorities controlled the Fund. It was financed by the proceeds of the local tax on business transactions originally set up in 1941 but now considerably developed. A general tax of 1.5 per cent on all business transactions was now made compulsory throughout the country, and the total revenue was divided up between the Commune, the Department and the national Equalisation Fund. The Fund was controlled by a committee representing all local authorities which allocated the Fund between the authorities. The procedure adopted by the committee will be dealt with later.[1]

In 1949 the standard tax of 1.5 per cent was increased to 2.7 per cent for the products of vertically integrated firms, but the normal tax remained at 1.5 per cent. Also, the *conseils municipaux* were empowered to make a special addition to the tax for their own use. The maxima allowed them were an addition of .25 per cent on the normal tax and .5 per cent on the tax on integrated firms. A *conseil municipal* can levy a lower rate if it wishes, on condition that a round percentage is used to avoid administrative difficulties.

The Equalisation Fund is the latest and most comprehensive system yet devised both for providing local authorities with additional revenue from national sources, and for sharing out burdens more fairly. It will repay closer study later.

SOURCES OF LOCAL REVENUE [2]

The importance of local government finance in national finance is immediately evident from the published figures:[3]

[1] For further details of the Fund, see below, p. 185.

[2] In 1938 there were 124 francs to the £, and 1948–52 approximately 1,000 to the £.

[3] On opposite page, in tabular form, are the resources of Communes and Departments for 1938 and 1948 with their percentages. The figures, in million francs, are taken from pp. 176–177 of the *Inventaire de la situation financière au 1er. novembre*, 1949. *Imprimerie nationale*. Annex to the budget of 1950.

before 1939 the total of the budgets of all local authorities was consistently about a quarter of the State's budget. This percentage decreased to about 12% immediately after the war, but by 1950 it had risen to a new high level of 30%. In 1950 the Communes spent 330,000 million francs, and the Departments 171,000 million, making a total of 501,000 million francs compared to the state budget of 1,629,000 million francs. In the same year state grants and subventions came to about 15%. This is an important item, but before considering state aid in detail, the additional centimes and the local taxes must be examined, as these still constitute the bulk of the local authorities' revenue.

Additional centimes

Until the war the additional centime was the staple resource of local authorities; in 1918 it provided them with 9,902 million francs out of a total revenue of 26,792 million francs (33%). By 1947, however, there had been a sharp decline in the relative importance of the additional centimes, which then accounted for only 32,600 million francs out of the total budgetary figure of 150,000 millions (22%).[1] This decline is due to the inelasticity and rigidity of the present system for calculating the additional centime.

Before 1918 the additional centime was based on four taxes all relating to real and personal estate. These four taxes were assessed by state officials, and the citizen paid as tax a percentage of the value of his property; i.e. if a house was assessed at 200 francs, and the state tax voted by Parliament was 4 per

	1938			1948		
	Communes		Departments	Communes		Departments
Additional centimes	5,069 :	33%	4,833 : 42%	18,500 :	14%	34,000 : 30%
Octrois	1,180 :	8%	—	—		—
Local taxes	2,213 :	14%	210 : 2%	73,000 :	54%	14,000 : 12%
Estates	576 :	4%	92 : 1%	3,000 :	2%	150 : 1%
Commercial and industrial services	1,142 :	8%	—	7,500 :	5%	—
Grants and subventions	1,753 :	12%	2,997 : 26%	15,000 :	12%	39,000 : 34%
Loans	—		3,038 : 26%	6,000 :	4%	16,000 : 14%
Miscellaneous	3,204 :	21%	485 : 3%	13,000 :	9%	10,000 : 9%
TOTAL	15,137		11,655	136,000		113,150

[1] Communes 14 per cent and Departments 30 per cent.

cent, the citizen would have to pay 8 francs to the State. The amount which the state tax yielded in a Commune or Department formed the basis for calculating the additional centime. For every franc of this state tax which the citizen paid to the State, he had to pay in addition a certain number of additional centimes to the Commune (or Department). The local *conseil* was free to decide how many additional centimes it would raise; if it raised one additional centime then the citizen paid one centime to the Commune (or Department) for every franc he paid to the State; if it raised 6 additional centimes then he paid 6 centimes to the Commune for every franc he paid to the State. When calculating the amount of money the Commune would require, the *conseil municipal* would work out the yield from one additional centime, and called this the *value* of the centime. Thus if the State collected from the citizens of a Commune 5,000 francs, the value of the centime was 50 francs (i.e. 5,000 centimes). The *conseil municipal* had no control over the value of the centime, but it could decide how many additional centimes it would raise (i.e. the *number* of centimes). If, in the above instance, it decided on 30 additional centimes, the yield to the Commune would be 30 × 50 francs = 1,500 francs. It could therefore vary its revenue from this source by the *number* of centimes it voted.

The financial reform of 1917 (when income tax was introduced) abolished these four sources of revenue as far as the State was concerned, but the needs of local authorities were met by continuing the former system in a modified form. The whole system of additional centimes is now based on the legal fiction that the State continues to levy the old taxes.

The basis for calculating the *value* of the centime is the revenue the State would have collected each year if it really levied the pre-1918 taxes. This " revenue " is called the fictitious principal, and it varies only in so far as the assessed value of the property on which it was based varies from time to time. In fact, reassessment amounts to amending the land registers as new property is built, as old property is demolished, or as land is put to another use.[1] A slightly more realistic method of assess-

---

[1] G. Assémat: *La crise des finances communales et départementales.* Berger-Levrault, 1930, p. 38.

ment is used for the *patente* and the *contribution mobilière*, but real values are nowhere accurately reflected. This can be seen from the following table[1] of the fictitious principals at various times :

in million francs

	built-on land	un-built-on land	personal estate	business licences
1913	81	120	83	118
1931	134	87	154	378
1945	182	106	190	283
1949	197	107	195	564

The fictitious principals have no relation to the value of the franc or to current purchasing power, and only the *patente* has any tendency to rise as the taxpayer's real wealth increases. This unreality would be a relatively minor matter were it not that there is no longer any relation between assessments and the real value of the assessed property: consequently the ability of the owners to pay has to be ignored. Some people, though few, are burdened with disproportionately high charges, whereas others escape lightly. The increase in the fictitious principals shown above merely reflects the construction of new buildings, evaluated and taxed according to 1917 standards.

For a single local authority there will be small variations from time to time, and consequently the value of the additional centime will also vary slightly. For example, in the Commune of Le Puy (Haute-Loire) in the space of three years after the war the value of the centime rose steadily as business activity settled down and construction went ahead.[2]

Fictitious Principals.

	1947	1950
Built-on land	101,332	107,243
Unbuilt-on land	4,946	4,893
Personal estate	84,456	90,740
Business licences	232,520	400,820
	423,254	603,696

[1] From the *Inventaire financier*, p. 499.
[2] From the annual budget of Le Puy, 1950.

M

The value of the additional centime in Le Puy in 1947 was therefore 4,282 francs, and in 1950 it was 6,036 francs. It will be seen from the above figures that Le Puy is an urban Commune (hardly any unbuilt-on land) and that as the remaining land was built on so the fictitious principal for unbuilt-on land declined in favour of the fictitious principal for built-on land. It will also be seen that the *patente* is the only part of the tax which increases with the increasing wealth of the Commune. Naturally this fact provoked the allegation that business activity was penalised, and therefore a law in 1950 made the *patente* as unrealistic as the others by crystallising its fictitious principal at the 1948/49 figure.

Each year the Controller of Direct Taxation sends to each Mayor the *tableau des anciennes contributions directes*, from which the Mayor can count the value of the additional centime in his Commune. This *tableau* is naturally used for estimating the value of the Department's additional centime as well. Collection is in all cases made by the administration of Direct Taxation.[1]

To face up to modern conditions local authorities have to levy many hundreds of additional centimes, in order to raise sufficient revenue to meet their costs. In 1913 the average number of additional centimes levied by Communes and Departments was 66 and 78 respectively; by 1938 the numbers had risen to 596 and 616; from 1946 to 1949 the increase registered was from 1,486 to 3,860 for the Communes, and from 1,879 to 6,742 for the Departments. At the present time, therefore, there are a good proportion of local authorities who have consistently to raise well over 10,000 additional centimes. This is an extremely cumbersome method.

Since 1948 local authorities can only levy three kinds of additional centimes; those for ordinary expenditure, those for servicing the municipal or departmental debt, and those for extraordinary expenditure. Previously a wide variety of additional centimes were allowed for particular purposes, but of these

---

[1] In most budgets the State levies a charge on the authority as reimbursement for the work done by state officials in assessing and collecting the grant, and this is normally deducted from the outset in calculating the potential revenue.

special centimes only the highway centime still exists, and this will be explained later.

Finally, all local budgets require the approval of the appropriate tutelage authority if the local council levies more than 80 additional centimes for the combined ordinary and extraordinary budgets and for servicing the debt. In practice this means that all local budgets require approval.

A word should be said about the Departments of Bas-Rhin, Haut-Rhin, and Moselle, in Alsace-Lorraine; where, since 1945, a modernised form of additional centime has been introduced. The main difference is that the principals on which the taxes are levied are " real " and not fictitious, based on current rateable values. This modernised method removes many of the objections touched on above, and M. Lainville considered that it was a precedent which should be followed throughout France.[1] But since financial reform has been a matter of urgency for every Parliament since 1900, M. Lainville's advice may not be taken yet awhile.

Local Taxes

As the relative importance of the additional centime has declined, local taxes have risen in size and importance. Revenue from them had risen from 1,156 million francs in 1938 to 44,000 million francs in 1947, a new proportion of 33 per cent[2] of the total budgets. Several of these local taxes can only be raised by Communes, and even when Departments are empowered to levy them, in practice few do so; local taxes, therefore, certainly represent a proportion much higher than 40 per cent in the average communal budget.

These taxes are so varied that no rigid classification is possible, but for the sake of convenience they can be grouped under three main headings: (i) those which are added to taxes already levied by the State on its own account; (ii) those which the local authority is obliged to impose by law; and (iii) those which are within the discretion of the local authority itself.

(i) There are three main taxes where the local authority can tack its own levy on to that of the State. Their collection is

[1] Lainville describes the system in detail; op. cit.; pp. 41–49.
[2] Communes 54 per cent, Departments 12 per cent.

optional and they are collected with the state tax and returned to the local authority after a deduction for administrative expenses. The first of these taxes is important since it is on the *real* income obtained from property; it is levied on the sources of wealth on which the additional centime is calculated, but this time the taxable wealth is the real income obtained from these various sources and approximates to an income tax; in a largely agricultural country assessment of money incomes is extremely difficult because of the opportunities for false returns; property has a tangible merit. This tax, unlike the additional centimes, can be levied on one or several types of property, and the local authority is competent to decide which shall be taxed. An element of discretion implies a chance for discrimination, and victimisation is relatively easy in smaller Communes where a mere handful may be owners of land and be taxed, while many may own their own houses and escape scot-free. For this reason tutelage authorities are particularly vigilant for abuse of power when a *conseil municipal* decides to impose this tax on one type of property alone.[1]

The two other taxes in this category are taxes upon furnished accommodation and lodgings, and upon the rent of hunting, shooting and fishing rights. The local authority cannot raise more than a quarter of the state tax, except when so authorised by the *Conseil d'État*.

(ii) There are several taxes which are mandatory upon Communes. A striking, but not very fruitful one, is the tax on dogs; it ensures a steady moderate sort of return, and it is so graded that fancy lap-dogs are charged more than house and sheep dogs.

An important tax, both from the revenue it produces and for the use to which it is put, is the tax on public entertainments. Not only is it obligatory, but one-third of its revenue must be devoted to the needs of Welfare Centres (*bureaux de bienfaisance*) and other charitable institutions in the Commune, hospitals and hospices excepted. The rate levied for any particular type of entertainment varies according to the category in which it falls; theatres, races, cinemas, casinos and outdoor enter-

[1] Lainville: op. cit.; p. 69.

tainments are each treated separately, and for each category there are four different rates. The *conseil municipal* (subject to prefectoral approval) decides which rate to apply, and if the revenue obtained is not sufficient for its purpose a higher rate can be levied; similarly an existing rate can be down-graded. This tax produced nearly 5½ milliard francs in 1949.

The second tax of importance in this group is on the sale of alcohol. Originally this was a communal tax which could be added on to a state tax, but in 1942 the State doubled the rate the Commune could levy, and at once ceased to raise the tax on its own account; in effect, this meant that the entire previous tax now went to the Commune. The tariff to be applied in a Commune is decided by the *conseil municipal*, subject to prefectoral approval. The maximum rate of tax varies according to population, and it is progressive in the largest towns. In 1949 it raised 1,356 million francs.

The last tax worth mentioning in this group is a local stamp duty required from all property and financial transactions. It is, however, compulsory only in Communes of over 5,000 inhabitants. It varies from .5 per cent to 1.5 per cent of the value of the business done. An obvious criticism is that it would favour the larger and wealthier Communes, since few smaller rural areas have transactions of any value; business would be done in the cantonal capital where the solicitors live. To remedy this defect, the Department can levy this tax in Communes with under 5,000 inhabitants, and the *conseil général* redivides the revenue between the Communes according to its own formula. Small Communes find it a valuable and stable source of revenue. The Departments of Côtes-du-Nord, Ardennes, Eure, Gironde, Indre-et-Loire, Maine-et-Loire and Bas-Rhin take advantage of this system, and have created what amounts to a departmental equalisation fund for small Communes.

(iii) The third broad group of local taxes is raised at the discretion of the local authority itself; some can only be levied by the Commune, but the great majority can be raised by both Commune and Department. The only distinction within this group is that between taxes levied for general purposes (properly called *impôts*) and those charged for services rendered. In the latter group a tax can be imposed for disposing of household waste, for paving the road, for street-cleaning, and for performing certain administrative services. These taxes are peculiar in that only the cost of the service rendered should be recovered.

Next come a variety of unrelated taxes such as those on domestic servants, horse-carts, balconies, mechanical musical instruments, hawkers, gas and electricity installations, and public meeting-places. The limits within which these taxes can be raised are fixed by Ordinance, and the maxima can only be exceeded with the permission of the *Conseil d'État*. The collection and assessment of these taxes varies considerably; for some the departmental Director of Direct Taxation is responsible, for others the Director of Indirect Taxation, and for yet others the municipal administration and the *receveur municipal*. When the Department levies a tax on the same matter as a Commune, its method of assessment is binding on the municipal authority. For example, if the Department assesses the value of balconies according to the distance they project over the street rather than according to their cubic capacity, then the Commune must do the same.

The last important local tax does not fit into any of the above categories: it is a special tax (or group of taxes) levied for the maintenance of communal highways. This tax has a long and curious history and it is unique in that it can be paid either in money or in kind. A certain number of days' work on the roads or a money payment in lieu thereof can be required from every male between 18 and 60 resident in the Commune and paying taxes, and from every draught animal and cart. The cash equivalent of a day's work is fixed for the whole Department each year by the *conseil général*. Until just before the war the choice of work or money lay entirely with the individual, but so many chose to work that Mayors found themselves with too many men and not enough material, too many donkeys and no steamroller, too many carts and nothing to put in them. In 1938, therefore, Parliament authorised *conseils municipaux* to demand money for a certain proportion of the tax. When a *conseil municipal* votes one day's work the tax-payer has an option as to how he will pay; but if two or three days are voted he retains his option only for the first day, and the *conseil municipal* can demand a money payment for the remainder. If a fourth day (the maximum) is voted, the tax-payer again has an option for the last day. The same number of days must be levied on men, animals or carts. This system is called a *prestation*, and the human and financial resources it provides must be used for the upkeep of minor communal roads outside the urban area of the Commune.

The *prestation* can be replaced in whole or in part by a different road tax (*taxe vicinale*) which consists simply of raising additional centimes especially for the upkeep of roads. The advantage of this alternative is that it hits absentee landlords, and it is a popular substitute in large urban Communes.

Labour or money raised by the *prestation* or by the *taxe vicinale* in excess of requirements can be employed on rural roads (linking Communes together) and on the roads inside the Commune (urban roads). In the ordinary way these rural and urban roads are a charge upon the ordinary budget, but a *conseil municipal* can vote an extra day's *prestation* for maintenance work. Some attempt has been made to equalise the burden between Communes in the same Department; highway maintenance can be a greater liability in the remoter rural areas than it is in urban centres. Since 1920 therefore the *conseil général* has the authority to raise a day's *prestation* throughout the Department to be paid entirely in money; the *conseil général* divides the fund so obtained between the Communes according to its estimate of the Communes' needs, length of roads, size and density of population, and so on. The individual tax-payer can therefore be called upon to pay for anything up to four days' work on one set of communal roads, one day for another set, and one day for the Department.

Parliament has not forgotten that France has a high peasant population: by special dispensation a local authority can count the first day of the financial year for highway matters as November 1st rather than January 1st, so as to let the taxpayer take advantage of the relative idleness of the countryside after the harvest.

State Grants

As has been explained elsewhere the State makes automatic payments to local authorities to assist them to carry out their obligations in the fields of public assistance and education. These grants will not be considered here. Controversy about state grants centres on the politics of optional grants, whether granted for constructive schemes or for balancing local budgets.

State grants were limited for a long time to assisting local authorities who left alone would have been unable to fulfil their legal obligations, for example, in providing primary schools. Later, grants were used deliberately to stimulate the modernisation of backward areas, for example, schemes for the electrification of rural areas and for the construction of irrigation canals. The list of matters for which state aid is nowadays granted includes reafforestation, silos, town-planning, physical education centres, dispensaries, sanatoria, training schools for nurses, municipal abattoirs and roads " of agricultural importance ". Many grants have also been made to aid local authorities' campaigns against social evils such as venereal disease, cancer and tuberculosis. No coherent plan, however, emerges from all this activity, and there is nothing comparable to the elaborate system of encouragement and control that has existed in Great Britain for some time.[1]

The French system now amounts to this. Any work of local interest which would in the ordinary way justify the local authority raising a special loan, is *ipso facto* eligible for a state grant.[2] The grants are made by the relevant Ministry from the funds allowed it annually by Parliament; thus, the Ministry of Public Health helps to construct nursing homes, the Ministry of Education schools, the Ministry of Agriculture rural roads, and the Ministry of the Interior water, gas and electricity distribution schemes. The Minister of the Interior has allowed individual Prefects to grant small sums for public works; other Ministers have been asked to follow suit so as to reduce the burden of central administration and planning.

A standard scale of charges for each type of work is fixed by

[1] Cf. J. Boulouis: *Essai sur la politique des subventions administratives.* 1951, p. 317.
[2] Lainville: op. cit.; p. 127.

the Ministries, and grants are allowed accordingly. The grant cannot exceed a certain proportion of the total cost of the scheme as fixed by law; an inter-ministerial ordinance, however, can raise this limit in special cases. The scale of permitted charges and the size of the State's grant are calculated according to the size of the authority, the number of people to be served by the project, the financial situation of the authority, and above all the probable value of the project to the area or region compared with alternative schemes.

The plans prepared by the local authority must be submitted to a technical committee of the Ministry concerned before any work is begun and before any resources are committed. The Minister has to approve the scheme, and the local authority must accept any alterations proposed by the committee. Technical control continues from beginning to end of the building operations, and the scheme, when finished, is subject to examination by ministerial experts to see that specifications have been met. In addition, the Ministry's officials and also representatives of the Ministry of Finance exercise close financial control to see that the grant does not get mixed up with the general fund of the local authority. If a grant is not used within a fixed period it must be returned intact to the Treasury. In practice the officials of the Ministries in the Department assume responsibility for both technical and financial control except in the case of regional schemes, and the system is not so imposing and top-heavy as a formal description makes it appear.

Such policies have serious disadvantages: central Ministries tend to have a predominant role in determining the direction of local authorities' expansion; co-ordination is lacking and it is extremely difficult to plan ahead. The alternative to direct state control is to confide the control of national funds to an elected authority, and this is what the Equalisation Fund has done.

The Equalisation Fund was set up in 1948 to replace the former grants for " expenses of general interest " and the special *subvention d'équilibre*. The Fund is financed from the local tax on business transactions.[1]

The revenue from this tax is redistributed between local authorities in four stages. First, a proportion of the money

[1] See above, p. 174.

raised is automatically returned to the Commune and Department in which the tax was collected. Where the Commune in which the tax was collected has fewer than 10,000 inhabitants it receives back 60 per cent, and the Department in which the Commune is situated 15 per cent. Where the population of the Commune is between 10,000 and 100,000 it gets back 65 per cent, and Communes over 100,000 receive 70 per cent. Communes in the Department of the Seine get back 75 per cent. Departments in all these cases receive 15 per cent.

Second, Communes which have had their revenue from state grants decreased by the introduction in 1949 of the new system have the right to compensation; this no longer comes to the full amount, and soon this prior charge will disappear.

Third, the law of March 27, 1951, guaranteed every Commune an annual revenue of 800 francs per head of population (the figure was later raised to 1,300 francs), and in 1952 an analogous guarantee was extended to the Department amounting to 400 francs per head. As a corollary, Communes whose revenue per head of population was above the national mean were required to hand over the difference to the Equalisation Fund.

These three stages are fixed by law, and leave no discretion to the body responsible for administering the Fund. The final stage of redistribution, however, is entirely in the hands of the Committee controlling the Fund.

This Committee comprises 19 members, of whom fourteen are representatives of local authorities. There are four Presidents of *conseils généraux*, seven Mayors representing the Communes (graded according to population), and two *rapporteurs généraux* of the *Ville de Paris* and the Department of the Seine respectively, a representative of the overseas Departments, and four senior officials of the Ministries of the Interior and Finance. The President of the Committee is a senior *conseiller d'état*. The elected representatives are elected by their fellows in the same category; for example, there are three Mayors chosen by the Mayors of Communes of under 2,000 inhabitants, two by those of between 2,000 and 20,000, and so on. The Committee is elected every five years, and a member must resign if he ceases to hold his official position.

The Committee's task is to ensure an equitable allocation of the resources which come into the Equalisation Fund. At its first meeting the Committee decided that one-fifth of the Fund should be reserved for the Departments and that the remainder should go to the Communes. It established a formula designed to reflect the comparative financial difficulties of all the Departments on the basis of population, area, the value of the additional centime, the length of roads, and so on. So far it was relatively straightforward.

Each *conseil général* was in turn to allocate its share in three stages: the first 60 per cent to be divided between the Communes in proportion to the revenue each receives from other sources, and to the average income per head of the population. The second 35 per cent to be divided up according to revenue from communal estates, the length of roads, the size of the reconstruction programme, and the size and density of population. The final 5 per cent to be allocated in equal parts between the Communes, although variations were permitted at this stage to reflect the fixed administrative charges incumbent upon each Commune.

Beyond this the Committee preferred to leave the *conseils généraux* considerable freedom in allocating the funds between the individual Communes. Several mathematical formulae were devised to fit varying cases, and the *conseil général* could choose between them.

A fair example of these formulae was

$$p\left(T - t + \frac{R - r}{K}\right)$$

where p represents the population of the Commune, T the result of dividing the available fund by the number of inhabitants in the most favoured (i.e. greatest income per head) Commune in the Department, t the same operation for the Commune under consideration, R the mean income per head of population obtained from communal property in the most favoured Commune in the Department and r the same operation for the Commune under consideration. K is an index figure representing the cost of administering the communal estate; it can be determined by the *conseil général*.

This simple formula could be made more complicated by adding other factors; for example, the value of the centime in

relation to the population, and other niceties. Different formulae were available for each of the three stages of the allocation
between the Communes, but the *conseil général* could, if it
desired, use the same one throughout, or change from one to
another, or alter the index figures arrived at by increasing or
decreasing them by 10 per cent.

Not unnaturally the system gave rise to some difficulties. In
several cases *conseils généraux* were baffled and did not know
what they were supposed to do. Other *conseils généraux*,
quicker to perceive the possibilities, chose the formulae which
most favoured the larger and influential Communes.

The Committee met again in 1950 and decided not to change
its formulae, as it believed that practice and prefectoral advice
would soon make for easier comprehension and more intelligent discussion. The Committee however condemned the
favour shown by some *conseils généraux* to the richest and most
influential Communes, and to avoid a recurrence they limited
their discretion. No sums were to be allocated from the first
60 per cent of the fund to any Commune whose annual revenue
was above the national mean as defined by an inter-ministerial
ordinance each year. The second stage was subject to the same
restrictions, but under pressure the Committee agreed to allow
the *conseils généraux* discretion in making allowance for active
constructive work in the Commune. The Committee urged the
conseils généraux deliberately to use this part of the fund to
encourage Communes to modernise and develop their areas.

In 1949 (its first year of operation) the total sum raised by
the tax on business transactions was 92,368 million francs,
and by 1951 it had increased to 125,756 million francs. In 1949
the amount directly allocated to the local authorities in whose
area the tax had been collected came to 73,488 million francs,
and in 1951 108,830 million. The amount paid as a prior charge
to compensate local authorities for loss of revenue in 1949
amounted to 15,580 million francs; but by 1951 this prior charge
had declined to a mere 2,755 million francs. However, when in
1951 a second prior charge was introduced guaranteeing a
minimum revenue per head of population in the Communes,
this amounted to 5,337 million francs; in 1952 this figure will be
substantially increased since the allocation per head has been

raised for the Communes and the Departments have received an analogous guarantee.

In 1949 the sum remaining in the Equalisation Fund available for redistribution by the Committee amounted to 3,300 million francs, and in 1951 to 9,834 million. This is a good deal less than its original supporters had hoped for, but like many other schemes it has suffered from the vagaries of French political life. The Fund had a bad send off from which it is only now recovering. Parliament, after agreeing to its creation in 1948, threatened to vote it out of existence again before it had come into operation, but sums were written into the 1949 budget to allow it to get started, and Parliament agreed to this. With such instability of purpose there is little that either the Administration or the local authorities can do.

The Fund has also suffered from the pressure of the large Communes who benefit less than do their poorer brethren. The compulsory prior charges are a leakage of considerable importance, and though the Committee has, by dint of energetic protest, been able progressively to reduce the compensation paid for loss of revenue, the introduction of a guaranteed revenue per head of population has brought back many of the vices inherent in the Common Funds. There is a genuine conflict of interest between the small rural Communes and the urban business Communes. The former receive more from per capita grants, while the latter benefit most from a percentage allocation of the revenue collected in their areas. There is probably no satisfactory solution to this problem.

Two reforms suggested as an interim measure are to abolish the compulsory levy on the wealthier Communes and the tax on business transactions in the smallest Communes. It is argued that the actual revenue obtained from these sources does not warrant the administrative burden involved.

The mechanics of the Equalisation Fund have been dealt with at some length since it is the culminating point in an important tendency in local finance. Local authorities' dependence on the State will diminish considerably if a representative body outside the state hierarchy is given control of a sufficiently large fund to bridge the gap between local authorities' actual income and their desirable expenditure. Few challenge the

State's right to decide how and when to bestow extraordinary aid for special projects, but it is regarded as essential for the local authorities to be more independent than at present where ordinary finance is concerned.

THE BUDGETS OF LOCAL AUTHORITIES

There is an important difference in the substance of the budgets of the Communes and those of the Departments. They have different obligations, and although they both draw upon the same financial resources already described the relevance of each source of revenue is markedly different. Whereas the Commune relies to a very great extent upon the additional centimes and local taxes, the Department draws its principal income from those sums received from various quarters for its work in the field of public assistance.

This can be seen from a condensed version of the budget of the Department of the Rhône in 1949.

INCOME

ORDINARY BUDGET	francs
Ordinary additional centimes	927,364,672
Departmental taxes	273,754,349
Common funds (*fonds communs*)	10,000
Revenue from gifts and foundations	1,635,949
Revenue from administrative services	4,400
Ordinary resources for minor road maintenance (*vicinalité*)	5,286,733
Ordinary resources for public assistance	2,223,173,153
Miscellaneous receipts	55,641,867
	3,486,871,123

EXTRAORDINARY BUDGET	
Extraordinary additional centimes	203,080,966
Loans	247,682,000
Extraordinary resources for work on local railways, departmental tramways and motor-buses	1,500,100
Extraordinary resources for minor road maintenance ..	20,643,235
Miscellaneous receipts	70,844,580
	543,750,881

TOTAL BUDGET	..	4,030,622,004

Public assistance accounts for some 63 per cent of the ordinary budget: this revenue comes from annual fixed contributions made by the State, from the contributions made by the Communes to the Department for the use of hospitals and for their maintenance, for clinics, free medical assistance and aid to the homeless, aged, infirm and orphans, and from the payment of fees by private patients.

Departmental taxes raised only some 8 per cent of the ordinary revenue, whereas ordinary additional centimes made a substantial contribution, some 26 per cent of ordinary revenue. The extraordinary revenue, destined as it was in large part for capital expenditure, was derived principally from loans and from extraordinary additional centimes. Additional centimes (both ordinary and extraordinary) make up some 28 per cent of the total budget.

EXPENDITURE

ORDINARY BUDGET		francs
Departmental buildings		19,797,800
Rented property		1,106,000
Departmental equipment		1,077,000
Personnel and administration		152,111,400
Departmental highways		508,891,000
Public assistance		2,754,160,538
Wards of the Department	246,648,341	
Child welfare	45,020,000	
Free medical assistance	909,117,500	
Aid to old, infirm and incurables	1,011,958,964	
Assistance to the family	25,880,000	
Maternity grants	3,350,000	
Protection of public health	11,236,000	
Lunatics	436,536,338	
Miscellaneous	64,413,395	
Departmental archives		2,559,000
Grants in aid to Communes		21,426
Encouragement of art, science and letters		1,534,597
Encouragement of commerce, agriculture and industry		9,020,040
Public education		9,309,046
Miscellaneous		27,283,276
		3,486,871,123

EXTRAORDINARY BUDGET

Departmental Debt	139,135,574
Acquisition and construction of buildings	163,123,168
Acquisition and replacement of equipment	1,510,425
Use of gifts made to the Department	20,000
Construction and alignment of departmental roads ..	149,517,781
Construction of local railways and departmental tram routes	1,500,000
Contribution of Department to state schemes	61,042,000
Contribution of Department to communal schemes ..	27,901,933
	543,750,881
TOTAL BUDGET ..	4,030,622,004

If the budget is taken as a whole, 68 per cent of all expenditure is on one branch or another of public assistance, and work on departmental highways takes the relatively high proportion of 16 per cent, of which a fair part is on new construction. The burden of debt has diminished considerably since before the war, and inflation has done its work. The 3 per cent of total expenditure on personnel and administration is misleading since all the senior and many of the technical officials in the Department are paid by the State, although they work for the Department—the Prefect, Sub-Prefects, *trésorier payeur général*, and so on. On the other hand expenditure on property partly offsets this, as the Department has to provide residences for the Prefect and Sub-Prefects, offices for several state administrations, and to maintain and repair many buildings housing state services such as the law courts, the police barracks and certain educational institutions.

From the political rather than from the financial point of view there is a certain interest in comparing the draft budget prepared by the Prefect with that finally voted by the *conseil général*. The elected body increased expenditure in the ordinary budget by 40 million francs, and decreased the extraordinary budget by 134 million, a total reduction of 94 million francs. Expenditure was increased on personnel and administration, on free medical assistance, on aid to the old and infirm and on the encouragement of arts and industry; the Prefect's proposals for buying new property were decreased, and the *conseil général* made a sharp reduction in highway maintenance and construction work. With the tightening of financial resources and the proportion of income taken by obligatory charges, many enlightened local authorities endeavour to limit expenditure on fixed overheads in order to create for themselves sufficient resources to develop social and cultural work. This is the field where *conseils généraux* nowadays have the greatest scope for initiative.

Whereas the Department of the Rhône is in some general sense a representative Department, although wealthier and more important than most, there is no such thing as a representative Commune. The immense range in size from the *Ville de Paris* to tiny hamlets is too great to permit any valid generalisation. Comparison between Communes of roughly the same size is also dangerous, since so many questions are involved: is it rural or urban, industrial or agricultural, and so on. The budget of the Commune of Strasbourg for 1948-9 is given here as a single illustration but as no more.

INCODE

INCOME

ORDINARY BUDGET				francs
Ordinary additional centimes	..	..	..	305,495,000
Local taxes, compulsory and facultative		..	..	621,043,000
Receipts from commercial and industrial municipal monopolies	..	..	..	161,277,000
Receipts from concessions of public services	..	..	176,905,000
Communal estate	..	..	..	90,056,000
State grants and automatic subventions ..	..	..	360,759,000
Miscellaneous receipts	..	..	..	33,065,000
				1,748,600,000

EXTRAORDINARY BUDGET				
Extraordinary additional centimes	..	..	..	6,436,000
Loans to be raised during the year	..	..	..	10,000,000
Extraordinary state grants ..	..	..	..	76,000
Non-recurring income from communal estate	..	..	77,725,000
Miscellaneous extraordinary receipts	..	..	..	48,353,000
War-damage payments	..	..	..	7,010,000
				149,600,000
				1,748,600,000
TOTAL BUDGET		..		1,898,200,000

Local taxes were by far the most important single item of revenue, some 32 per cent, not far short of the total state aid and the additional centimes, 35 per cent. Strasbourg received 306 million francs from the Equalisation Fund during the year; that is about 80 per cent of the state aid it received: thus the Fund's importance to local authorities can be appreciated. The other grants were mostly of an automatic nature, for education, social services, and so on.

EXPENDITURE

ORDINARY BUDGET	Personnel	Materials	francs Expenses
Administration	431,826,000	25,588,000	—
Justice	—	—	572,000
Police	7,352,000	6,171,000	—
Fire and protective services ..	29,533,000	7,443,000	—
Public health	96,442,000	34,310,000	300,000
Urban roads	91,692,000	88,568,000	—
Minor communal roads ..	—	1,100,000	—
Abattoirs and markets ..	14,071,000	18,012,000	—
Industrial & commercial services	—	—	174,740,000
Communal estate	35,982,000	44,397,000	
Education	76,168,000	90,496,000	—
Public assistance..	56,593,000	17,422,000	134,930,000
Grants to other bodies	—	—	17,683,000
Cultural services and ceremonies	—	—	168,115,000
Miscellaneous expenditure ..	—	—	79,094,000
	839,659,000	333,507,000	575,434,000

TOTAL ORDINARY EXPENDITURE : 1,748,600,000 francs.

EXTRAORDINARY BUDGET	(francs)
Debt service	21,527,000
Acquisition of equipment	43,725,000
Acquisition of land	750,000
New construction and major repairs	57,300,000
War damage	7,010,000
Miscellaneous extraordinary items	19,288,000

TOTAL EXTRAORDINARY EXPENDITURE : 149,600,000

TOTAL BUDGET : 1,898,200,000 francs.

Personnel accounts for nearly half the ordinary budget and 44 per cent of the total budget; this is a very heavy prior charge on communal resources. The expenses of the industrial and commercial services are for reservoirs, municipal baths, municipal *pompes funèbres*, maintenance of the port of Strasbourg, and so on; they are in large part offset by the revenue received from the public for these services and from the concessionaires. Expenses under the head of public assistance are to cover both direct payments to the sick and needy living at home and contributions towards the departmental services to care for these people. Nearly a half of the total grants to other bodies went towards the upkeep and preservation of Strasbourg cathedral, while the remainder was for scholarships and charitable and educational institutions. The municipal theatre accounted for 112 million francs of the total spent on cultural services; the rest went to the museums, library and archives.

The figures quoted here are taken from the budget as it was originally passed by the *conseil municipal* at its budgetary session (*budget primitif*). If, and when, it becomes apparent during the year that the original estimates will be insufficient, the *conseil municipal* has to meet again and vote a supplementary budget (*budget supplémentaire*) to make good the impending deficit. In the present instance total expenditure had to be increased by 492 million, of which the wage bill accounted for 136 million. The cost of equipment rose by 60 per cent, while construction and major repairs showed a three-fold increase on the original estimate. More than a quarter of the deficit was covered by borrowing from banks and savings societies, 44 million from special state grants and 42 million from further additional centimes. By the end of the year the Commune was still left with a deficit of 241 million francs to be carried over into the following year. In recent years, with labour pressure, rising costs and inflation, many communal budgets, although balanced in the first instance, cannot remain so to the end of the year.

CONCLUSION

The present system of local finance is complex, unjust and inefficient. Its complexity is in large part due to historical accident, though generations of Parliaments cannot lightly escape the charge of negligence. It is estimated that local authorities can impose nearly 200 different taxes, many of them of virtually no importance, but many of them involving the tax-collecting administrations in a great deal of labour.

Any reform of local finance must first concentrate upon the present system of additional centimes. Three new taxes based on the real income and value of property, rents, and trading activities, would not only remove many injustices but would also ensure that in the future the tax yield would be related to the evolution of the economic situation. Many minor taxes could also as a consequence be abolished.

Second, there seems to be a strong case for a more rational division of expenditure between local authorities and the State. Local authorities should not, for example, be called upon to maintain law courts, an essentially national service. It would seem reasonable for the State to continue to assist local authorities in works which require large capital outlay, and which may either benefit large sections of the population (for example drainage schemes) or may be long term projects ultimately to improve the national economy (for example, afforestation). But the present semi-autonomy of various Ministries to finance their own services only leads to waste and inefficiency. In the financial as in the political field there is much to be said for reinstating the Ministry of the Interior as the predominant authority in all matters affecting local government.

CHAPTER SEVEN

The Organisation of Paris

THE Paris conurbation covers the whole of the Department of the Seine and also parts of Seine-et-Oise and Seine-et-Marne. This is known as the Paris Region. More precisely, however, Paris is the *Ville de Paris*, a single Commune, confined to that area which until the present century, lay within the fortifications of Paris. The walls have now been demolished but the boundaries have not been extended. The Department of the Seine comprises 80 smaller Communes as well as the *Ville de Paris*, but the latter is the core of the Department and this immense conurbation cannot be assimilated into the general pattern of local government in France.

The Department of the Seine, although the smallest in France, contains 4¾ million people, or ⅛ of the total population. Of these, 2¾ million live in the *Ville de Paris*. In 1950 the budget of the Department of the Seine was 30 milliard francs and of the *Ville de Paris* 42 milliard, while 50 per cent of all the taxes paid in France come from the Department of the Seine. Something like a third of all the industrial and commercial activity of France is carried on in this area.

This economic and social predominance would alone call for some modification in the administration of the area, and in fact they are reinforced by the political importance of Paris as the capital and by the revolutionary tradition of the Parisian people. Successive revolutions have shown that he who rules the streets of Paris rules France.

For all these reasons no French Government has been prepared to grant to Paris the same degree of local autonomy as to the rest of France. The laws of 1871 and 1884 do not apply to the Department of the Seine or the *Ville de Paris*. They are

instead governed by a special set of laws. Both the *conseil
général* and *conseil municipal* have reduced powers; the *Ville de
Paris* has no elected Mayor and municipal administration is in
the hands of state officials, while several departmental services
are under state control. There is a special police organisation
for the whole of the Department of the Seine under the
direction of a special authority, the Prefect of Police. Baron
Haussmann, Prefect of the Seine under the Second Empire,
went to the root of the matter: "the capital belongs to the
Government."

This chapter will deal first with the territorial sub-divisions of
the Department of the Seine and of the *Ville de Paris*; next
with the executive of the city (which is also the executive of the
Department); third with the elected authorities of both the
Ville and the Department; and finally with local bodies of a
special nature.

TERRITORIAL SUB-DIVISIONS

The Department of the Seine comprises 81 Communes; the
Ville de Paris and what are known as the 80 suburban Communes. The suburban Communes are, with a few exceptions
chiefly relating to the *police municipale*, administered according
to the general pattern; the *Ville de Paris*, on the other hand, has
a very special form of internal organisation.

The *Ville de Paris* is divided into 20 *arrondissements* each
comprising 4 *quartiers*. The *quartiers* are of negligible administrative significance, and although they were originally more or
less homogeneous localities their social significance has been
nearly eliminated by the development of an advanced urban
society.

The *arrondissement* is essentially an administrative sub-
division. Built up from the *quartiers* it is not an entirely artificial
unit but its administrative function has kept its boundaries less
fluid than the social life and status of any section of a city can be.
However, the *arrondissements* were originally drawn up to
allow for existing differences in social and political climate and
conditions, so that the Administration might more conveniently
deal with several comparatively homogeneous areas. Moreover,
once the *arrondissements* were used as areas for certain admin-

istrative services, they automatically assumed some degree of cohesion.

In each *arrondissement* there is a *Mairie* which is in many respects similar to the *Mairies* in the Commune of Lyons;[1] it is a centre for limited administrative functions, but the principal centre of municipal government is the *Hôtel de Ville* in the middle of Paris. Each *Mairie* houses minor administrative services such as the registry of births, marriages and deaths, the local magistrate (*juge de paix*), the Commissariat of Police for the *arrondissement* and a staff responsible for any other branches of municipal government specially delegated by the *Hôtel de Ville*.

It will be remembered that in Lyons the *Mairies* were headed by Assistant-Mayors elected by the *conseil municipal* from among its own number and appointed to the particular *Mairie* by the Mayor of Lyons. In Paris the Mayors of the *arrondissements* are not elected but are appointed by the Minister of the Interior on the recommendation of the Prefect of the Seine. In fact one of the few limitations on the Minister's choice is that they must *not* be members of the *conseil municipal* of Paris. Far from being elected representatives of Paris, they may well be Deputies and Senators from the far ends of France.

THE EXECUTIVE

There are three executive authorities in the Department of the Seine. First there is the Prefect of the Seine himself, who has, with some exceptions, all the powers of the ordinary departmental Prefect. In addition he is the head of the municipal administration of the *Ville de Paris*, and exercises in that area all the powers held in other Communes by the Mayors. There is no Mayor of the *Ville de Paris*. Second there are the Mayors of the suburban Communes, whose normal authority does not differ from that of any ordinary Mayor except where one of the two Prefects has special jurisdiction. Third, there is a special police authority, the Prefect of Police, who exercises all the police powers normally held by a departmental Prefect (*police générale*) and, in the *Ville de Paris*, all the police powers normally possessed by the Mayor in an ordinary Commune (*police*

[1] See above, p. 89.

municipale). He has special control over certain aspects of police administration throughout the Department, and over some aspects of *police municipale* in the suburban Communes.

The Prefect of the Seine

The Prefect of the Seine can properly be regarded as holding the highest post in the *corps préfectoral*. Like all Prefects, he is nominated by Decree on the recommendation of the Minister of the Interior, and he ranks as *hors classe*. Although the Minister is as free when appointing the Prefect of the Seine as when appointing any other Prefect, he usually chooses a man from the ranks of the *hors classe* Prefects and generally one of the most senior of those in service. The position is one of great moral eminence and personal responsibility, and it is doubtful whether any other state official has comparable prestige and authority.

The Prefect of the Seine is like any other departmental Prefect in that he is the executive head of the Department and also the representative of the State in his area; but there is one exception, that the *police générale* is outside his control. This is an important derogation from his powers, which in other fields are substantially greater than those of the ordinary departmental Prefect.

He has much greater control over the decisions of his *conseil général;* moreover, as will be seen later, the powers of the *conseil général* of the Seine are very closely defined, and it has a greatly reduced field of autonomous action. Many decisions normally taken by the *conseil général* are, in the case of the Seine, the province of the Prefect himself, who often does not even need the consent of the *conseil général* before acting. Another important factor is that the *conseil général* of the Seine is not allowed to elect a *commission départementale;* the powers of the *commission* are instead vested in the Prefect.

The exceptional position of the Prefect of the Seine as head of the municipal administration of the *Ville de Paris* invests him with a whole set of communal responsibilities with which the ordinary Prefect is only indirectly concerned as tutelage authority. The Prefecture of the Seine is the *Hôtel de Ville* of the *Ville de Paris*, and from it the Prefect of the Seine directs both the departmental and the municipal administrations. As head of the municipal administration his authority exceeds that of any other communal head. The *conseil municipal*, like the *conseil général* of the Seine, has its powers strictly delimited by law. He is in a very strong position *vis-à-vis* the Mayors of the *arrondissements*, who can properly be regarded as his administrative agents, since they are liable to instant dismissal by the Minister of the Interior on the advice of the Prefect of the Seine. Finally, the municipal services which he controls and directs are incomparably greater than those of any other city in France, and his decisions consequently have far greater repercussions.

The Prefect of the Seine is assisted by two Secretaries-General, both of whom are also Prefects (of the first and second class), and by a *directeur du cabinet*, who is a Prefect, third class. The administrative services of the Prefecture/*Hôtel de Ville* are divided between the Secretaries-General, one of whom is responsible for social and economic affairs, and the other for administrative and technical services. There are nine principal Directorates: of finance, technical services, personnel, social affairs, commerce and industry, architecture and town planning, general administration, departmental affairs and municipal affairs. All but the last two Directorates deal indiscriminately with both departmental and communal affairs; however, there are certain attached services which are specifically municipal in character, among them the municipal bank (*crédit municipal*), a special highways division, street cleaning, primary education, and so on, while some are purely departmental, such as the transport system (RATP)[1] and public works. Annexed services, like the RATP and town planning, do not live in the Prefecture but are scattered in various parts of the *Ville de Paris* or the Department, and some have several subordinate branch offices. Under the control of the Prefecture there are also the offices of various *syndicats intercommunaux* in which are grouped all or some of the Communes of the Department. The principal services dealt with in this way are gas, water, electricity and *pompes funèbres*. The *Ville de Paris* does not belong to any of these *syndicats;* instead it has special contracts with the national gas, water and electricity companies and it has its own funeral undertaking services, the *pompes funèbres de Paris*.

[1] *Régie Autonome des Transports Parisiens.*

Other special services are contracted out to private individuals or companies: sewage disposal, markets and abattoirs, swimming pools, sports stadiums and certain types of cheap housing schemes are dealt with in this way. They are all municipal services, and outside the *Ville de Paris* these matters are of course within the jurisdiction of the suburban communal authorities.

The administrative personnel of the Prefecture of the Seine and the *Hôtel de Ville* are all, except the clerks and manual labourers, officials from the national cadres of the Prefectures, the *chefs de division*, *attachés* and *secrétaires administratifs*. Municipal administration in the *Ville de Paris*, therefore, is carried on by state officials; it is the only instance of its kind.

Various powers are delegated by the Prefect of the Seine to the Mayors of the *arrondissements* of the *Ville de Paris*. These are assisted by Assistant-Mayors (*adjoints*) numbering between two and six according to population.[1] Neither the Mayors nor the Assistant-Mayors have any police powers, and practically no ordinary powers of municipal government. They are responsible for the services normally undertaken by the Communes on behalf of the State: registering births and deaths, celebrating civil marriages, keeping statistics and certifying official documents; they prepare and keep up to date conscription records and electoral lists and have certain duties to perform in relation to the public assistance and public health services; they preside over the *bureau de bienfaisance* and the local school committees of the *arrondissement*, and they are directly responsible to the Prefect of the Seine for all their actions and have no independent powers.

It will now be seen that the use of the title Mayor in these circumstances is extremely misleading, for there are virtually no similarities with the Mayor of the ordinary Commune. The post has a certain honorific value likely to attract minor provincial Senators and Deputies. For some years after the Liberation several of these posts were held by Resistance leaders of the Left, and they gave good and able service and devoted more time to the job than had formerly been the practice. But they were alleged to have been involved in the demonstrations against General Eisenhower in 1951 and were dismissed by the Minister.

[1] There are also additional Assistant-Mayors (*adjoints supplémentaires*) in the very large *arrondissements*.

The Prefect of Police

Control of the streets of Paris means control of the Government of France; consequently the police organisation in Paris has always been quite exceptional. In the first place the size of the police force itself is much greater per head of population than anywhere else in France. Secondly the Paris police is the only autonomous police force in France, and its head, the Prefect of Police, owes allegiance only to the Minister of the Interior, and is completely independent of the state police. Finally, in the Department of the Seine all the police powers normally possessed by the departmental Prefect (*police générale*) together with virtually all the municipal police powers in the *Ville de Paris* (*police municipale* of an ordinary Commune), are entrusted to the care of one man, the Prefect of Police, who also has exceptional powers of police tutelage over the Mayors of the suburban Communes. The Prefect of Police is strengthened still further by the fact that he commands his own independent police forces and is not, like other Prefects, entirely dependent upon nationally organised forces. His position is unique, and he holds great responsibility and immense powers.

Like any other Prefect he is appointed by Decree on the advice of the Minister of the Interior, and he is nearly always one of the most senior members of the *corps préfectoral*. He ranks as an *hors classe* Prefect, and like the Prefect of the Seine receives higher allowances than the other Prefects. He has a special residence in the *caserne de la cité* known as the Prefecture of Police, and this block of buildings houses the various services which are under his control. He is assisted by a *directeur du cabinet* who is a third class Prefect and by the Secretary-General of the Prefecture of Police who is usually either a first or second class Prefect.

The Prefecture is divided into three main Directorates, roughly corresponding to the main sub-divisions of the *Sûreté Nationale*.[1] First there is the Directorate of the *police municipale*, counting some 18,000 uniformed policemen who are responsible for public order in the streets, traffic, demonstra-

[1] See: *L'Organisation de la Police de France: Etude schématique présentée par le Secrétariat Général de la CIPC à Paris.* (International Police Commission.)

tions, public meetings, and so on. They are divided between 20 district police stations (*commissariats d'arrondissement*) in the *Ville de Paris*, and 25 area police stations (*commissariats de circonscription*) in the suburban Communes. An emergency reserve is kept in the *caserne de la cité*. When circumstances require, the Prefect can requisition and deploy two special regiments of the *gendarmerie* known as the *Garde Républicaine*. These regiments, numbering some 2,000 men, also form the ceremonial guard for public ceremonies, for the residence of the President of the Republic and for the legislative assemblies.

The second Directorate is that of the *Police Judiciaire*, consisting of 2,000 men responsible for discovering crimes and apprehending criminals; it also has six special brigades for crime, assaults, morality, abortion and juvenile delinquency, highway robberies, and a special brigade for executing warrants for arrest. This Directorate also has a Judicial Identity Department to identify recidivists and centralise criminal records.

The third Directorate is roughly equivalent to the Special Branch, and is known as the *Renseignements Généraux*. Its task is to collect any material on social, economic or political matters which is likely to be of interest to the Prefect of Police or to the Government, and it claims to be able to discover the details of private associations, political machinations or the past life of public or private individuals concerned with politics. Its files will undoubtedly be of great importance to future historians.

The Prefecture of Police also has several technical Divisions: laboratories for examining food and drink offered for sale, forensic medicine laboratories, veterinary services, an inspectorate of weights and measures and a financial section for dealing with fraud. The fire-services of the *Ville de Paris* come under the Prefecture of Police.

With such an administrative machine the Prefect of Police must ensure the peaceful life of Paris and of the national Government.

The dual role of *police municipale* and *police générale* means that the Prefect of Police is responsible for an immense range of subjects: any civil catastrophe or emergency, whether it be a riot, flood or epidemic, is his province for action, and he has to regulate many public activities in the interests of public order; for example, the markets, the quality of meat, the medical fitness of taxi-drivers, and so on. In six months in 1951 the Prefect of Police had to deal with a work-to-rule movement by taxi-drivers, a lengthy strike of all butchers in the Paris area, evictions of squatters, mass demonstrations by Algerians, Communists, students, Gaullists and Pétainists, eight plastic bomb outrages and the national elections for the *Assemblée Nationale*, in addition to the ordinary work of preventing crime and detecting offenders, of public health, public hygiene and public morality. It is not surprising, therefore, to find that on some occasions in the past Prefects of Police have exercised very considerable political power over the Government of the day.[1] This is usually the result of a series of weak Cabinets and ineffectual Ministers of the Interior, which can place the Prefect in a position where he is bound to act continually on his own authority without adequate supervision.

The division of responsibility between the Prefect of the Seine and the Prefect of Police is rather blurred, notably regarding the regulation of public health, markets and highways. The general principle is that the Prefect of the Seine makes the permanent regulations required for the smooth and efficient operation of these services, while the Prefect of Police enforces those regulations. The Prefect of the Seine lays down the general conditions under which markets and fairs can be held while the Prefect of Police is responsible for good order, the quality of goods offered for sale and fair dealing. The Prefect of the Seine maintains the highways, lays down building regulations, licenses hawkers and administers the cleansing department; the Prefect of Police is responsible for the free movement of traffic and the safety of pedestrians on the highway. The Prefect of the Seine controls the normal public health services such as the disinfection and vaccination services, the salubrity of private dwellings and the care and safety of beggars and lunatics; the Prefect of Police is responsible for preventing public nuisances, for the salubrity of furnished lodgings and hotels, for preventing the spread of contagious diseases and for protecting the population against epidemics.

Conflicts of competence between the two administrations

[1] For example, M. Jean Chiappe, Prefect of Police 1927–February, 1934.

inevitably arise. The Prefecture of the Seine is in favour of the extension of outdoor markets and weekly fairs, since traders and public benefit from them and the municipal treasury receives welcome contributions from licences and rents. The Prefecture of Police, however, views them with a jaundiced eye since they are always a potential menace to public order and they require continual supervision and inspection. Again, on one occasion the inhabitants of the rue de Ménilmontant complained to the Prefect of Police that the *vespasienne*[1] in their street was a public nuisance. After due enquiry the Prefecture agreed and proposed a new site for the offending edifice in the neighbouring Boulevard de Belleville. However, the construction and repair of public conveniences is charged on the municipal budget and the Prefect of the Seine refused to pay out the half a million francs estimated cost of removal. The *vespasienne* remained where it was.[2]

Difficulties of this sort are, however, normally resolved by consultation between the services affected, or, in the event of further difficulties, between the two Prefects personally. In the last resort the Minister of the Interior will decide what shall be done, and his word is law for the Prefects.

The actions of both Prefects are always liable to public question and debate in the *conseil général* and *conseil municipal*, and they or their Secretaries-General are, seated below the President in the council chamber, present throughout the sessions. Thus both prefectoral administrations have a keen interest in avoiding protracted disputes which might otherwise provoke ruthless interrogation by a militant chamber.

The Suburban Communes

The 80 suburban Communes of the Department of the Seine are in principle governed in exactly the same way as any other Commune in France. They are divided into the two *arrondisse-*

[1] Outdoor urinal. According to Larousse they were named after the Emperor Vespasian who levied a tax on them. But when they were first built they were called " Rambuteaux " after the Marquis Rambuteau, Prefect of the Seine, 1833–48, who introduced them. There is reason to believe that he endowed them with their present title in order to save his own name. See Pierre-Henri: *Histoire des Préfets*, Paris, 1950, p. 140.

[2] Reported in *Le Monde:* January 8–9, 1950.

ments of Saint-Denis and Sceaux, but since 1880 neither of these has had a Sub-Prefect so that all the Communes come directly under the tutelage of the Prefects. These Communes vary considerably in importance and size, ranging from Boulogne-Billancourt with 100,000 inhabitants to Rungis with under 500. In general, however, despite their picturesque names, they are urban Communes housing the overspill population of the *Ville de Paris*. In most places it is difficult to determine the technical boundaries between the *Ville* and the surrounding Communes.

Such irregularities as there are in the organisation of the surrounding Communes are the direct result of the special powers of the two Prefects in Paris. It has already been explained that the Prefect of Police and not the Mayor controls several branches of the *police municipale* in these Communes; moreover, the Prefect of the Seine, who shares the responsibility for tutelage, tends to be more vigilant than the ordinary departmental Prefect. His authority is further enhanced by the fact that he personally decides many matters which would normally be the province of the elected *conseil général*.

The Communes are responsible, like any others, for their own individual municipal services, and for the major utility services (excluding transport) there are very large *syndicats intercommunaux*. All the Communes belong to one *syndicat* for the distribution of electricity, 58 to one for *pompes funèbres*, for water 68 Communes join with 70 from Seine-et-Oise and Seine-et-Marne, while for gas 72 join with 61 from the same neighbouring Departments. The Communes which do not belong to these *syndicats* make their own separate arrangements.

THE ELECTED AUTHORITIES

The Conseil Municipal

The *conseil municipal* of the *Ville de Paris* is the largest body of its type in France. Until 1935 there was one councillor for every *quartier*, or 80 in all. The variations in the size of the *quartiers* resulted in serious inequalities in this system of representation, and over many years there were vociferous complaints. The Law of April 10, 1935, increased the number of councillors to 90 and allocated the new seats between the most heavily populated *quartiers*. As a result of these modifications there is no longer any necessary connection between a councillor and a *quartier*. After the Liberation a new system of representation was instituted, and now (for electoral purposes) the *Ville de Paris* is divided into six constituencies, each comprising several *arrondissements* and each returning between 14 and 17 councillors. The rules governing eligibility and elections are virtually the same as for the rest of France, except that no Mayor or Assistant-Mayor of an *arrondissement* is eligible.

The sessions of the *conseil municipal* are different from those elsewhere. There are four sessions each year: the first in February or March, the second between May and July, the third in November and the fourth in December, the last two being run together into one continuous session. The first two must each last at least ten days, and the last two not more than six weeks in all. Only the Prefect of the Seine can call an extraordinary session, and the councillors themselves can never decide by a simple majority to do so, although if a third of them demand one the Prefect's refusal must be accompanied by reasons and is subject to appeal to the Minister.

The Prefect and the Minister have far greater potential disciplinary powers over the *conseil municipal* of Paris than elsewhere in France,[1] and although these are rarely invoked they have a deterrent effect.

The internal organisation of the *conseil municipal* is much more complex and highly developed than is usually the case. Each year the *conseil* elects a President, four Vice-Presidents, four Secretaries and the *syndic*.[2] The President of the *conseil municipal* can be regarded as the elected civic head and he usually represents the *Ville* on official occasions. This right was for long contested and it is only some fifty years that he, rather than the Prefect of the Seine, has done so. On the whole

---

[1] The Prefect can suspend the *conseil municipal* for two months, the Minister for up to a year. The Prefect is bound to suspend it if it publishes proclamations. The President of the Council of Ministers can dissolve it by Decree and replace it by a nominated commission for up to three years before holding new elections. In fact the *conseil municipal* has never been dissolved.

[2] Responsible for the management of the premises used by the *conseil*. By custom he also acts in the same capacity for the *conseil général*.

the presidency carries greater prestige than power; he presides over the sessions, he has a seat as of right on several of the most important committees of the *conseil municipal*, and he is responsible for the good order of the *conseil*'s sessions. But he is dependent on the Prefect of Police for police assistance if circumstances ever warrant it. A long tradition whereby the presidency was changed each year to avoid giving a political complexion to that post, has been broken since 1945; Pierre de Gaulle was re-elected by the Gaullist majority three years running before deciding to retire.

Most of the work of the *conseil* is not done in the public sessions at all, but in the six large standing committees (*commissions*), between which all the councillors are divided. Each committee deals with a variety of subjects, but they can roughly be classified as Finance, Administration and Police, Highways, Education and Fine Arts, Public Assistance and Public Health. Each committee has fifteen members and each elects its own president, who is normally one of the more influential councillors. These six presidents of the committees have considerable influence in the affairs of the *conseil*. Each of the committees is a miniature *conseil municipal* reflecting in its composition the political alignments of the whole body. Their importance can be judged by the fact that some 80 per cent of the decisions taken by the *conseil municipal* are merely formal votes to ratify proposals of the committees. It is, as elsewhere, illegal to delegate powers to these committees, and they are technically only study groups, but the pressure of work on the *conseil municipal* is so great that without the valuable work of these committees the full *conseil* would be swamped.

Over and above these standing committees there is a *comité du budget*. This is a committee of the whole *conseil*, but has a special standing body (*commission du budget et du personnel*) composed of senior councillors. This small body examines in detail the draft municipal budget presented by the Prefect of the Seine and the budget of the Prefect of Police, before they are laid before the *comité du budget;* and its report saves valuable time by centering discussion quickly on the important and controversial points. The budget is voted by chapter by the whole *conseil*. Discussion of the several items gives the councillors

O

ample opportunity to discuss all aspects of municipal administration, to review broad issues of future policy and to delve into details of past administration.

In addition to the standing committees there are three other types of committee set up by the *conseil municipal*. There are the " special " committees, to deal with one particular subject such as town planning or child protection; these can be set up *ad hoc* but many are more or less permanent. Next, there are mixed committees on which members of the *conseil municipal* sit together with members of the *conseil général* to discuss matters of common concern such as transport and unemployment. Finally, councillors of the *conseil municipal* and members of the administrative services of the *Ville de Paris* can sit together in " administrative " committees to deal principally with technical problems like drains. These three types of committee are subsidiary to the six standing committees, and the councillors are nominated by the appropriate parent body. Altogether there are about 90 of these subsidiary committees.

Until 1939 the *conseil municipal* of Paris, like all others, was empowered to discuss and to take decisions upon all matters of communal interest; but whereas its field of discussion was the same, a much larger proportion of its decisions required the approval of the tutelage authorities. The Decree Laws of April 21, and June 13, 1939, cut down the scope of the *conseil municipal* of the *Ville de Paris*. These laws specifically enumerated those particular matters of communal interest which henceforth the *conseil municipal* of Paris could discuss, and this list named only the most important items of communal administration. It included the budget, the imposition and rates of local taxes, raising of loans, grants to other bodies, creation of new communal services, participation in *syndicats intercommunaux*, legal proceedings involving sums above a certain level, markets, highways, monopolies conceded by the *Ville de Paris*, use of communal property and the sale of communal property above £1,000.

It must be understood that although the *conseil municipal* could discuss and take decisions on all this list, an insignificant proportion even of these decisions were executory without the further approval of the tutelage authorities. Tutelage remained stricter for Paris than for any other *conseil municipal*. It will be remembered that elsewhere in France, where the *conseil municipal* was empowered to take a decision that decision was executory *unless* the law specifically required tutelage approval. The converse is true for Paris. For Paris, in all matters not included in the list, the Prefect of the Seine could act without the consent of the *conseil municipal*, whose intervention is restricted to questions, motions on the budget and demands for information in the council chamber.

It is not always clear who is the tutelage authority for Paris in any particular instance. In most matters the Prefect of the Seine is competent, but many important matters like the budget must be passed by the Ministers of Finance and of the Interior. In some cases the *Conseil d'État* and even the *conseil de préfecture* of the Seine have to be consulted. Various other Ministers, especially those of Public Health, Public Works and Transport, have considerable powers when the subject dealt with is within their competence: for example, the Paris transport system is firmly in the hands of officials of the Minister of Public Works, and the Minister of Health has extensive control over the institutions and organisation of Public Assistance in the *Ville de Paris*.

It is with some justification that the *conseil municipal* of Paris complains of its subordinate role. In no circumstances do the elected representatives of Paris control municipal affairs as do the Mayors and Assistant-Mayors in the other Communes of France. All but a few trivial decisions require the approval of state officials, and they alone can execute those decisions. But powers taken from the *conseil municipal* do not always go to increase the authority of the Prefect of the Seine, since he in turn is under close ministerial control.

The root of the matter is that Paris is the capital and seat of government of all France, and its administration is therefore considered to be of more than local concern. The size of its budget alone would justify some extra degree of control, and shortcomings in many of the municipal services would undoubtedly adversely affect the work of the national Ministries. To balance its disproportionately large budget each year it requires substantial state aid, and so long as this is so the Ministries, and especially the Ministry of Finance, will naturally insist on their right to have the last word on most major issues.

The Prefect, consequently, frequently finds himself championing the *conseil municipal* before the Ministers. His position means that he must face two ways at once, alternately advocating the cause of the *conseil municipal* and justifying to it the decisions of the Ministers. This is a critical test of personality, and the result often is to bring the Prefect and the *conseil municipal* closer together and to breed respect and mutual sympathy.

The Conseil Général

There are special laws which regulate the elections, organisation and jurisdiction of the *conseil général* of the Seine. Its composition is unique in that the 90 municipal councillors of the *Ville de Paris* are of right members of the *conseil général* without further election. The other 60 members of the *conseil général* are elected according to a system of *scrutin de liste* with proportional representation based on five large constituencies each covering several suburban Communes. Because of its integration with the *conseil municipal* of Paris, the *conseil général* is re-elected in its entirety every six years at the same time as the *conseil municipal* instead of half every third year as in other Departments. Also, its sessions coincide with those of the *conseil municipal* of the *Ville;* that is, in February or March, between May and July, in November and in December. This contrasts with the two annual sessions normally held in April and October. The *conseil général* of the Seine can hold extraordinary sessions under the same conditions as the other *conseils généraux*.

The internal organisation of the *conseil général* is very similar to that of the *conseil municipal* of the *Ville*. The whole assembly elects its own President, four Vice-Presidents, four Secretaries and the *syndic*. Its members are divided between six standing committees, each of which deals with a variety of subjects but which may be styled the committees of Finance, Public Health, Public Assistance, Police, Education and Fine Arts, Highways, Water and Estate, and Housing and Town Planning. There is a similar system of special, administrative and mixed committees in addition to the budget committee of the whole house. No powers can legally be delegated to these committees which are supposed only to examine proposals and make recommendations, but in practice, as with the *conseil municipal*, the whole assembly ratifies a great number of the committees' recommendations without debate. The committees of the *conseil général* of the Seine are exceptionally important owing to the absence of any *commission départementale* to act on its behalf between sessions. An Ordinance of April 13, 1945, gave any standing committee the right to meet at any time between sessions if a majority of its members so desired: on these occasions they are convened by their own presidents and not by the Prefect.

Before 1939 the *conseil général* was empowered to deal with all matters of departmental interest in the same way as in ordinary Departments, with the proviso that many more of its decisions were subject to the approval of the tutelage authorities. The importance of the Department of the Seine, the wealth of its inhabitants, the number of large and influential social institutions, the size of the public utility services and the extent of departmental property, all meant that the activities of the departmental assembly of the Seine covered an immensely larger field than any other.

The Decree Laws of 1939 which restricted the *conseil municipal* also severely limited the activities of the *conseil général*. A list was drawn up to include all matters which the *conseil général* was empowered to discuss: this list certainly included the most important matters of departmental concern, but as with the *conseil municipal*, anything that was not included in the list lay within the jurisdiction of the Prefect of the Seine. Since this law the *conseil général* has lost the right to decide on a variety of fairly important subjects, including buying property, the creation of public assistance institutions, leases of departmental property of under 18 years duration, concessions of public services of less than 10 years, and so on. A further limitation on its powers is the provision that the departmental budget must not be voted by items but by broad chapters, thus leaving the Administration free to transfer funds from one item to another in the same chapter. Naturally the most important matters like the budget or loans require the consent of the *conseil général*, and its members have complete freedom to demand information from the Prefect and to criticise and oppose any action taken by him; the discussion of the budget also gives the councillors ample opportunity of reviewing and criticising policy. In all, however, the *conseil général* is in a much worse position than the *conseil municipal;* it has less cohesion, its work, though wide and influential, seldom bears upon matters of immediate and vital importance to the population (except in transport and housing), and it is less openly political in character. Few, if any, councillors of the *Ville de Paris* are nominated for election by their parties unless they are first and foremost active politicians; several members of the *conseil général* on the other hand owe only nominal allegiance to a party. Its work is consequently less spectacular and more studied, but for that same reason it does not hold its public. As with the *conseil municipal,* its best work is done in the committees where there is no gallery and no temptation merely to rant.

The relations of the *conseil général* with the Prefects are similar to those of the *conseil municipal,* and generally lead to a *modus vivendi* tolerable to both sides. In 1950 the *conseil général* showed its teeth when it refused to vote its budget after the Ministries had drastically reduced various credits it had allowed for optional services. This reserve weapon had never been used before, and it had the desired effect of forcing restoration of a fair part of the cuts.

Both elected assemblies of Paris would be virtually consultative bodies if the laws relating to their conduct were to be strictly applied. In fact, their influence is considerable; because, apart from any other consideration, France is not an authoritarian country, and the Administration welcomes the active participation of elected representatives. Every endeavour is made to eliminate differences in the committees, and policies usually bear the mark of compromise between administrators and councillors working together in private.

It is also well to bear in mind, as the Administration must, that Paris attracts the attention of all political parties, not only because of the electoral importance of the Paris constituencies but also because of the unique political influence of Paris on the government of the country. No party can afford to ignore Paris,

and the national party machines are always liable to intervene
in the politics of the assemblies, and ultimately to provoke
questions to Ministers in the national Assemblies.

SPECIAL ORGANISATIONS

Some administrative organisations in the Paris Region are
without parallel in the rest of France: others have their counterparts elsewhere but have special powers in Paris. Brief mention
must be made of these special services owing to their practical
importance.

(i) The *conseil de préfecture* of the Seine and the organisation of the Public Assistance services are in principle the same as
their counterparts elsewhere, but they are both distinguished by
their wider powers and by their greater importance to the State.
The *conseil de préfecture* of the Seine was excluded from some
of the provisions of the reorganisation by the laws of 1926, with
the results that it alone remains based on a single Department
and that recruitment is different. Of the total of ten councillors,
half the members of the *conseil de préfecture* of the Seine must be
presidents or first class councillors promoted from other *conseils de préfecture*, a quarter must be members of the *corps
préfectoral* (Prefects and *hors classe* Sub-Prefects with a law
degree), *auditeurs* of the *Conseil d'État* or law teachers from the
universities, and a quarter from the *attachés* in the Ministry of
the Interior who possess a law degree. The *conseil* is divided into
two sections, each working independently and each with its own
president, who may be either a specially nominated *conseiller*
or a *conseiller d'État*.

The *conseil de préfecture* of the Seine has greater administrative powers than any other and its opinion must be sought
by the Prefects on several cases, notably the division of police
expenditure between the suburban Communes and the *Ville de
Paris*, and on the terms of contracts for new construction at
municipal or departmental expense, and for large repair work.
It has the usual juridical functions, together with extra powers
over the contracts entered into between the Administration and
public services. Naturally, the concentration of the national
administrative services, the many large public corporations, and

the size of the municipal and departmental administrations, give rise to an exceptional amount of administrative litigation, and enhance the practical importance of the *conseil de préfecture* of the Seine.

(ii) The Public Assistance institutions of Paris are governed by special laws[1] and are quite unique in scope and influence. Several of the hospitals and homes have as long a history as the capital itself, being foundations of old monastic and nursing orders. There are now some 80 different homes, hospitals and institutions with 45,000 beds. In 1951 the total budget was some £32 million, made up of receipts from rents, contributions from Communes and from the Department, payments for and by patients and from the tax on entertainments.

In addition to the institutions themselves there are the *bureaux de bienfaisance* in each *arrondissement* of the *Ville de Paris*, which are under the general direction of the Mayors, administered by the members of the municipal administration with the aid of investigators (*commissaires enquêteurs*) and lady visitors (*dames visiteuses*).[2] There are special agencies responsible for orphans and neglected children, and there are ten childrens' hospitals. In all there are between 25,000 and 30,000 persons employed by the Public Assistance of Paris, including administrative and medical personnel, technical staff and workmen. The head of the whole organisation, the Director General, is appointed by the President of the Republic, and the Secretary-General by the Minister of Public Health on the advice of the Prefect of the Seine. An advisory body (*conseil de surveillance*) of 32 members, partly official, partly nominated, meets from time to time under the presidency of the Prefect of the Seine. The senior administrative staff are appointed to office by the Prefect of the Seine from a list drawn up by the Director General; all other personnel are appointed directly by the Director General.

The Public Assistance of Paris is under the administrative and financial tutelage of the Ministers of the Interior, Finance

---

[1] Especially by the Law of January 10, 1849, subsequently modified.

[2] The suburban Communes are responsible for their own *bureaux de bienfaisance;* most of them are attached to one or more of the hospitals of the Public Assistance of Paris.

and Public Health, and under the technical supervision of the Minister of Public Health alone. The rates to be charged in the institutions are fixed not by the *conseil général* as is normally the case, but by an interministerial ordinance on the recommendation of the Prefect of the Seine.

(iii) One of the most famous public institutions in Paris is the *crédit municipal*. Originally founded in 1777 by Necker, it is closely associated with the Public Assistance of Paris. It is essentially a charitable and philanthropic organisation and it advances sums against all sorts of security. Before 1919 the *crédit municipal* had to make over to the Public Assistance of Paris all the profits made during its operations, but since that date it has been allowed to keep a fair proportion in reserve and for current needs. It advances money against real and personal property for varying lengths of time at an interest rate of between 5 per cent and 8 per cent. A special storage charge is made for pianos, motor-vehicles and heavy furniture. Rather more than 75 per cent of its transactions involve less than 200 francs a pledge. It is also a savings bank prepared to pay 2 per cent on all deposits. When it needs more working capital it raises special short term bearer loans at between 3 per cent and 5 per cent. It is important to remember its charitable origin: clothing taken as pledge is not infrequently returned to its owners without repayment, especially in severe weather.

Besides the central office of the *crédit municipal* in the Rue des Francs Bourgeois, there are three main branches and fourteen bureaux scattered throughout the city, employing some 600 people. The Director is appointed by the Minister of Finance and the Secretary-General by the Prefect. They are advised by a *conseil d'administration* composed of members of the *conseil municipal*, the Prefect of Police, representatives of the Public Assistance of Paris, and ordinary citizens under the presidency of the Prefect of the Seine.

(iv) The other notable public body without parallel elsewhere is the Transport Monopoly (*Régie Autonome des Transports Parisiens*). With the extension of the metropolitan area this service has increased tremendously in size and importance, but it has been a continuous source of trouble. On political and social grounds the Government has always been reluctant to increase fares, and the transport budget has been continually in deficit since 1918. The deficit is shared by the *Ville de Paris*, the Departments of Seine, Seine-et-Oise and Seine-et-Marne, and the State; but the State's contribution is limited by law to 15 per cent. There are repeated strikes for more pay, energetic protests by the elected assemblies on behalf of their electors at any increased tariff, and a consistent refusal by the State to cover any more losses. Before 1948 the elected assemblies exercised considerable control over the transport system; the Law of March 21, 1948, reorganised all the services as a *régie autonome* under the close control of the Minister of Public Works. The technical and administrative heads are senior officials of the Ministry, and although the assemblies are represented on the board of the holding company they are always in a minority, and the decisions of the board require the Minister's approval.

CHAPTER EIGHT

Conclusion

THERE are several criteria for estimating the strength and worth of local government in various countries. The most general are tests of freedom, popular participation and efficiency. It may be instructive to examine French local government in the light of these three criteria, though it must be remembered that both definitions and standards are relative.

Firstly it is customary to measure freedom in local government by the extent to which local affairs are regulated by local elected bodies. French government is usually characterised quite simply as centralised. This misconception is not surprising. Most foreign students of French affairs naturally concentrate on national politics, which is hardly the best introduction to the reality of local administration: on the other hand, many French scholars who concern themselves with political institutions are jurists by training, and are interested in legal concepts rather than political reality.

The term centralisation is often used to describe both the transfer of decisions on local affairs to central Ministries, and the subordination of local decisions to the agreement of a state official. This dual sense is not always clearly distinguished, and in England they often amount to the same thing. In France the distinction is very important. The large majority of Communes have practically no contact with the centre, except on the rare occasions when they wish to join a *syndicat intercommunal*, when they wish to raise a very large loan, and so on. All Communes are subject to one or more members of the *corps préfectoral*, and if centralisation means the subordination of local decisions to the agreement of state officials, then French local government is highly centralised. But it is centralisation in which the centre is the departmental Prefecture and not Paris, and this alters the picture a great deal. The state official who deals with local matters is resident in the area, aware of local difficulties, easily approachable, and fully informed, and he has effective control in his area over the officials of all other central services. Indeed, the real centre for most Communes is even closer to home, in the Sub-Prefecture. The slow and infuriatingly impersonal process suggested by the term centralisation is far from being an accurate picture of French local government.

It may be said that, since the Prefect is the direct subordinate of the Minister, the reality of close central control is merely camouflaged by the interposition of a local state official: there is some justification for this. It is possible for the Minister to ensure a uniform policy throughout the country by issuing a directive, and this is done on all issues of national importance. The internal history of France has often been so disturbed as to require immediate measures to be taken throughout the country without the risk of conflicting loyalties and unwilling instruments. In ordinary circumstances ministerial Circulars leave much to prefectoral discretion, and many deal with matters of routine and are of no public interest. On practical grounds alone the Minister is well advised to leave many matters to his subordinates in the Departments. Social, political, and economic circumstances vary so much from one part of the country to another that orders phrased in minute detail would frequently be impractical, and raise opposition.

It is possible to argue that local control of education and the police forces is the really valid test of freedom in local government, and that since both these services are under state direction France is by definition a centralised country. The removal of these two very important services from local elected control undoubtedly weakens French local authorities in comparison with their English counterparts, but it is unrealistic to imagine that " education " and " police " have the same social and political significance in France as in England. The conflict between Church and State for influence in the educational field is still a struggle for political supremacy in which opposing philosophies are bitterly engaged. It is a matter in which Bishops openly acclaim tax-strikes against the State, and

Prefects are expected to know the secret convictions of teachers.

It is difficult to estimate just how deep-rooted this antagonism is, and in many cases perhaps only the *curé* and the *instituteur* really believe in it. In other places, however, education is a real battleground—for example, in the Vendée and in Alsace—and it has a real political significance: and even where it probably has not, councils and politicians behave as if it had. This may be unpalatable, but it would be a danger to public order if local authorities in France had the same educational powers as in this country.

Similarly with the police: if England had had five régimes overthrown by force in just over a century, her authorities would also be very conscious of the desirability of central control over the country's security forces. In addition, the results of local control over police forces in the United States are not likely to convince the continental observer of the essential rectitude of local authorities. The Mayor of Marseilles may be less free than the Mayor of Chicago, but at least the citizens of Marseilles do not have to pay for his licence. It is obvious that in any evaluation of political institutions, weight must be given to the characteristics which distinguish one country from another.

When the second criterion, that of popular participation, is applied, a different balance has to be struck between England and France. The paradox is that although local authorities possess greater powers in this country, there is more interest in local matters and more vitality in local government in France. There are several reasons for this. The first and most obvious is the smallness of very many Communes and their isolation from even the departmental capital. Many Communes have fewer inhabitants than an English parish and are as remote as villages in central Wales. Yet they have powers of self-government such as no parish council possesses, and naturally local attention is more concentrated and local politics are more personal.

This personal element holds good throughout the local government system, and it is certainly one of the most fundamental causes of its vitality. In the Department, the concentration of authority in the person of the Prefect focuses attention on him: he personifies the State, and he is credited with formidable powers and influence in high places. When a general police ordinance appears, when a school is opened, when the Commune's budget is returned and when a subvention is granted, *M. le Préfet* appears either in person or in print. None who see him or experience his influence can plausibly maintain that local affairs are arranged by an impersonal administrative machine. The correct antidote to bureaucratic government is to require the man who administers to justify his decisions publicly. This not only stimulates public attention but also brings to the fore more dynamic administrators.

The concentration of executive municipal authority in the Mayor also personalises the processes of local government. The Mayor is the centre both of local politics and of municipal activity. These politics frequently have nothing in common with national political struggles except the names of the parties, and are genuine contests between conflicting local personalities about local policies. In provincial France apathy towards the activities of the National Assembly is often offset by the vigour of local strife.

Local political affairs are the more active because the Department is normally the constituency for national elections, and the sympathy and support of municipal and departmental party associations is more important to the prospective candidate than the approbation of the central party organisations. This is evident in the readiness of local personalities to set themselves up as rivals of the nominees of their own parties if they consider that they still possess a predominance of local sympathy. Anyone who aspires to a political career must build up his influence by his activity in local affairs, and the municipal and departmental *conseils* are the natural testing ground for active and ambitious men.[1] When such men become Deputies and Senators they take with them to Paris the marks of their origins, and many of their electors consider them as delegates sent to protect and forward local interests, rather than as rep-

[1] This is less true for the Communist Party, which often takes men from industrial life and politics and trains them in the bureaucracy of the Party, than for the other parties. The MRP also have several prominent members who have emerged by other means; frequently from the Resistance.

resentatives of France. In these circumstances self-interest recommends the local men of business to take some part in local political affairs in order to have the ear of their Deputy should that become necessary.

It should be added in passing that this exercises a baleful effect on national government, and emphasises the predominance of the "country" over the "town": the result is a divergence between economic importance and political power. It is curious to find that active interest in local politics may be related to instability in central government.

It is not easy to define "efficiency in administration". It seems to mean in practice the prompt, smooth and predictable passage of matters requiring decision to a known authority, who can and does take those decisions on his own responsibility. This is a simplification of a complex process, but it furnishes the principal criteria of promptness, smoothness and predictability.

The greater part of local administration in France is efficient in this sense. The concentration of communal and departmental executive power in the hands of the Mayor and the Prefect greatly facilitates the prompt and orderly despatch of business: each is unchallenged master of his subordinate officials, and the Prefect, as representative of the State, can command the allegiance of all the state officials throughout the Department.

The concentration of state and departmental services in the departmental capital facilitates joint policies as well as quick decisions, while the Prefect's tutelage powers over the Communes of a Department ensure a uniformity of practice in matters of common importance, and speedy and knowledgeable assistance to municipal authorities when they are involved in complex legal or political situations. Even more accessible than the Prefect is the Sub-Prefect in every *arrondissement*, who is constantly on hand to advise municipal authorities on administrative and financial details, and to a great extent mitigate the difficulties of many small Communes which have only a skeleton administrative staff.

The codification of laws is an important element in ensuring prompt, smooth and predictable administrative practice. The basic laws on municipal and departmental administration state precisely the division of responsibilities and powers. Additional and amending laws have complicated the picture, but rarely beyond a point where they can be settled at the Prefecture, and never without clearly specifying the exact course of appeals. Here the work of the administrative courts and the advanced development of administrative law play an important part. The courts provide an efficient channel through which pass cases of disputed powers or alleged violations of the law: strict limits are fixed to legal delays at each stage of the appeal. The whole system benefits the Administration itself, and also gives to the public the assurance that the Administration is working according to established and therefore non-arbitrary rules.

There are, however, factors which pull the other way and hinder the prompt, smooth and predictable despatch of business.

Foremost of these is the present system of local government finance. The inelasticity and unreality of the additional centimes hinders the rational development of local resources; administrators are seriously handicapped if they have to base their calculations on a legal fiction. Further, the rules governing the award of state subventions vary considerably, and complex financial calculations have to be made before even a rough estimate of future grants. Even when this has been done there is no guarantee that the National Assembly will continue to allow adequate sums in the Budget, or to follow a consistent plan for state investment in works of local interest and for the expansion of local resources. The instability and incoherence of central government seriously damages the efficiency of local administration, since local authorities are often prevented from making long-term plans. But the National Assembly is inescapably responsible for the whole national Budget.

Nor can the administration of the large Communes be really efficient while their budgets continue to be under the control of several different Ministries. The budget of the *Ville de Paris* has, in recent years, been repeatedly returned to the municipal authorities eight or nine months after the beginning of the financial year, during which time the Ministries scrutinised the details. Any alterations which they require must be inserted in a budget already three-quarters dead. Interministerial control is neither prompt nor predictable, and the smoothness of local administration suffers accordingly. The development of the

Equalisation Fund, the general adoption of the revised system
of additional centimes in use in Alsace-Lorraine, and the
reorganisation of central financial tutelage, would all diminish
the present uncertainty of local finance, and they are reforms
which are long overdue.

Another obstacle to administrative efficiency in local government is the illicit interference at higher levels of Deputies and
Senators. For several reasons the problem is less acute under the
Fourth Republic than it was under the Third, but it still remains
troublesome. The assumption that decisions will be taken
objectively by a predetermined authority does not always hold
good.

The most satisfactory way of lessening the occult power in
administrative affairs of Deputies and Senators is undoubtedly
to increase the autonomy of local authorities. The division of
powers between the local elected bodies and the Administration
allows the former in the last resort to escape the full burden of
their responsibilities. They may decline to risk the hostility of
their electors by taking politically distasteful measures, with
the assurance that the Administration will ultimately have to
take them instead; or they may propose aggressive and im-
practicable actions, knowing that the Administration will never
allow them to be carried out.

The French tend to take for granted the essential irrespons-
ibility of local elected bodies, and accordingly to insist on administrative safeguards against it: in fact these safeguards
themselves hinder the growth of a full sense of public responsibility.

Lastly, there is the question of the appropriate areas for
local government, which has caused much discussion in the
last decade. It is argued that many of the present Communes are
too small to be efficiently or economically administered. Many
Communes are incapable of providing even the most elementary
public services except through *syndicats intercommunaux*. The
real problem is not that they are inefficient in what they do, but
that they do not do nearly enough. As has been seen, however,
this is a question of some delicacy. The *conseils municipaux* of
these Communes undoubtedly reflect the opinions of their
electorate when they refuse to go beyond the bare necessities of

P

essential services; state subventions are not bait large enough to overcome the ingrained suspicion of the peasants for the State and all its works.

After much debate some measure of agreement seems to have been reached. More extensive use (under proper safeguards) should be made of the right of the *Conseil d'État* to insist on Communes joining *syndicats intercommunaux:* this should be accompanied by a closer scrutiny of conditions in the smaller Communes, and whenever serious shortcomings are found, the Commune should be amalgamated with its neighbour as a *section* of a Commune. Neither of these policies can be expected to have rapid results, but they seem to offer some hope of increasing efficiency with the minimum interference with the principle of local representation.

The problem of the Department is more difficult. Its very existence testifies to the fact that the French do not in principle object to " artificial " areas of local government. Experience has shown that the concentration of administrative services in one town, the primacy of one state official over all others in the area, and a strong elected authority, are together sufficient to give to an area originally lacking in " natural " unity a genuine social and political homogeneity. Critics who have argued that the Department is too small to be an area of modern admin- istration have advocated the creation of Regions, each com- prising several Departments: each Region would have its own administrative centre, and the present unstandardised service regions would, as far as possible, be made to conform with the administrative Region. A return has even been suggested to the old Provinces. The experiments in regional government since 1939 have, however, evoked so much hostility that it is im- probable that any further extension of regional administration is now politically feasible.

The truth is that the Department is too important politically ever to be changed while the present system of parliamentary government is retained. Beside that basic fact pleas for greater areas of administration on grounds of efficiency are doomed to failure. For one thing, there is not much inclination in France to regard efficiency as the sole criterion in any form of government, and the cares of administrators are considered as secondary to the interests of politicians and the wishes of the administered. The present system of separate regions for separate services is only tolerable because the Department is used as a further area of devolution in which the normal administrative and political processes are still predominant.

The politicians' argument is shrewd and realistic. We in England are accustomed to a good deal more administrative centralisation than are the French, and insist on assuming that administration is in some way separate from politics; consequently we refuse to acknowledge the need for special political and judicial control over administrative officials. Accordingly we tend to judge the creation of new administrative regions almost entirely in terms of administrative convenience and efficiency. The French see in them new areas of uncontrolled power, too large for effective local political control. The standardisation of regions under a regional Prefect, combined with the eclipse of the Department, would entail a complete revision of the political machinery of the country. Quite possibly this would have beneficial results in Parliament, but the present vitality of local government would be lost.

The French do not believe in benign and incorruptible officials, and they have a very realistic idea of what constitutes power in the State. Their history shows them that no administrator has ever had a vested interest in freedom, but that some politicians have.

SELECT BIBLIOGRAPHY

THIS bibliography lists the principal works consulted. In addition several reviews are of great value for studies on specialised aspects of local government. The *Revue du Droit Public*, the *Revue Administrative*, the *Revue de Législation et de Jurisprudence* and the *Revue Politique et Parlementaire* are especially to be noted. M. Rolland indicates in the text of his *Précis* many specialised studies to be consulted on particular aspects of administrative law, and M. Doueil lists in his bibliography the most important articles and short studies which have appeared in the last decade. The libraries of the Faculties of Law in the various university towns contain a wide variety of doctoral theses which are of great value and are too frequently and quite unjustifiably ignored by students of French affairs.

LAW

P. DUEZ: *Les actes de gouvernement*. Paris, Sirey, 1934.

M. HAURIOU: *Précis élémentaire de droit administratif*. 5th edition, Paris, Sirey, 1943.

G. JÈZE: *Principes généraux de droit administratif*. Paris, 2 vols.

R. MASPÉTIOL ET P. LAROQUE: *La tutelle administrative*. Paris, 1931.

M. PRÉLOT: *Précis de droit constitutionnel*. Paris, Dalloz, 1949.

L. ROLLAND: *Précis de droit administratif*. 9th edition, Paris, Dalloz, 1947.

M. WALINE: *Traité élémentaire de droit administratif*. 6th edition, Paris, Sirey, 1951.

CODE ADMINISTRATIF: Paris, Dalloz, 1950.

ADMINISTRATIVE COURTS

J. ALIBERT: *Le contrôle juridictionnel de l'administration au moyen du recours pour excès de pouvoir*. Payot, 1926.

R. BETTINGER: *Le conseil de préfecture, juge du contentieux départemental et communal*. Paris, Sirey, 1935.

P. DE FONT REAULX, R. DURNERIN, J. MARIZIS: *Les conseils de préfecture; organisation et compétence*. Paris, Sirey, 1937.

B. OLIVIER-MARTIN: *Le Conseil d'État de la Restauration*. Paris, Sirey, 1941.

TROUILLAS: *La responsabilité des administrations publiques en matière de police*. Thesis, Paris, 1943.

THE COMMUNE

M. ARAGON: *Les administrateurs communaux et intercommunaux.* Paris, Sirey, 1935.

P. BERTRAND: *Le statut du personnel communal.* Paris, Sirey, 1946

J. BOULONNOIS: *La réforme municipale.* Lachèvre, Pontoise, 1946.

P. DOUEIL: *L'administration locale à l'épreuve de la guerre 1939-49.* Paris, Sirey, 1950.

R. MASPÉTIOL: *L'organisation municipale.* Paris, Sirey, 1934.

R. LAINVILLE: *Vers la réforme municipale.* Paris, Sirey, 1946.

R. NESTOR: *Le contrôle du Préfet sur l'administration communale.* Thesis, Paris, 1931.

J. ROY: *L'administration intercommunale: le problème des petites communes.* Thesis, Bordeaux, 1944.

P. H. TEITGEN: *La police municipale générale.* Thesis, Nancy, 1934.

THE DEPARTMENT

Annuaire du Corps Préfectoral, et de l'Administration Centrale. Paris, Charles-Lavauzelle, 1950.

J. GANDOUIN: *La constitution et la réforme de l'organisation départementale et communale.* Thesis, Paris, 1950.

P. GUERRINI: *Origines et pouvoirs du Secrétaire Général de préfecture.* Thesis, Lyons, 1938.

LOMBARD: *Le rôle financier du Préfet.* Thesis, Paris, 1937.

R. MILLET: *La France provinciale; vie sociale, moeurs administratives.* Paris, 1888.

MINISTRY OF THE INTERIOR: *Attributions des Préfets et Sous-Préfets comportant pouvoirs de décision.* March, 1948; Folio.

PIERRE-HENRY: *Histoire des Préfets.* Paris, Nouvelles Éditions Latines, 1950.

Rapport présenté par l'Inspection Générale pour l'organisation et le personnel des préfectures departementales. Melun, 1942.

P. RIX: *Le Secrétaire Général de préfecture.* Thesis, Toulouse, 1938.

THE REGION

J. BANCAL: *Les circonscriptions administratives de la France.* Paris, Sirey, 1945.

M. BRUN: *Départements et Régions.* Paris, Presses Modernes, 1939.

J. LEGRAND: *Les essais d'administration régionale.* Thesis, Paris, 1950.

P. GAY: *Le Préfet régional.* Paris, Sirey, 1942.

FINANCE

J. BOULOUIS: *Essai sur la politique des subventions administratives.* Paris, Colin, 1951.

R. LAINVILLE: *Le budget communal.* 7th edition, Paris, Sirey, 1951.

MINISTÈRE DES FINANCES: *Inventaire de la situation financière 1913-1949.* Paris, 1949. (First published 1946.)

A. POMME DE MIRIMONDE: *La Cour des Comptes.* Paris, Sirey, 1947.

L. TROTOBAS: *Précis de science et législation financières.* 9th edition, Paris, Dalloz, 1947.

PARIS

M. BARROUX: *Le département de la Seine et la Ville de Paris; notions générales pour en étudier l'histoire.* Paris, 1910.

M. FÉLIX: *Le régime administratif et financier du département de la Seine et de la Ville de Paris.* 2 vols., Paris, Rousseau, 1945.

Organisation et attributions des services du département de la Seine et de la Ville de Paris. Paris, Imprimerie Municipale, 1950.

Organisation et attributions des services de la Préfecture de Police. Paris, 1946.

RAYMOND-LAURENT: *Paris: sa vie municipale.* Paris, Godde, 1938.

P. VÉZIEN: *Les services publics industriels dans la région parisienne.* Thesis, Paris, 1940.

INDEX